Men's Discourses of Depression

Men's Discourses of Depression

Dariusz Galasiński

palgrave
macmillan

First published 2008 by
PALGRAVE MACMILLAN
Houndmills, Basingstoke, Hampshire RG21 6XS and
175 Fifth Avenue, New York, N.Y. 10010
Companies and representatives throughout the world

PALGRAVE MACMILLAN is the global academic imprint of the Palgrave Macmillan division of St. Martin's Press, LLC and of Palgrave Macmillan Ltd. Macmillan® is a registered trademark in the United States, United Kingdom and other countries. Palgrave is a registered trademark in the European Union and other countries.

ISBN-13: 978–0–230–50752–4 hardback
ISBN-10: 0–230–50752–2 hardback

This book is printed on paper suitable for recycling and made from fully managed and sustained forest sources. Logging, pulping and manufacturing processes are expected to conform to the environmental regulations of the country of origin.

A catalogue record for this book is available from the British Library.

Library of Congress Cataloging-in-Publication Data
Men's discourses of depression / Dariusz Galasinski.
       p.   ;   cm.
   Includes bibliographical references and index.
   ISBN-13: 978–0–230–50752–4 (hardback: alk. paper)
   ISBN-10: 0–230–50752–2 (hardback: alk. paper)
   1. Depression in men—Patients—Language.   2. Discourse analysis.
   [DNLM: 1. Depressive Disorder—psychology.   2. Men—psychology.
   WM171 G146m 2008]   I. Title.
   RC537.G335 2008
   616.85′270081—dc22   2008016158

10   9   8   7   6   5   4   3   2   1
17   16   15   14   13   12   11   10   09   08

Printed and bound in Great Britain by
CPI Antony Rowe, Chippenham and Eastbourne

To my life

Contents

Acknowledgements   viii

1   Men, Depression and Discourse Analysis   1
2   Discourses of Depression   23
3   The Experience of Autonomy (of Depression)   44
4   At Arm's Length. The Not-So-Depressed Self   58
5   Life Illness. Depression and the Accounts of Everyday Life   75
6   Normal Biographies. Depression and the Life Story   90
7   The Timeless Self. The Inevitability of Depression   106
8   Lesser Men. Depression and the Model of Masculinity   121
9   Men's Imperatives. Men, Depression and Work   136
10 Rejections. Men, Depression and the Family   151
11 Insight and Suffering: A Linguist's View of
    Psychopathology   169

Notes   181
References   182
Index   209

Acknowledgements

This book would not have been without those who decided to share their suffering with me. First and foremost, my thanks go to the men who agreed to be interviewed.

I would also like to thank those who showed the humane and positive side of psychiatry: Piotr Baranowski, Zbyszek de Barbaro, Zbyszek Ćwiklinski, Agata Dimter, Dominika Dudek, Jola Robak and Maryna Rostworowska, who were not only kind enough to help me with my research but also persuaded me to change my anti-psychiatric sentiments. My special thanks to Zbyszek de Barbaro for answering my first e-mail and to Jacek Bomba, the head of the Department of Psychiatry of the Jagiellonian University, for letting a linguist in.

I am indebted to Justyna Ziółkowska, who agreed to talk about men's depression with me, letting me forget about her doctorate for a while.

And to Ola, Michał and Ania, for letting me off.

1
Men, Depression and Discourse Analysis

... where no man can go at all

We, men, are under constant pressure to prove our masculinity. The exploits of the heroes of the popular TV or cinema, together with their divine six-packs, bulging biceps, square jaws and hair in all the right places are quite enough to make you feel green with envy and inadequate. If this were not enough, the good guys, just like us, really, always succeed in whatever they put their minds to. They never crack under pressure, always find this last-minute solution to save the day and are able to get on the high horse and ride into the sunset with a woman of their dreams, who could not only win the Miss Universe competition hands down but has, if need be, an IQ of 250. But the charge *to boldly go where no man has gone before* sometimes appears so very very difficult. For in 'real life' men do crack under pressure, life hurts them, they do feel sad, powerless, helpless. They come up nowhere near to the ideal set by the society of what it is to be a man.

This book is about such men. It is about men who feel and are unable to satisfy the Western requirement that men be active, enterprising, always tough and powerful. I want to write about experiences of men who are powerless and weak, men who somehow cannot 'get a grip' despite just about everybody around expecting them to. This is a book about men in depression. I am interested in exploring what it means for them to have an illness which undermines the very core of what it means to be a man. The overarching argument I shall develop is that the experience of what psychiatry calls depression is intrinsically linked to gender and thus masculinity. There is no depression outside being a man (or woman for that matter). I shall argue that this might have profound consequences both for the psychopathology of depression and its therapy.

1

Proposing that the experience of depression is gendered, I shall focus on two lines of argument. First, I am interested in how men position themselves in relation to their illness. What does it mean to be depressed, how does depression relate to their selves, their biography, their life? Thus, I am interested in the lived version of depression and its experience. Second, I shall explore the relationship between illness experience and masculinity. I am interested in men's positioning with regard to depression, the dominant model of masculinity and their families. What does it mean to be a depressed man, what does depression do to masculinity?

Beforehand, however, I need to clarify my 'starting points', the assumptions I shall be making with reference to four major research issues. Thus in what follows, I shall briefly review the current psychiatric thinking on depression and its experience, and I shall position my considerations in relation to debates on gender and masculinity. I shall then discuss literature on masculinity, health and depression in particular. I shall finish by laying down my approach to discourse analysis, and suggest how it might be useful in the exploration of mental illness.

Depression

As one might expect, there is vast literature on diagnosis, course, prognosis, therapy and aetiology of depression, or, as psychiatry would have it, the depressive episode (coded by the World Health Organisation as F32 for a single episode and F33 for a recurring one), and impossible to review here. A summary of psychiatric thinking on depression is offered by the National Institute of Clinical Excellence (NICE), the United Kingdom's watchdog of clinical practice. NICE (2004) says that depression is a wide spectrum of mental health problems characterised by lack of positive affect, such as lack of enjoyment or interest in ordinary things or experiences. Although the institute does acknowledge that distinguishing between 'normal' sadness and depression remains problematic, it is the additional symptoms that help make the distinction. Importantly, however, the low mood is typically unreactive to circumstance.

This is a narrative summary of the diagnostic criteria offered by the World Health Organisation's International Classification of Diseases (ICD) (WHO, 1993). The ICD constructs depression in terms of three diagnostic criteria, two of which must be present:

1 depressed mood to a degree that is definitely abnormal for the individual, present for most of the day and almost every day, largely uninfluenced by circumstance, and sustained for at least 2 weeks;

2 loss of interest or pleasure in activities that are normally pleasurable;
3 decreased energy or increased fatigability.

Depression is classified into three degrees of intensity. In the mild episode there 'should' be one or more symptoms present from the additional
ones, giving a total number of symptoms of at least four; in the moderate
episode, at least six; in the severe one, at least eight. Those additional
symptoms include loss of confidence, unreasonable feelings of self-
reproach, recurrent thoughts of suicide, excessive or inappropriate guilt,
indecisiveness.

The World Health Organisation states that depression affects 121 million people worldwide, is the fourth leading contributor to the global
burden of disease in 2000 (second for people between the ages of 15
and 44) and is projected to be second by the year 2020 for all ages and
both sexes.[1] Papakostas and associates (2004) add that depression was
shown to account for a 23-fold increase in social disability and 5-fold
increase in short-term work-disability. In 1994, about 51 million Amer-
icans aged 18 years and older were diagnosed with some form of mental
illness of which just under half were 'mood disorders' (especially depression) (LeDoux, 1998). A survey of six European countries reported that
17 per cent of the population had experienced depression in the previous six months (Lepine *et al.*, 1997); yet, Paykel and associates (2005)
give an even higher estimate of 32 per cent for women and 17 per cent
for men. Over a longer duration, 10 per cent of the US population had
experienced major depression in the past year and between 20 and 25
per cent of women and 7 and 12 per cent of men will suffer from clinical
depression in a lifetime (Segal *et al.*, 2002).

Depression as cultural

However, within psychiatry itself there is a significant opposition both
to the psychopathological nosology (see Chapter 2) and to the notions
of depression as a mental disorder. It is quite uncontroversial to say
that psychiatric categories are not natural kinds (e.g. Kirmayer, 2005;
Zachar, 2000; also Cooper, 2004). In other words, they do not refer to
diseases that naturally occur in the world, but they are practical categories which help describe and deal with distress. In this sense the two
main psychiatric diagnostic manuals are public policies (Sadler, 2005b).
Moreover, given the perennial problems with what constitutes normality, the decision whether a condition is a mental disorder is partly a value
judgement (Barilan and Weintraub, 2001; Cooper, 2004; Fulford, 1989),
underpinned by the personal values and expectations of the individual

clinician (Corin, 1996). In addition, the currently dominant biological thinking of depression (i.e. suggesting that depression is caused by a chemical imbalance in the brain, and particularly decreased levels of serotonin) is just one of the options, and, as history of the disease and its various types coming into or out fashion (McPherson and Armstrong, 2006) shows, there is no reason to believe that it is the 'ultimate' in understanding depression.

Yet, the diagnostic criteria which are to capture mental distress in all people in all situations are challenged much further. Much criticism has been made of the progressive loss of lay conceptualisations of distress in favour of biological models (e.g. Fabrega, 1996; Kleinman, 1995, 1988b; Miller, 2005) and lack of inclusion of the patient's perspective (e.g. Mezzich, 1999; Schmolke, 1999), normally coupled with postulates for inclusion of the social sciences in nosological considerations (e.g. Fabrega, 2005; Lewis, 2000).

Jenkins and Kleinman (1991) stress that all psychopathological considerations, including those of threshold and duration of what counts as a disorder, are ultimately grounded in culturally specific and locally defined judgements about what constitutes abnormal behaviour. Pilgrim and Bentall (1999) second this, pointing out that dominant discourses of psychopathology assume mental illness to be trans-historical and trans-cultural, while the clinician operates in an atypical social setting, having a superior epistemological status, as he/she is equipped with the 'warranting voice' (Gergen, 1989) of the dominant discourse. And yet, this clinician must refer to the lay account of distress in order to make his/her judgement, an account which is inherently indeterminate (Jenkins and Kleinman, 1991)!

There are also critiques which challenge the notion of depression itself. This line of criticism is associated particularly with Kleinman (1986; also Kleinman and Good, 1985), whose research undermined depression as a biological condition showing its social origins. Lutz (1985) points out that judgements referring to it are grounded in the wider beliefs, knowledges and attitudes towards emotions which themselves are cultural constructs (on social constructionist approach to emotions; e.g. Harré, 1986; Harré and Parrot, 1996; Harré and Stearns, 1995; Lupton, 1998). It is the insistence that normality involves positive affect which is at the core of the notion of depression, and the lack of the 'pursuit of happiness' is deemed particularly deviant (Lutz, 1985). Moreover, Kleinman (1996) points out that most research on depression is carried out on those in psychiatric treatment – a self-selected minority of people who decided to seek professional help, not necessarily because of sadness.

As cultural and social expectations place different emphases upon different emotional states and their intensities (Manson, 1996; also Falicov, 2003; Schieffelin, 1985), depression, whatever it might be, happens in the social context in which the distressed person is submerged. This might be the macro-context of not only, say, social class (Blair, 1993) or gender roles (Crowe, 2002), but also the particular situation in which he/she is in. People's decisions as to whether they are ill or not are socially situated and based both on considerations of the local context in which they operate and on their expectations of themselves and those that others are perceived to have of them (Radley, 1994; Radley and Billig, 1996). In this view, depression is nowhere near a 'medical condition', but a social condition underpinned by a variety of discourses outside psychiatry (Fee, 2000b) and resulting from complex decision processes happening well before a formal diagnosis can be made (see also Keys, 1985), during which, incidentally, most of this 'personal' aspect of depression will have disappeared (Casey and Long, 2003; Rowe, 1978).

Such debates are an important context in which depression should be seen. Whether biological or not, depression is also social. And even though the men I interviewed were all psychiatrically diagnosed to have a depressive episode, this in fact does not guarantee consistency or even similarity of their experience (see e.g. Kirk and Hsieh, 2004; Kirk and Kutchins, 1988). Yet, I am interested in those experiences that made them seek psychiatric help and which psychiatry calls the depressive episode. Moreover, they all shared the need to seek psychiatric help and had to deal with the problems and stigmas associated with a (particular) psychiatric diagnosis and psychiatric treatment. More importantly, I am going to juxtapose my informants' experiences with the diagnostic pronouncements. I shall show their 'lived translation' into narratives of depression. In this way I shall attempt to juxtapose the discourses of psychiatry with those of lived experience of mental distress.

Gender and masculinity

I have discussed the issues of gender and masculinity in my earlier work (Galasiński, 2004), and here I would like to offer a summary of where I stand with regard to issues of gender and masculinity. Most importantly, I take an anti-essentialist view of gender identity, thinking of it not so much as a fixed state, but, rather, a process of becoming.

Connell (2002, also 2000) proposes that gender is a social structure within which the society handles the human body and it is within such a social structure that people construct themselves as men or women.

Starting from the act of gender endowment – 'It's a boy' – a human subject is put into a regulatory frame within which he performs masculinity (Butler, 1990), or it is performed for him, especially at the beginning of his life (McIlvenny, 2002a). Masculinity is achieved in situated conduct (West and Zimmerman, 1987; see also Cameron, 1997; McIlvenny, 2002b). Changing perspective, Morgan (1992) proposes that masculinity is something that is done (see also Whitehead, 2002); Brittan (1989) adds that masculinities are always local and subject to change (for a review of definitions of masculinity, see Connell, 1995; also Clatterbaugh, 1997).

This is the first understanding of masculinity I subscribe to. It is an accomplishment in the local situation, a gender identity, always provisional, always subject to change (e.g. Barker and Galasiński, 2001; Kerfoot, 2001). The other is related to social representation. Ochs (1992) proposes that masculinity refers to patterns of behaviour that become associated with being male or female (also Edley, 2001; Tannen, 1999). They are social constructs reducing masculinity to biology, or some non-negotiable identity core, underpinned by perceptions of biologically based 'sex categories' (West and Zimmerman, 1987). In other words, these are ideologies of men and masculinity, idealisations which can be aspired to as much by men as by women (Bordo, 1997). In this understanding, masculinity has little to do with the locally constructed masculine identities, even though it might, of course, act as a regulatory frame in which social actors construct themselves. Such ideologies are constructed by both individual and public discourses, with various social and communicative purposes, with various audiences. They are unlikely to be homogenous and without contradictions (e.g. Chapman, 1988; Edwards, 1997; Rutherford, 1988). In this sense, of course, one can speak of a number of masculinities coming into interaction with such social factors as historical location, age and physique, sexual orientation, education, status and lifestyle, geography, ethnicity, religion and beliefs, class and occupation, culture and subculture (Beynon, 2002: 10). But one could also add disability, illness, military service, imprisonment, trauma, political system and probably a number of other, more micro-scale, contexts (Galasiński, 2004).

In my earlier work (Galasiński, 2004), I rejected the notion of masculinity as a set of practices, social (Barrett, 2001; Pujolar, 2000; Walker, 1994; Whitehead and Barrett, 2001a) or linguistic (Coates, 1997, 1999; Lakoff, 1973; Mulac *et al.*, 2001; Tannen, 1998; for critique, see Talbot *et al.*, 2003). There is no need to repeat the argument here, so let me just say that as analysts, we shall be able to observe certain patterns in social or linguistic behaviour, constructions of identities and the like.

Men do make use of such discourses, practices which they associate with masculinity – this is indeed why we normally would expect men to be dressed in particular clothes, in a particular way. My argument, however, is that while people speak 'the way one speaks', that people dress 'the way one dresses', it does not mean that such practices are linked to masculinity in some sort of essential way.

To sum up, I view masculinity in two dimensions. On the one hand, it is to do with the locally negotiated identities, always provisional, always in a state of flux. It is men's performance of being a man, always done anew, always in a particular local context. Unless they are playing, I think women cannot perform masculinity in this sense, inasmuch as men cannot perform femininity. On the other hand, masculinity is a social construct, a gender ideology, a society's way of associating certain practices with gender. Here masculinity can be seen as a configuration of social practices, but these practices are not there to be read off what men say or do, they are mediated by the society's ideological constructs.

Men and health

There is a consensus in the literature on health and gender that in the developed world men do not fare very well with regard to their health. They not only die significantly younger than women, but more men die of the leading causes of death than women; they also commit considerably more suicides (Cochran and Rabinowitz, 2000). Men are considerably more likely to engage in risk-taking behaviours (Bennett and Bauman, 2000; Fong *et al.*, 2001) and are less likely to report illness (Addis and Mahalik, 2003; Galdas *et al.*, 2005), both facts having significant impact upon their health outcomes. Verbrugge (1989) points out that while women's morbidity tends to be limited to less serious conditions, men have higher prevalence of such fatal conditions as heart disease or arteriosclerosis. Needless to say, men perceive their health as good also more frequently than women (Hearn and Kolga, 2006).

The statistics offered in the literature are quite frightening, if you are a man. A few facts given by Courtenay (2000) make the point forcefully. He states that men in the United States not only suffer from more severe chronic conditions, but they have higher death rates for all 15 leading causes of death. Men's age-adjusted death rate for heart disease is twice higher than women's, with 75 per cent of those dying of the disease before the age of 65 being men. Men account for higher incidence of seven out of ten most common infectious diseases. In addition, men receive significantly less time from their doctors than women and are provided with briefer explanations (Weisman and Teitelbaum, 1989); they also receive less advice (Friedman *et al.*, 1994). Roter and Hall (1997) have stated that it has never been found that women receive less information from their doctors than men. This can be juxtaposed with findings that men's use of health services is perceived within the dominant discourses of masculinity, with women constructed as responsible for men's health (Lyons and Willott, 1999; Seymour-Smith *et al.*, 2002).

The Gender Equity Project report (Men's Health Forum, 2006) in the United Kingdom says that men are significantly more likely to be overweight and consequently suffer from co-morbidities of overweight and obesity. They are also twice as likely as women to die from the ten most common cancers affecting both sexes. Also in childhood boys do not fare very well (with some evidence that higher men's mortality starts prenatally, Bräher and Maier, 2001). Sixty per cent of all sudden deaths in the United Kingdom occur in boys. Boys are twice as likely to be killed in pedestrian accidents (Men's Health Forum, 2006).

Although the Social Focus on Men report (Mill *et al.*, 2001) proposes that British men's mental health is better than women's, the United Kingdom's Commission for Healthcare Audit and Inspection report, *Count Me In* (2007), shows that significantly more men are admitted to hospitals than women (5:4 ratio), with the ratio rising to approximately 4:1 when referrals via criminal justice routes are considered. About twice as many men as women were noted with learning disabilities (ibid.). While it is frequently recognised that men's health is under-researched (e.g. Hearn and Kolga, 2006), especially in its social aspect (Lee and Owens, 2002), men's mental health is lagging even further behind (Robbins, 2004). Indeed, notably, a recent overview of men's health (Sabo, 2005; see also Connell, 2000) does not discuss men's mental health problems. Still, Singleton and her associates (2000) show that although more women in the United Kingdom suffer from neurotic disorders (including anxiety, depressive, obsessive-compulsive and panic disorders), more men are diagnosed with personality disorders, substance abuse and psychotic disorders. It must be noted, however, that men are regarded as consistently underreporting psychosocial problems (Möller-Leimkühler, 2002; O'Brien *et al.*, 2005). Almost twice as many mentally ill men as women (28 per cent compared with 15 per cent women) were classified as enduring severe lack of social support (O'Brien *et al.*, 2002).

More generally, Pilgrim and Rogers (1999) comment that while female mental health problems are likely to be treated by 'soft' psychiatry, those of men are treated by its 'harsh' end. They also point out (Rogers and Pilgrim, 2003) that there are very few discussions focusing specifically upon men's mental health, while the focus upon female mental health results in underestimating both the content and prevalence of psychiatric problems in men.

Even though this state of affairs is recognised as in need of much more research (Galdas *et al.*, 2005), mostly it is explained by the dominant ideology of masculinity in which males are socialised. As New (2001) argues persuasively, men can be victims of the very gender order that gives them privilege (see also Emslie, 2005; Sabo and Gordon, 1995). The stereotype of the tough male who does not succumb to difficulties, including those of his health, is thought to prevent men from accessing health services (White, 2001). Indeed, there is consensus in the literature on masculinity that it is socially linked to action and particularly to employment (Willis, 2000; Willott and Griffin, 1996, 1997; also Hood, 1993; Mattinson, 1988). Illness cannot and does not feature in such a model and a healthy male identity equals a strong one (Riska, 2004). Indeed, Pollack (1998) reports that men are more likely to deny depression as they fear it would jeopardise their self-image. In a nutshell, there is some consensus that at least part of men's price for their more powerful position in the society is their poor health (also Courtenay, 2000; Rosenfeld and Faircloth, 2006), with medical services reinforcing the model and demedicalising male behaviour (Riska, 2002, 2004). Evidence from research into men's experiences of illness suggests that at least some illnesses are seen as challenging masculinity. And while it might be expected in the case of impotence (Oliffe, 2005), testicular cancer (Gurevich *et al.*, 2004) or prostate cancer (Chapple and Ziebland, 2002; Oliffe, 2006), it is perhaps less obvious in the case of depression, which is often experienced as unmasculine (e.g. Brownhill *et al.*, 2005; Warren, 1983; see also below). Indeed, Levant (1996) proposes that a new framework for a psychological approach to men should question the traditional norms of the male role (also Miller and Bell, 1996; White, 2002).

Both research and medical practice still face the problem of men's invisibility. There is of course significant literature recognising men as gendered subjects with regard to health (e.g. Courtenay and Keeling, 2001; Hearn and Pringle, 2006b); yet, recognising men as partaking of gender structures is still more a postulate rather than a fact taken for granted (e.g. Gutmann, 1997; Schofield *et al.*, 2000). Moreover, Annandale and Clark (1996) argue that by subscribing to the cultural notions of men's strength, researchers and other health professionals contributed to the 'invisibility' of men's poor health. Nicholson and associates (1999) showed that clinicians felt more confident in their information about mothers rather than fathers; men's emotional distress after pregnancy loss was reported to be ignored (McCreight, 2004). Szymczak and Conrad (2006) demonstrate how age and disengagement from traditional masculine roles contributed to older men's concerns being ignored. This view of men and masculinity is exacerbated by the common (but questionable, see Galasiński, 2004) assumption that men are unable to speak of their experiences (Pinnock *et al.*, 1998) and particularly their emotions (Grossman and Wood, 1993; Heesacker *et al.*, 1999). Indeed, there is a sizeable literature which takes the alleged men's lack of emotionality at the level of mere assumption (e.g. Clare, 2001; Horrocks, 1994; Middleton, 1992; Seidler, 1994). Some researchers choose to medicalise the alleged male inability to be in touch with their emotions and talk about men in terms of 'alexithymia' (e.g. Honkalampi *et al.*, 2000; Levant, 1998).

Men and depression

Although it is commonly stated that incidence of depression in women is up to twice as high as in men (for British data, see Mill *et al.*, 2001; for discussion of US and international data, see Cochran and Rabinowitz, 2000; see also Singleton *et al.*, 2001), Rogers and Pilgrim (2003) remind us that the picture is different when gender categories are unpicked. Unmarried men, for example, are over-represented in the prevalence of depression (ibid.). There is also consensus that depression in men is often undiagnosed and untreated (although some researchers point out that it might concern depression in general, Higgs, 1999). Pollack (1998) states that 65 per cent of verified depression in men was undetected and undiagnosed (also Aneshensel *et al.*, 1987; Angst and Dobler-Mikola, 1984; Potts *et al.*, 1991). Moreover, while Real (1998) says that the rise in depression rates is greater amongst men, it is accepted that male drug and alcohol abuse, gambling, sex addiction and so forth can be understood as forms of behaviour that act as a defence against overt depression (Busfield, 1996; Giddens, 1991; Real, 1998).

Finally, if depression underlies more than half of suicides (Möller-Leimkühler, 2003), men's significantly higher suicide rate might also be a factor in the lower prevalence of depression among men (e.g. Johnstone, 2000; Rogers and Pilgrim, 2003). Thus in the United States, three out of every four suicides are committed by white men (Moscicki, 1997), with older men (over 75) committing 15 times more suicides than women of the same age (Kennedy *et al.*, 1995). Although, at various rates (in the United Kingdom 'only' three times as many men commit suicides than women; ONS, 2007), men commit more suicides in practically all countries (Hawton, 2000). In view of such data, one must see claims that the lower prevalence of depression in men has something to do with men having fewer 'real-life problems' with astonishment (for a critical discussion, see Prior, 1999).

Despite that, calls for gender-sensitive assessment of depression (Cochran, 2006; Cochran and Rabinowitz, 2003; Kilmartin, 2005) are largely unheeded. For the most part, the existing literature takes up men's depression in studies of gender differences in which gender is mostly associated with biological sex, one of the demographics which informants are asked to provide. Depending on one's stance, one can find both literature arguing that men's and women's depression does differ from each other (e.g. Hänninen and Aro, 1996; Möller-Leimkühler *et al.*, 2004; Rutz *et al.*, 1997; Winkler *et al.*, 2004; also Pollack, 1988; for review, see Winkler *et al.*, 2005) or that it does not (e.g. Klose and Jacobi, 2004; Nolen-Hoeksema, 2001; Vedel Keesing, 2005). It must be said, however, that the studies do not necessarily have to be mutually exclusive, as researchers focus on core or other symptoms, or simply focus on gender differences in filling out particular instruments (e.g. Hammen and Padesky, 1977; Steer *et al.*, 1989).

More generally, there is a tendency within social and critical approaches to psychiatry and mental illness (e.g. Busfield, 1996; Johnstone, 2000) and depression in particular (e.g. Stoppard, 2000; Stoppard and McMullen, 2003), as well as in more mainstream psychological and psychiatric work on depression (e.g. Brown and Harris, 1978; Kennedy *et al.*, 2004), to focus (explicitly or implicitly) upon women's mental health problems. In fact, I am aware of only one academic book-length monograph devoted to men's depression (Cochran and Rabinowitz, 2000).

Experience of depression

When I was reviewing the literature on depression, I was struck by its vastness, yet I was even more surprised by how minuscule within it is the literature on the experience of the illness. It is quite notable that a series of *Handbooks of Depression*, edited by various scholars, do not take up the issue of the patient perspective or their experience (see e.g. Beckham and Leber, 1995; Gotlib and Hammen, 2002; Kasper *et al.*, 2003; Paykel, 1992; Power, 2004). Depression in such literature is represented as sets of features attributed to people, as if they were their more or less inherent faculties which can be measured by a myriad of psychiatric instruments. So, depressed people are characterised by a number of social and emotional dysfunctions (Rottenberg and Gotlib, 2004); vulnerability (Teasdale and Dent, 1987; Zuroff *et al.*, 2004); antithetical interpersonal scripts (Demorest *et al.*, 1999); low physical, role and emotional functioning (Stewart *et al.*, 1989); and long-lasting deficits in psychosocial functioning (Hays *et al.*, 1995). Even lay theories of depression can be measured (Furnham and Kuyken, 1991), while various scales can be compared and assessed (Faravelli *et al.*, 1986).

To put it radically, I do not think psychiatric instruments offer much more than insight into how people fill them in. They offer very little, if any at all, insight into the illness and its experience (also Galasiński, 2008; Nicolson, 1995; Stoppard, 2000). Indeed, Coyne and Gotlib (1983) point out that there is little evidence that what depressed people think has anything to do with how they are portrayed to think on standardised instruments. Such research also ignores the fact that it is the diagnosis itself which can cause significant emotional disturbance which can, in fact, be of greater importance than the symptoms which the instruments are claimed to measure (Kilian and Angermeyer, 1999; Lester and Tritter, 2005; Sayre, 2000).

Indeed, Karp (1996) criticises the existing research on depression for silencing the voices of those in depression, even though, as Stoppard (2000) posits, the knowledge about depression is ultimately held by the people suffering from it. Burr and Chapman (2004) also make this point by showing that South Asian women negotiated their symptoms of depression in ways which allowed them better access to health care. Pollock (2007), on the other hand, demonstrates how accounts of depression were negotiated with the need to maintain face and privacy.

Now, such arguments demonstrate an acute need for research offering in-depth insight into experiences of depression as part of a larger narrative of life experiences, situating depression in its lived context with the foci and relevancies as they appear to those who tell the story, rather than driven by a diagnostic schedule or criteria. Thus, McMullen and Stoppard (2003) show that social and economic circumstances were a significant aspect of how women in depression experienced their illness. Depression could not be seen outside everyday life – financial difficulties, unemployment, relationships and lots of other considerations people in depression, just like the rest of us, face on a daily basis (also McMullen and Stoppard, 2006; Sundquist *et al.*, 2004). The two researchers add that focusing on the socio-economic conditions of women's lives has the potential of preventing depression (McMullen and Stoppard, 2003). I shall demonstrate in this book that the argument could easily be extended onto men's lives.

Incidentally, if doctors are reported to medicalise depression (Thomas-McLean and Stoppard, 2004), and, on the other hand, patients attribute quality of care to doctor–patient communication (Gask *et al.*, 2003), it seems that exploring the 'stories of depression' with their own relevancies can be seen as directly relevant to improving the care depressed patients receive. Similarly, a study by Rogers and her associates (2001), showing that depression is experienced (both by patients and doctors) as too large and complex to square into the primary health care system, demonstrates the need to account for the experience of depression outside the medical and medicalising model.

The largest number of studies in what little has been written on experiences of depression concerns women. In addition to feelings of aloneness and isolation (Scattolon, 2003) and the discourses of the flawed self (McMullen, 2003), researchers report attempts to 'normalise' depression. Depressed women prefer not to see themselves as mentally ill, likening depression to physical illness (Stoppard and Gammell, 2003), or see it as a result of 'normal' life stress (Scattolon, 2003; also Kangas, 2001). Yet, Stoppard (1997) writes that women's accounts are also ridden with uncertainty as to what is happening to them and why, adding that they reflect experts' medicalised formulations of depression and thus raising questions as to the status of such narratives. The important aspect of such research is that depression is shown as narrated in the social context of its experiences by women who are afforded certain subject positions from which they can offer their narratives (Crowe, 2002).

In his study, Karp (1996) shows, among others, constructions of depression as having a life on its own (see also Chapter 3) as well its impact upon the identities of those suffering, forcing redefinitions of the self, as the illness progresses from what he calls 'inchoate feelings', through acceptance of a problem and a crisis, to the stage of coming to grips with the illness.

I have found three studies explicitly exploring men's experiences of depression (Brownhill *et al.*, 2005; Emslie *et al.*, 2006; Heifner, 1987; but see Smith's (1999) account his own experience of depression). The researchers agree that depression is seen by depressed men in terms of the dominant model of masculinity and the men's non-conformance with it. Strength, control and independence were all values which the interviewed men strived for. Depression is not so much seen in medicalised terms, but, rather, at the backdrop of what Connell (1995) called 'hegemonic masculinity'. This book takes this research further. While I shall confirm this overall finding, I shall also argue for a more nuanced understanding of men's experiences of depression, offering at times alternative interpretations, arguing that it might not always be useful to see the speaking subject in terms of gender.

Moreover, the major shortcoming of this research is that it focuses predominantly upon the content of what is said by the informants. Although I have no doubt that it provides useful and interesting insights into men's experiences of depression, the research overlooks an important aspect of depression narratives: its lexico-grammatical form. This book aims to redress it. The discourse analytic approach I am taking here offers insight both into *what* my informants said and crucially, into *how* they said it. Discourse analysis is a powerful tool in understanding how people engage with and construct reality, including their own experiences. It also provides insight into how they construct their identities in relation to both the social environment in which they find themselves and how they experience it and themselves in it.

Discourse analysis

This book is about how people talk and the discursive resources they avail themselves of. I am interested in how they narrate their illness, themselves in their illness, their lives and those close to them. I assume that all those experiences are predominantly discursive. Following Bauman (1986), it is not the world which is the material of the narrative; rather, it is the narrative from which the world is abstracted. In what follows, I am going to offer a brief account of a model of discourse analysis with which I have sympathy (for a much more comprehensive discussion, see Barker and Galasiński, 2001). The review I offer here is based upon the earlier one, although some accents have changed.

I situate my analyses in a constructionist approach to discourse, and within its critical strand. Thus I draw upon a tradition in discourse analysis which is an amalgamation of a number of approaches, including critical linguistics (Fowler, 1991; Fowler *et al.*, 1979; Hodge and Kress, 1993), social semiotics (Hodge and Kress, 1988; Kress and van Leeuwen, 1996), sociocultural change and change in discourse (Fairclough, 1989, 1992, 1995, 2003) and socio-cognitive studies (e.g. van Dijk, 1993, 1998). Linguistically, it is anchored within systemic-functional linguistics (e.g. Halliday, 1994, 1978; Halliday and Hasan, 1985), which complements the analyst's self-reflexivity (Wodak, 1999) and can help reduce the arbitrariness of interpretation by anchoring it in the linguistic form itself.

I take a textually oriented approach (Fairclough, 1992). Thus, I focus upon the content and the form of stretches of discourse, with an interest in both the semantics and syntax of an utterance, as well as the functions of what is said within the local context, and the social actions thus accomplished. I understand discourse as a form of social practice within a sociocultural context. Language users are not isolated individuals, but they are engaged in communicative activities as members of social groups, organisations, institutions and cultures. To a considerable extent they speak the way one speaks, the way it is appropriate (in many senses of this word) to speak. I am therefore interested in discovering the 'discourses of depression', the ways in which the experience of a particular disease is made social through the process of narrating it.

The following assumptions I make about discourse are relevant here.

1. Discourse is socially constitutive. It enters into a 'dialectical' relationship with the contexts in which it occurs; so, as much as it depends on its context, it also creates social and political 'realities' (Fairclough and Wodak, 1997; van Leeuwen and Wodak, 1999). One does not have to refer to the notorious case of homosexuality as a former mental disease (Kutchins and Kirk [1999] tell an extraordinary story of how it was demedicalised) in order to argue that such 'traditional' diseases as schizophrenia or anorexia came to existence only after they were created by the dominant discourses of modern psychiatry. Although it has a much longer history (Radden, 2000), the modern understanding of depression does not exist outside discourse. For if the next editions of, say, the International Classification of Diseases contain a different set of criteria for diagnosing the disease, it will simply change. This kind of analysis I shall employ predominantly in Chapter 2, where I shall be analysing dominant psychiatric discourses of depression.

2. Discourse is a system of options from which language users make their choices. The construction of any representation of 'reality' is necessarily selective, entailing decisions as to which aspects of that reality to include and how to arrange them. Each selection carries its share of socially ingrained values so that representation is socially constructed (Hall, 1997; Hodge and Kress, 1993) and alternative representations are not only always possible, but they carry divergent significance and consequences (Fowler, 1996). Nevertheless, texts seek to impose a 'preferred reading' (Hall, 1981) or a 'structure of faith' (Menz, 1989) upon the addressee.

What is important to note is that optionality of discourse refers both to the linguistic form (the notorious 'terrorist' vs. 'freedom fighter' opposition), and also to the content of what is being communicated. As more and more social scientists claim to analyse 'discourse', linguistic discourse analysis tends to focus more upon the form of discourse. Yet, content is an important aspect of our analyses and it should not be thought of as marginal. Thus, in addition to the analysis of the form of what my informants said, I shall also be using a hermeneutic-like interpretation of discourses in terms of the context in which they were submerged (see Titscher *et al.*, 2000). It is particularly in this perspective that I shall discuss how my informants constructed, more or less explicitly, their masculinity or their relationships.

3. Discourse is ideological. The selective character of representation leads to the view that it is through discourse and other semiotic practices that ideologies are formulated, reproduced and reinforced. I understand the term ideology as social (general and abstract) representations shared by members of a group and used by them to accomplish everyday social practices: acting and communicating (Billig *et al.*, 1988; Fowler, 1985; van Dijk, 1998). These representations are organised into systems which are deployed by social classes and other groups 'in order to make sense of, figure out and render intelligible the way society works' (Hall, 1996: 26), while at the same time they are capable of 'ironing out' the contradictions, dilemmas and antagonisms of practices in ways which accord with the interests and projects of power (Chouliaraki and Fairclough, 1999). And it is with the ideological nature of discourse in mind that I shall be particularly interested in how my informants constructed both depression itself and their selves in relation to the illness. The argument of the dominant model of masculinity which underpins what my informants said will be made within this perspective.

4. Finally, I assume that text – the product of what one says or writes – is intertextual. Texts are full of other texts, accessing them for stylistic, ironic effect or for ideological message. Intertextuality can be intentional, but it also can be unwitting, which suggests that certain texts have a dominant role in how certain contents or experiences are constructed. Here I shall be looking for evidence that the narratives of my informants draw upon certain texts or formulations, particularly in their accounts of illness. Particularly then, I shall be interested in evidence of medicalisation, the dominance of the medical view of reality over a lay one (e.g. Ballard and Elston, 2005).

What I shall not be interested to find, however, is a 'language of depression' in the sense of trying to find some linguistic or discursive markers of the illness. I reject the analyses such as that of Fine (2006), who claims to find characteristics of depression in language. It is practically impossible to make an assessment as to, say, how much or how fast people should speak in order to make a claim that in depression these faculties are decreased. It is also quite difficult to make definitive claims as to what affect in language is supposed to look like in depression or outside it, with negative thoughts in language being just about unassessable.

Discourse, mental illness and qualitative research

The final element of the background I am laying out here is my view of the relationship between mental illness and discourse analysis. In her Foucauldian analysis of the *Diagnostic and Statistical Manual of Mental Disorders* (DSM) of the American Psychiatric Association (APA), Crowe (2000) suggests that the *Manual* is not so much based on the concept of mental disorder, but, rather, on the implicit assumptions of what constitutes normal behaviour. This 'normality' underpinning the DSM is not only very much Western, but in some cases underpinned by the neo-liberal ideology. Parker and his associates (1995) in turn point out the non-transparency of psychiatric terminology introduced by the DSM as a vehicle of not only constructing disorders, but also providing an emotional and evaluative frame which is imposed upon the person who is labelled with it. In the same vein, Hepworth (1999) challenges the assumptions made by women in psychiatric discourses of anorexia nervosa, while Heinimaa (2000) unpicks the notions of 'self' and 'person' in psychiatric discourses, showing the ambiguities in their use.

Such general critiques are complemented by a number of discourse analytic studies taking up issues of psychotherapeutic and psychiatric practices, such as interviews, diagnosis, note taking. In one of the fullest studies of psychiatric practices, Barrett (1996), a psychiatrist and anthropologist, reports on his ethnographic study of a hospital ward caring for patients diagnosed with schizophrenia. Barrett shows, among other things, how the patient's experience is made irrelevant within the medical frame imposed upon it by such events as the diagnostic interview or the patient's notes (see also Mohr, 1999). Guilfoyle (2001) shows the relationship of power in the psychotherapeutic situation as imposing subjectivities on patients diagnosed with bulimia. Finally, such analyses lead to more positive studies of psychiatric discourses, showing the potential usefulness of discourse analysis in mental health research and practice. Harper (1995, 1998) posits that discourse analysis opens opportunities of negotiability of positions in psychiatric contexts, sensitising clinicians to the possibility of imposing 'illness identities' (also Coyle and Pugh, 1998), while Crowe and Alavi (1999) argue that accepting a patient's account of illness re-establishes his/her participation in the community of others (see also Speed, 2006).

It is the analysis of illness experiences with which I shall be mostly concerned in my argument here. As a thorough discussion of the nature of experience is well outside the scope of this book, I assume here that discourse is a primary platform on which experiences are structured, and expressed. Discourse analysis is therefore a primary and main probe into people's experiences. It is even more so in the case of mental illness.

Focusing upon patients' experience of illness is a response to repeated calls from researchers, both within medicine and in the social sciences, for the inclusion of the subjective into psychopathology (e.g. Haidet and Paterniti, 2003; Kleinman, 1988a; Shaw, 2002) as well as its validity as source of knowledge about illness (Beresford, 2005; Prior, 2003). Moreover, discourse analysis and its focus upon lived experiences of (mental) illness brings the recognition of the fact that there is no one rigid illness narrative, but that they fluctuate depending on the context in which they are told (Hardin, 2003), the aim with which they are told, varying from, say, constructing an illness experience and making it understandable to reconstructing life history (Hyden, 1997; also Frank, 1995; Skultans, 2000). Discourse analysis attempts to gain insight into the experience of mental illness in its high complexity.

Furthermore, if health can be seen as a narrative register (Roberts, 2004), it is precisely through the focus upon individual accounts that one can trace the process of creation of health identities (Fox and Ward, 2006; Frank, 2006), understand illness as suffering (Monks, 2000; Morse, 2001) and, more generally, understand the process of giving shape to the experience of illness (Good, 1994; Mattingly, 1998). As Bury (2001) suggests, an illness narrative offers a lived link between the body, the self and the society in which it is anchored, making only certain worlds more plausible than others (Plummer, 1995). Indeed, Fredriksson and Lindström (2002) report that allowing psychiatric patients to narrate freely results in different plot structures, ones which not only reveal but also might hide suffering. Finally, it is people's accounts that enable researchers to see how mental health patients make sense not only of their madness (Casey and Long, 2002, 2003) but also of the therapy and the healing process (Burr and Butt, 2000). Launer (1999) goes further, suggesting that a narrative-based practice enables both sides to agree on a story that makes sense both to the patient and to the doctor. Greenlagh and Hurwitz (1998) add that narratives not only set a patient-centred agenda, but they are also likely to challenge the institutionally valid knowledge (also Gwyn, 2002). Ingleby (2006) makes the point that the qualitative focus upon illness experience has the advantage of looking at people as active actors who actively interpret their experiences.

Indeed, Crowe (2002) and Stoppard (2000), referring to women's depression, and Hepworth (1999), commenting on anorexia nervosa, show discourse analysis as a powerful instrument in examining experiences of illness and psychiatric services. According to the studies by Van Staden (2002), as well as by Crowe and Luty (2005), Levitt *et al.* (2000) or Ridge and Ziebland (2006), on depression, and by Rudge and Morse (2001) on schizophrenia, discourse analysis can also be useful in the assessment of patients' recovery. And while Lysaker and his associates (2003) propose that it is narrative transformation which can be seen as an outcome in schizophrenia (see also an interesting transformulation of cognitive-behavioural therapy in discourse analytic terms done by Drew *et al.*, 1999), Davidson (2003) argues not only that recovery should not be seen in terms of reduction of symptoms (also Kirmayer, 2005), but, rather, that it should be negotiated by the patient's life narrative (also Svenaeus, 2000).

That does not mean of course that narrative research is the panacea to all problems of mental health research. Patients are not transparent actors who simply tell it like it is, whether to the doctor or the researcher. Chatwin (2006) points out that patients can self-censor, limiting themselves to elements directly relevant to their complaints; Charmaz (2002) notes that a narrative can be used to mask suffering. Moreover, Pilgrim and Rogers (1997) remind that mental health problems are not merely constructions and do have physiological aspects. Yet, my aim here is to shed some light on a crucial aspect of what it means to be mentally ill, the subjective experience of the illness, an aspect which is still significantly under-researched, yet one which constitutes the ultimate context for whatever psychopathological research claims of mental disorders.

Finally, throughout this book I predominantly use the word 'illness', rather than 'disease' (on the distinction, see Kleinman, 1988b). This is because I am mostly concerned with men's experiences of depression, rather than with how depression is described and conceptualised within the discourses of psychiatry or psychology.

The interviewees

This book is based upon a convenience sample of 27 semi-structured interviews I carried out with men diagnosed with the recurring depressive episode of mild or moderate severity (ICD F33.1-2; although two were diagnosed with bipolar affective disorder F31, both in the depressive phase at the time of the interview). At the time of the interview, all interviewees were undergoing voluntary psychiatric treatment for depression either in an out-patient clinic or in day-care centres (spending only mornings and early afternoons on the ward) where they were interviewed. I carried out my research in two university hospitals in Poland; all interviews were in Polish.

As it happened, all my interviewees were white, Polish, heterosexual, between the ages of 30 and 60. All were or had been (three were divorced) in stable relationships with female partners (usually, wives). There is no doubt that these characteristics of the sample have had an impact upon the kind of data I collected. Two points can be made, though. First, logistic, the practicalities of my research were such that I collected my interviews over the period of over one year (with six weeks of actually working as an intern in one of the hospitals). Although only two men declined to be interviewed, I managed to collect only 27 interviews. During my internship, coming to work every day and passing through an out-patient affective disorders clinic, I realised very quickly that the vast majority of patients are women and there are simply extremely few men who seek psychiatric help for depression. Given such conditions, it is extremely difficult to diversify the sample. Second is an academic one. With hindsight I am pleased with a very coherent sample of interviewees, which translated into the data which were very amenable to analysis. My informants offered insights into how men who espouse the dominant model of masculinity do actually relate to it. The tightness of the sample might also suggest that I have been able to talk to those men who most frequently seek help. But I do realise that I am not focusing upon gay men, single men or perhaps those who do not seek help and struggle with their depressions at home. The experiences of these groups of men still require researchers' attention.

The interviews I carried out concerned mostly experiences of depression, but also the men's relationships as well as their views on the illness, masculinity and recovery. Apart from two interviews (they were with the two least-educated men of the sample) which were shorter, all interviews lasted for about an hour. After recording them, all were transcribed, while the extracts I analyse here were translated into English.

The book's projects

Writing about men and mental illness is political. Inevitably, it raises issues of power, patriarchy or gender relations. This is why I want to make my political projects in the book explicit. The need to do so struck me when I was reading Cochran and Rabinowitz's *Men and Depression*. Towards the end of the preface, they express hope that their book would not be seen as politically provocative, noting their debt to researchers and clinicians exploring women's depression and insisting that men's depression is worth our attention. I found this statement extraordinary, yet I recalled my own experience of presenting a paper on men's emotionality a few years ago. The discussion was quite brief and consisted of one statement. A well-known scholar declared that men's emotionality might be important, but what is really important is to explore women's emotionality.

The first aspect of my political project is to restate the importance of research into men and masculinity, even those white, heterosexual and middle-aged. It is as important as that exploring women and femininity. I do accept that such men used to be the 'human universal' in research, yet, thankfully, we do know better now, also because it worked against the men themselves. There are plenty of issues relating to us white, heterosexual, middle-aged men (incidentally there are plenty of other adjectives that could be added here) that are not only interesting, but also important both to us and to the society. Our depression is one of them.

The second part of my political project is to reinforce Johnson's (1997) rejection of man as the all-purpose universal oppressor. Although many are, not all men are oppressors. There are also considerable numbers of men who are oppressed and vulnerable (also New, 2001; Taylor, 2006). Some are both, some are only oppressed. This book is about men who are oppressed, vulnerable, who are at their most powerless. They are also mentally ill, which in itself puts them on the margins of the society, and I hope to give them voice, or at least some voice. I want to reinforce the message that inequality, strife, vulnerability, marginality or powerlessness applies also to men. And given the dominant model of masculinity, it might be even more difficult for them to accept that.

Finally, even though this book is critical of psychiatry, I want to be taken as its critical friend. This book is not intended as yet another attack on psychiatry and its nosology. My argument is not meant to be anti-psychiatric. I believe that psychiatry is the most useful discourse of mental illness, useful also for those in distress. This does not mean that it cannot improve and learn from those who would like to enter into a dialogue with it. This dialogue, even though occasionally already in existence, on a larger scale is long overdue (Fee, 2000a).

The book is also a personal project. When I embarked on the research underpinning this book, I took up an internship in a psychiatric hospital. I wanted to see psychiatry from inside. Daily, I met people who were willing to share their misery, suffering, pain with me. The conversations and the interviews were sometimes more difficult for me than for them, yet I appreciate their willingness to help me write my book very much. All who agreed to be interviewed expressly hoped that what they had to say would help understand depression better and help others like them in coping with it. I do hope I shall do justice to their expectations.

Overview of the book

This book consists of three parts. Part 1 (Chapters 2 and 3) takes up the issue of depression. While in Chapter 2 it is explored as a construct of dominant psychiatric discourses, in Chapter 3 I discuss how my informants constructed it in their narratives. In Part 2, I am interested in how the self partakes of the experience of depression. Thus, in Chapter 4, I focus on how depression is attributed to the self, demonstrating that the relationship is never easy. The self is never explicitly constructed in terms of depression, but, rather, a number of distancing strategies are used. In Chapter 5 I look at the accounts of everyday life in my corpus. Contrary to my expectations, the informants' narratives focused on actions, rather than on their psychological states. In Chapter 6 I explore my informants' biographies. Once again, contrary to what I expected, depression is not a 'disruption' in the biographies of the men I interviewed; rather, it is a milestone, on a par with others. Chapter 7, the final in Part 2, takes up the constructions of the 'timeless self' my informants used to account for their depression, showing it as inevitable, rather incidental in their lives.

Part 3 of the book is concerned with issues of masculinity in the narratives I collected. Chapter 8 explores the relationship between depression and masculinity and discusses the challenge the illness poses for my informants' gender identity. In Chapter 9, in turn, I take up depression's relationship to work, a crucial aspect of the dominant gender ideology, demonstrating that work is seen as a crucial aspect of recovery. Chapter 10, finally, shows the difficult relationships my interviewees have with their families, for the most part feeling rejected by them. The concluding chapter both takes stock and shows the significance of discourse analytic research into the experience of mental illness for psychiatry. I also suggest extensions of the argument onto issues of insight as well as suffering.

2
Discourses of Depression

Introduction

In the previous chapter I introduced the dominant understanding of depression and its critiques. Yet, I have seen psychiatric discourses as mostly 'transparent' (even though subject to critique), as merely carrying information about a disorder which is 'out there' to be viewed, diagnosed and treated. In this chapter I explore depression as a discursive construct. Taking on board two instances of mainstream psychiatric discourse, I shall analyse how they construct the illness. I shall then consider how both these findings impinge upon the discourses I collected in my research, both in terms of their viability in institutional context and in terms of their own form.

Discourses of psychiatry

I am interested in how the diagnostic criteria of the depressive episode are stipulated by the current (10th) version of the World Health Organisation's *ICD-10 Classification of Mental and Behavioural Disorders: Diagnostic Criteria for Research* in its original English version and in its Polish translation (WHO, 1998). I shall then look at the Beck Depression Inventory (BDI), one of the most commonly used self-assessment tests for diagnosing the severity of depression.

The two documents operate at different levels. The ICD-10 is intended for a global audience and is the 'ultimate' guideline for how to diagnose depression (rivalled in range only by the American Psychiatric Association's *Diagnostic and Statistical Manual of Mental Disorders*, currently in its fourth edition). The BDI, on the other hand, is intended as an elicitation device, in a particular local context. They both present an institutional view of depression. The former is a description of what depression is and what it should be seen as, and in that sense it is direct-ive, not only descriptive. It is meant to be *the* epiphany of the 'current thinking' on depression. The latter is designed to be a text which facilit-ates the clinician in assessing the severity of depression, through which he/she can harvest the symptoms and assess their severity. It is supposed to be a transparent conduit between what the patient feels or experiences and the psychiatrist.

But as much as this is what the texts are supposed to do, linguistic-ally, things are considerably more complicated. The ideological potential of discourse applies also to such texts which are culturally expected to be neutral. Textbooks (e.g. Apple and Christian-Smith, 1991), laws (e.g. Gibbons, 1994), diagnostic manuals (Crowe, 2000) and questionnaires (see below) are all known to represent reality from a particular ideology-laden point of view. All these texts are guided by the 'interest' (see Kress and van Leeuwen, 1996) of the sign-maker. Their authors make selections as to what they see as the criterial aspects of the represented objects along-side with and in addition to the choices which are to reflect the overall intellectual ideologies underpinning, in the case of the ICD and the Beck Inventory, psychiatry and its research.

Diagnostic manuals

There are two international diagnostic manuals used commonly by the international mental health community: the *ICD-10 Classification of Mental and Behavioural Disorders* prepared and published by the World Health Organisation and the *Diagnostic and Statistical Manual of Mental Disorders*, prepared and published by the American Psychiatric Associ-ation. As I said above, they are far from merely classification catalogues. As the clinical part of the ICD-10 stipulates (WHO, 1992), it was designed for clinical and educational use by psychiatrists and other mental health professionals.

There is much literature on the status, kinds, uses and forms of classi-fication of mental disorders. Needless to say, the evaluations of the two manuals range from pronouncements of them becoming a conceptual framework for diagnosis (Bertelsen, 1999) and major and helpful step for psychiatry (e.g. Cunningham Owens, 2000; Jablensky, 1999), an agreed text based on current empirical data (Frances and Link Egger, 1999; Nathan and Langenbucher, 1999), through studies aiming to improve the classifications (e.g. Maj, 1998; Regier *et al.*, 1998; Strain, 2005) and those rejecting the manuals' reliability (Kirk and Kutchins, 1994; also studies in Kirk, 2005), to accusations of creating diseases (Kutchins and Kirk, 1999; Parker *et al.*, 1995). As a thorough review of the literature is well outside the scope of this chapter, I shall briefly point to some of the critiques which are relevant for my exposition here.

There are two main lines of criticism levied at the diagnostic manuals. First, as I have already mentioned in Chapter 1, both manuals are charged with removing both the individual's experiences of distress and the social context in which the individual operates (there are studies defending this, though, e.g. Wakefield *et al.*, 2002). Kraus (2003) goes as far as saying that the traditional diagnosis is prejudiced against what the patient actually says, orienting itself towards the disease rather than the person, a point seconded by J. Phillips (2005), who argues that the clinical goals are in contradiction with those of the manuals (also Berganza *et al.*, 2005; Mezzich and Berganza, 2005). Gottschalk (2000), finally, posits that if the current understating of self is in terms of changeability, the psychiatric classification prevents us actually from acknowledging it (also Corin *et al.*, 2004). Despite arguments that diagnostic criteria are not to be true or false but useful or not (Beckham *et al.*, 1995), the other line of criticism challenges the classifications' clarity. Parker (2004) says that the guidelines are uninformative for clinical use and display a disturbing lack of rigour (also Kirk and Hsieh, 2004; Pilgrim, 2007; van Praag, 2002). Such critiques are coupled with statements that psychiatric classification is an attempt to establish expertise over mental health illness (McPherson and Armstrong, 2006), with pressure stemming from insurance companies (Cooper, 2004).

For one reason or another, it is the DSM (currently in its revised fourth edition) which is seen as particularly tendentious and downright harmful by the critics. Kutchins and Kirk (1999), under the telling title of *Making us crazy*, quite convincingly, I think, even if somewhat tendentiously, show the *Manual* as creating rather than describing diseases based on arbitrary decisions, not to say a whim of the executive committee, or, occasionally, a vote. The critique shows a document which is immersed solely in the dominant psychiatric discourse. With the critics' focus on the DSM, the ICD has got off quite lightly in comparison, with the criticisms of the classification reflecting largely those which are made of classifications in general. Yet, the ICD, as much as the DSM, cannot be seen as a better or more transparent way of representing mental diseases. It is underpinned by a certain perspective, a dominant view of what counts as a mental disease or what is the role of the clinician.

Now, in the preface to the *ICD-10 Classification of Mental and Behavioural Disorders: Clinical Descriptions and Diagnostic Guidelines* (WHO, 1992), Sartorius posits that the *Classification* is a response to a growing need to improve the diagnosis and classification of mental disorders followed since the 1960s. Thus after much debate and consultation, field trials in 40 countries and extensive testing in 32 countries the final draft of the 'manual' appeared. There are two versions of the manual: the *Clinical Descriptions and Diagnostic Guidelines* (CDDG) and the *Diagnostic Criteria for Research* (DCR), but the latter is recommended to be consulted with the former, as it is only the former that contains the clinical concepts upon which the classification is based and the commentary. As the authors indicate, however, these elements are not 'essential for diagnosis' (WHO, 1993: 1) and this is exactly why I decided to focus upon the DCR version of the classification. I am interested to see the 'bare' minimum of the criteria required to diagnose the disorder. And while I accept that the commentary puts the criteria in some context (I shall return to this below), it is the criteria themselves which are the backbone of the diagnosis (they are said to be somewhat more restrictive here, ibid.: 2). Finally, I am going to focus on the 'positive' criteria, and ignore the exclusion clauses, as I am going to ignore the somatic syndrome in the case of depression, wanting to focus upon the criteria of diagnosing the prototypical depression.

I also decided to offer a brief comparison between the 'canonical' English-language version of the ICD and the Polish translation of the text. The two versions of the text should not only offer *exactly* the same criteria, but they should also be synchronous ideologically. As I shall demonstrate below, such claims cannot be supported even as an aspiration. The two versions differ quite considerably, which, I would propose, is quite ironic, given the implied claims of the universalness of the diagnostic criteria.

Depression according to the ICD

The most suspiring statement in the description of the depressive episode (F32) is its first sentence:

> G1. The depressive episode should last for at least 2 weeks.

It is surprising, of course, because of the word *should* (not uncommon throughout the classification, incidentally), which modalises the proposition (Halliday, 1994). And thus, instead of a yes-or-no statement (does it last for two weeks or not?), we have more of a 'perhaps' sentence. Modalisation introduces an aspect of degree. Halliday (ibid.) stipulates that there are two kinds of degree: probability (the spectrum between possibly and certainly) and usuality (sometimes to always). Although for the most part *should* introduces the latter, it also implies the former. So while the depressive episode normally lasts, or is expected to last for two weeks or more, there might be exceptions and the first thing I am tempted to say is that there goes the restrictiveness claimed by Sartorius at the beginning of the volume. But things are even more complicated.

The formulation opens the possibility of the question of who gets to decide whether what the patient presents is the depressive episode or not. Although the answer to the question is not explicit, one could surmise it is the researcher/clinician's decision that is given most weight. The second point is that the implied author of the text positions themselves as someone who will not (or cannot) introduce a clear rule. Introducing the degree usuality, the word also introduces an element of expectation, rather than certainty, on the part of the author. In this way, the ICD's assumed authority is undermined.

Communicatively, the *should* is a hedge. Brown and Levinson (1987) define hedges as particles, words or phrases that modify the degree of membership of a predicate or noun phrase in a set. They say of the membership that it is partial, or true only in certain respects, or that it is more true and complete than might be expected. Such expressions as *a sort of, rather, technically* (as in *Technically, it is depression*) are referred to as hedges. Brown and Levinson (1987) point out that some hedges cover the entire force of an utterance. When words such as *should* qualify the force of statements in this way, they become weaker or, implicitly, their authors become less certain of what they say.

This weakness of the claim continues when additional symptoms of the episode are introduced:

C. an additional symptom or symptoms from the following list *should* be present (emphasis mine).

Yet, interestingly, the claims made by the ICD were suddenly strengthened. The mild depressive episode (32.0) is introduced:

A. The general criteria for depressive episode (F32) must be met.

B. At least two of the following three symptoms must be present.

The introduction of *must* strengthens the claim and introduces a deontic dimension (i.e. obligation) into the activities of a diagnostician. Thus, in order for the mild depressive episode to be diagnosed, the previously stated criteria *must* obtain. What is quite fascinating is that the only 'positive' criterion of F32 is, actually, the time component (G1) and only that particular criterion *should* be met. What appears is that the authors are at their most forceful in reference to a criterion with regard to which they are actually pretty uncertain.

But what of the other use of *must*? Two of three of the following criteria must obtain:

1   depressed mood to a degree that is definitely abnormal for the indi-
    vidual, present for most of the day and almost every day, largely
    uninfluenced by circumstance, and sustained for at least 2 weeks;
2   loss of interest or pleasure in activities that are normally pleasurable;
3   decreased energy or increased fatigability.

The ambiguity of the criteria is quite striking. What exactly constitutes an abnormal mood? What exactly is most of the day and how many days constitute 'almost every day' of two weeks? These are decided by a number of assumptions based on social expectations of what a person 'normally' is or does, or likes. It also assumes that people measure time in weeks, which, while perhaps obvious in Anglo-Saxon societies – note for example the weekly pay, weekly organisation of school and university activities – might be less pronounced in other places.

Now, the adverb *definitely* is designed to countermand the fuzziness of the criteria. It is supposed to introduce some firmness of the decision which is not to be based on a whim, but on good grounds. Yet, there are no such grounds – the difference between a mood which is *abnormal for the individual* and the mood which is *definitely abnormal for the individual* is that of, shall I say, spin. The adverb does not actually offer any solution as to how to identify abnormality, which, as Fee (2000a: 6) proposed, is 'harshly relative'.

But the most important aspect of the criteria is, I think, the linguistic form in which the symptoms are rendered. Invariably put as nouns, they are rendered as things. Clinicians are to look for, among others, loss of confidence, unreasonable feelings of self-reproach, recurrent thoughts of suicide, excessive or inappropriate guilt, indecisiveness. Such complex, dilemmatic, extended-in-time processes such as losing one's confidence or thinking about killing oneself are rendered as these obvious, clear, unproblematic objects to be spotted by the clinician. What exactly con-stitutes indecisiveness: inability to buy a house or a tee-shirt? When does the process of weighing up the pros and cons of things being indecisive-ness? There are of course no answers to such questions. Moreover, these nominalisations (i.e. rendering actions and processes as things) make the symptoms more objective, almost universal, as if a suicide thought of John, a farmer in England, were like the suicide thought of Andrzej, a businessman in Poland, or Manuel, a professor in Spain, and as if they were individual thoughts – one here, one there, just to constitute recurrence.

Remarkably, the clinical guidelines of the CDDG (WHO, 1992) do not offer any advice as to how to translate these 'objects' into practice, stressing the clinical judgement of the person making an assessment. And so the core of the ICD's construction of depression is that depression is whatever the clinician decides it is. Despite the explicit claims of restrictiveness underpinned by claims of extensive testing, the DCR's pronouncement positions the clinician/researcher as taking the ultimate decision. Moreover, the power to decide is constructed as something largely unproblematic. The clinician/researcher is supposed to simply observe the symptoms and count them, from four to eight – depending on the severity of the episode.

There is no patient, no experience of illness, no distress. All that which happens with the person who comes for psychiatric help is reduced to a few 'objective' categories which the diagnostician can easily assess. There is no context, no individuality, despite the fateful phrase of the mood being 'definitely abnormal for the individual'. But the individual is never positioned as someone with a perspective. It is still the diagnostician which makes the assessment. The ICD constructs a version of psychiatry in which a patient is a set of symptoms which are to be harvested by the clinician. He/she is a transparent conduit of symptoms which are to be treated, as if these symptoms simply existed 'out there' or in the patient for all suitably trained to see. It is difficult not to agree with van Dongen (2000), who says that the clinical transformation of experience is a sign of psychiatry's powerlessness (see also Jaeger, 2003).

The Polish *DCR* – a change of perspective

The Polish version of the ICD-10 DCR was published in 1998. In the preface, the editors of the volume, two eminent Polish psychiatrists, Pużyński and Wciórka, make an explicit statement as to the translators' attempts to offer a translation as faithful to the original as possible. As with the English version, I shall start with the first sentence. Thus, while the original has *The depressive episode should last for at least 2 weeks*, the Polish version, in translation, reads

G1. The depressive episode lasts for at least 2 weeks.[1]

The difference could not be more striking. The Polish text removes the modalised sentence, the hedge on the temporal rule of depression introducing a 'weakness' in the auctorial voice. The Polish version is authoritative, introducing a clear rule, with yes-no certainty. The text constructs its author as having the ultimate power to define what the illness is and there is no hint of delegating this responsibility to the diagnostician. In fact, while the English-language version introduces both hesitation and obligation into the text, the Polish text removes these completely. Consistently, the speaking voice in the Polish DCR is that of an omniscient narrator. Thus in contrast to the original,

A. The general criteria for depressive episode (F32) *must* be met.

B. At least two of the following three symptoms *must* be present (emphasis mine).

The Polish version has

A. The general criteria for depressive episode (F32) met.

B. At least two of the following three symptoms are present.[2]

Now, the differences between the two versions cannot be explained by translation problems, and the fact that the English *should* is somewhat weaker than its Polish equivalent *powinien* making the tentativeness that the latter would have introduced into the Polish translation somewhat higher. There is little doubt that the original lack of authoritativeness could have been rendered by different means. The differences go well beyond those of translation.

Before I attempt an explanation, I would like to offer a story. I was visiting a friend of mine, a consultant psychiatrist in a large university hospital in Poland. We were walking through a ward when we were approached by a woman, who, as it quickly transpired, was also a consultant. My friend and she engaged in a professional conversation, as I was standing by. My presence was not acknowledged by the woman in any way. After a few moments my friend realised that I was being ignored and introduced me to his colleague as Professor Galasiński. The change in his colleague's behaviour was extraordinary. Not only did she greet me showing highest reverence, but started apologising for having to address her colleague rather than me. She assumed I was a professor of medicine and in one way or another she was in a relationship of professional dependence with me.

This story reflects to a considerable extent my experiences with the medical profession. The reverence I was offered was simply embarrassing.

As I started enquiring about it, all my acquaintances in the medical profession confirmed my impressions: Polish medicine is hierarchical in the extreme. This is indeed how I see the discursive shift between the original text and its Polish version. It is not so much a reflection on the state of Polish psychiatry or the competences of Polish diagnosticians. Rather, it accomplished, to use Billig and his associates' (1988) term, the intellectual ideology underpinning Polish medicine. The professor is always right. Even if he/she is not right, refer to the first statement. Given the status and hierarchical nature of Polish medicine, delegating any decision-making to rank-and-file diagnosticians simply cannot be done. The authority must lie with the psychiatric 'top brass'.

However, I am not claiming at all that the editors and translators of the ICD-10 DCR intentionally set out to make sure that it is they who are constructed as the decision-makers, that it is they who take all the decisions. Rather, I am saying that in the particular 'order of discourse' of a particular sphere of life (i.e. 'the totality of its discursive practices, and the relationships . . . between them'; Fairclough, 1995: 132), there are things which are simply unsayable. Even though there are all sorts of options in which things can be said, this choice is invariably socially structured (e.g. Chouliaraki and Fairclough, 1999; Fairclough, 1992). In other words, within the current configurations of practices, power relations and other social structures of Polish psychiatry, it is only the construction of the text, and its Polish editors in terms of authority, which is just about the only viable option.

The ideologies of psychiatry

Now, even toning this interpretation down, the fact remains that the two texts are at odds with each other and simply blaming 'bad' translation is not really an option. The analysis raises enormous problems for psychiatry and its claims to objectivity. The problems are twofold.

First, it confirms what is quite well known in linguistics and discourse analysis, but still protested outside, that the text of the ICD is not a transparent, atheoretical account of a disease, rather it is an ideological account of certain realities (also Moreira, 2003), whatever the status of those realities actually is. Thus, regardless of whether the disease exists independently of the classification, the text constructs a particular kind of disease, one which is to be assessed and decided upon by the clinician only, while the patient's experience is not even given a voice. Moreover, the analysis of the two versions of the ICD shows striking differences in the construction of the disease, in who is empowered to assess it, whose 'clinical judgement', problematic as it is, prevails. Rather than a standardised, internationally tested diagnostic manual, we in fact have two quite distinct manuals, with different world views underpinning them. Incidentally, the changes of the ideology also impact upon the actual formulations of the key criteria of depression. Even though mitigated in the clinical guidance, still the criteria are actually different!

The second problem is, I think, even more important. It shows what is supposed and claimed to be a discourse of an objective account of a disease, to be a socially anchored story. The texts not only reflect the 'current thinking', or the dominant discourses of what constitutes a mental disorder, but, crucially, they also reflect the 'current configurations' of institutional psychiatry. Not only is the ICD *a* story of mental disorders, it is subject to change by those who write themselves into it. And I am not saying at all that the English-language version is somehow superior to the Polish one, or vice versa; they are simply different. To say therefore that I have been analysing the institutional discourses of depression is quite an understatement. They are institutional also in the sense of conveying the power structures of institutional psychiatry. To put it bluntly, the diagnostic criteria actually depend on who writes them – a conclusion quite sobering given the claims to universality in the text.

Yet, there is also the question of how the differences in the two versions translate into psychiatric practice, as it would be implausible to assume that the texts are merely a dead letter that no one pays attention to. I can only offer speculation here, though. It seems to me that the crucial difference is in the rigidity of the diagnostic frame offered by the English and Polish ICDs. While the former delegates the decision to the psychiatrist, the latter does not offer any latitude, pre-empting any doubts it can. One could argue that this means that by allowing judgement, the English version might be more attuned to the patient and the context of their distress. The Polish version, it can be argued, stifles that potential. But then, such an argument assumes an ideal world in which all psychiatrists make sensible judgements and have actually the time to think hard about their patients. Yet, the world is not ideal; the hard pondering over the patient's experience is probably an aspiration only. The Polish version makes it easier – there are fewer hard choices to be made, some options have already been taken by the text itself. Speaking more generally, the English version shows more trust, while the Polish version prefers to err on the safe side.

The Beck Depression Inventory

The Beck Depression Inventory (BDI), now in its second version, is a self-assessment tool for gauging the severity of depression (Beck *et al.*, 1961; and for the second version Beck *et al.*, 1996). It is one of the most widely used and reputed to be a reliable and valid self-report measure of depression, for both patients in psychiatric care and the rest of the population (Nezu *et al.*, 2002). The second version of the scale, the BDI-II (Beck *et al.*, 1996), was designed to reflect the DSM-IV diagnostic criteria of the major depressive episode. Intended not to reflect any theoretical stance of aetiology of depression (Beck and Beamesderfer, 1974), it consists of 21 items, each to be answered by questions ranked from 0 to 3, representing severity levels from no symptom to the most severe. Needless to say, the BDI is one of scores of instruments designed to measure the intensity or kinds of depressive symptoms (see e.g. Lam *et al.*, 2005).

The psychiatric literature on the BDI focuses mostly upon its psychometric features, quoting the level of its reliability and validity (e.g. Beck *et al.*, 1988; Schotte *et al.*, 1997) and commonly applauds them (see e.g. Nezu *et al.*, 2002). Criticisms are relatively infrequent and focus mostly on what exactly the Inventory measures. Coyne (1994) suggests, for example, that the BDI might measure the level of general psychological distress rather than severity of depression and points out that the scores of BDI can be reduced drastically a few days after admission to hospital, although the patient might not have received any significant treatment (also Katz *et al.*, 1995; van Praag and Plutchik, 1987). Endler and his associates (2000) point out that the BDI might measure trait-like depression and, significantly, different aspects and levels of depression in clinical and non-clinical samples. In addition, Richter and his associates (1998) also indicate, among others, high item difficulties or doubtful objectivity of interpretation. Finally, there are also reports that the BDI might be interacted with differently, depending on gender and age of those who complete it (e.g. Aben *et al.*, 2002; Page and Bennesch, 1993; Wallace and Pfohl, 1995; see also Steer *et al.*, 1999).

However, such criticisms are made predominantly within the parameters set by the discourses of quantitatively oriented psychiatry and clinical psychology, taking an explicitly positivist research perspective. It assumes that questionnaires can gauge a 'psychological reality' of or in the people who complete them. They are looked at only as instruments which are to provide researchers data of 'good quality' and thus must be clear, accurate, complete and logical and must compute well (Gillham,

2000; also Conrad *et al.*, 1999). Even such stinging critiques of questionnaire research as Schwarz's (1999) which shows drastic inconsistencies
between the data collected via self-reports and other methods (see also
a classical study by Schuman and Presser, 1981) are aimed at improving
the failing instruments.

Within the qualitative perspective, questionnaires are criticised for
reproducing the researcher's view of the world, their assumptions, values,
beliefs, which in combination with the lack of any context depth results
in at best very partial data (Denscombe, 1998; Donsbach, 1997; Henn
et al., 2006). They do not offer access to the process by which people form
views or opinions, let alone their dilemmatic nature (Billig *et al.*, 1988).
Mishler (1991: 27) put it aptly by saying that 'by adopting an approach
that is behavioural and antilinguistic, relies on the stimulus-response
model, and decontextualises the meaning of responses, researchers have
attempted to avoid rather than to confront directly the inter-related
problems of context, discourse and meaning'. Robbins (2002: 213) adds
to this critique arguing that questionnaire data are an 'unknown mixture
of politeness, boredom, and a desire to be seen in a good light' rather
than offering insight into what the respondents actually think or feel.
The qualitative perspective rejects the ontological assumption of discovering reality via an instrument and stresses its social nature (Denzin and
Lincoln, 2000; also Denzin, 1989), just as Speer (2002; also Baker, 1997)
argues that questionnaires are a standardised means of constituting the
object of research, constructs which do not easily translate into lived
experience.

Such critiques are reiterated within psychopathology. In tandem with
general critiques of positivist psychopathology (see e.g. Barrett, 1996;
Kleinman, 1988a; also Parker *et al.*, 1995), criticisms of standardised psychological and psychiatric instruments view them as socially situated
texts (e.g. Drennan *et al.*, 1991) offering a difficult frame for mental distress (Barroso and Sandelowski, 2001). In a particularly forceful critique
of standardised psychological assessment, Rose (1989) goes even further,
pointing out that rendering subjectivity calculable and thus capable of
being documented and archived contributes to the overall apparatus of
governing the self. Finally, commenting on the process of constructing
and validating scales for measuring psychological distress, Masse (2000)
points out that it leads to denaturalisation and objectification of distress,
while at the same time to its decontextualisation and disembodiment
(also Wiggins, 2001).

That said, I have found practically no literature approaching such
instruments as institutionally empowered texts with which those who

complete them enter into interaction and thus as texts which open up interaction spaces within which the person must find herself/himself (Kozłowska, 2004). A notable exception is a study by Barroso and Sandelowski (2001) in which the authors interrogate the BDI in view of the interactions one of them had while administrating the questionnaire. They point out not only the difficulty their informants had with the BDI, but also the fact that their lived experience of depression could not be squared to fit into the scale. Furthermore, I have found no study taking the issue of discursive workings of psychiatric instruments in general and the BDI in particular. Thus, in the analysis below, I shall comment on three linguistic aspects of the BDI: lack of contextualisation, the linguistic perspective and its 'scaleness'.

Lack of contextualisation

The BDI displays a lack of fit between the questionnaire items and the potential experiences of the respondent. Take for example the question concerning the ease of decision-taking (Item 13, Indecisiveness). As I said before, an answer to the question of whether decisions are taken as easily as before cannot be made without recourse to what kind of decisions they are (decisions to buy things will obviously be dependent on the scale of the financial commitment) and in what context they are made. Two assumptions underpin the question: one is that the default way to take decisions is to take them easily, and the other that decisions of a certain kind will be taken in a similar fashion. Both are problematic to say the least. A promotion or demotion at work, let alone losing or getting employment, changes the context so crucially that one cannot possibly compare decisions taken in such extremely different situations. Bad decisions in the past are likely to influence the present process of decision-taking. Finally, it is perfectly natural and indeed sensible not to take decisions, like, to marry, to divorce, to have children, quickly or lightly. Incidentally, there are folk wisdoms that warn people against quick decisions, and advise a good period of thinking.

I would argue, therefore, that in order for such a question to be indicative of indecisiveness and suggest affective pathology, a person who completes the questionnaire not only must make a significant number of assumptions, but they must also be ones made by the question setter. Not only can it not be guaranteed, but it cannot even be postulated. Indeed, Brown (1991) suggests that it is only free narrating that will resolve the problem of question understanding; yet, even this does not resolve the issue of standardisation.

Linguistic perspective

Each language use carries its share of these ingrained assumptions, beliefs and values, so that the reality represented is also constructed ideologically (Hodge and Kress, 1993) from a particular point of view. It is this perspective which is projected by the BDI that I shall be interested in here. More specifically, I shall focus on what kind of communicative actions are imposed onto the respondent by the questionnaire, in what kind of positions (e.g. Harré and van Langenhove, 1999a) those who complete it are placed.

Consider the following zero options from a number of BDI items:

1-0 I am not sad.
2-0 I am not discouraged about my future.
5-0 I don't feel particularly guilty.
6-0 I don't feel I am being punished.
8-0 I don't criticise or blame myself more than usual.
9-0 I don't have any thoughts of killing myself.
10-0 I don't cry any more than I used to.

What is striking is that they are all in the negative. Thus, given the first person singular format, socially, they take the form of a denial. To explain – normally, when I make a positive statement, e.g. saying 'I am sad', I assume that my addressee has not got the information and, for one reason or another, would like to have it or I would like them to have it. This is the basis of Grice's Cooperative Principle (Grice, 1975), which stipulates, among others, that one should not say more than necessary. Things are different when we issue a negative statement. Normally, when I say that I am not sad, I assume that my addressee might have grounds to believe otherwise. By volunteering a statement in the negative, I perform a denial. And what the BDI does is ask the respondent to deny having certain symptoms. As the BDI co-constructs depression, how can you ever not be depressed?

The Beck Depression Inventory takes the point of departure of depression. It assumes that whoever completes it actually has depression, or at least has certain symptoms which count as contributing to depression. Yet, as the BDI was designed to gauge the 'severity of depression in psychiatrically diagnosed adults and adolescents' (see Beck *et al.*, 1996: 6), perhaps the assumption of depression seems less perturbing. But then, the assumption constructs every diagnosis of depression as correct, a position untenable in view of a relatively large body of literature on the problems faced by psychiatric diagnosis, including Beck's own classical studies (Beck, 1962; Beck *et al.*, 1962; see also Caplan and Cosgrove, 2004; Kleinman, 1988a; Sadler, 2005a). Incidentally, the perspective of depression taken in the BDI is underscored by the fact that even a nil score on the scale (i.e. the respondent denied having any symptoms tested by the instrument) still, according to the authors, indicates depression! But Beck and his associates (1996) note that the BDI has become 'one of the most widely accepted instruments (. . .) for detecting possible depression in normal [sic!] populations' (e.g. Dutton *et al.*, 2004; Lasa *et al.*, 2000). In such studies, quite obviously, the assumption of depression is simply unacceptable.

The questionnaire's use of the first person singular adds to the problem. Reading the questionnaire, the respondent is put in a speaking position. Taking the perspective of 'I', the scale is putting words in his/her mouth. Thus it is actually 'my' perspective, which is one suspecting that the world around me thinks that 'I' am depressed. 'I' might be tempted to deny it, but then, perhaps the world knows better, after all 'I' am completing the Beck Depression Inventory, given to me by my doctor.

BDI as a scale

Finally, is the BDI a scale, does it assess symptoms on scales of severity? Let me consider Item 3, purporting to measure the Sense of Failure (or, in the BDI-II, the Past Failure) in the patient (see also my analysis of the Polish version of the test, Galasiński, *forthcoming*). The item reads:

3.
0. I do not feel like a failure.
1. I have failed more than I should have.
2. As I look back, I see a lot of failures.
3. I feel I am a total failure as a person.

Let me first consider the structure of the four sentences. Two of them are introduced by superordinate clauses indicating a particular way of looking at the matter; the other two are not. Thus, options 2 and 3 are introduced by a predicate referring to a mental process (e.g. feeling, thinking or seeing; Halliday, 1994) on the part of the respondent. With this in mind, the items look as follows:

0. nil
1. nil
2. As I look back
3. I feel

Options 2 and 3 request the respondent to consider the failure in a particular way. In 2, he/she is asked to 'look back', to make a judgement as to their perceptions; in 3, they are told to 'feel', to make an emotional judgement about themselves. But, in 0 and in 1, they are simply asked to make the statement – without qualifying it. Thus, the item introduces three different perspectives of judgement and three different perspectives of representation of their failure. If the scale means that like is compared with like, there is no question of it here.

Recall also my earlier comments on hedging–communicative resources that modify the range of applicability of certain statements. Options 2 and 3 are precisely that. The speaker is asked to hedge, rather than commit themselves to what they say. And if it is easier to make statements by hedging them, as they do not commit to the speaker to what he/she says as much, then options 2 and 3 are actually tempting, precisely because they offer this half-committal position, although they are the choices of greatest symptomatic severity.

But things get even more problematic when one considers the 'core' of the options – the actual reference to past failures. Two aspects are important here. One is the actual representation of the failures and the other is the constructed relationship of the self to the failures. Let me consider them in turn. As above, the references vary:

0. failure
1. have failed
2. a lot of failures
3. a total failure

One might perhaps argue that the spectrum of 'failure – (a lot of) failures – total failure' is a scale of sorts; yet, it is clearly disturbed by option 1, where the failure is referred to by a verb. Still, I cannot quite see the difference between a failure and a total failure and what exactly is their relationship to many failures. But this argument cannot really be made without looking at the constructed 'I' and its relationship to the failures. Thus we have:

3.
0. I (do not feel like) a failure.
1. I have failed.
2. I see a lot of failures.
3. I am a total failure.

The hint of a scale of the above-mentioned spectrum disappears as one realises that the options ask about different things. For options 0 and 3 predicate failure of the person – they are statements made about qualities of the person who is speaking (or completing the BDI). They are quite different though. Option 0 constructs the self by reference to feeling and, as I said above, via a denial, whereas option 3 is an unqualified statement of being a failure. On the other hand, options 1 and 2 refer to actions. Option 1 is a direct statement of having failed, the speaker is said to have done something; option 2, in turn, introduces the speaker's active perception of his/her failures (although it is actually quite ambivalent whose failures option 2 refers to). To put it crudely, to be a failure (total or not) is quite different from failing and they are both different from seeing failures. The item simply cannot be thought of as a scale – the options refer to different things and they cannot be thought to gauge one symptom on a scale of severity. Although, I am focusing on only one item, it is not atypical. Similar analyses can be done with reference to Item 2 (Pessimism), Item 4 (Loss of pleasure), Item 5 (Guilty feelings) or Item 7 (Self-Dislike) and others.

The measuring tape . . .

The BDI is a result of psychiatric discourses similar to that of the ICD, as it is explicitly geared to test the symptoms of depression as stipulated by the APA's DSM-IV. The instrument is founded on the assumption that it is a transparent conduit between the patient and the clinician, a gauge which simply measures the severity without actually impacting on what it measures.

Yet, given the analysis above, such a claim is quite implausible. If you start from the perspective of depression, you are more than likely to get depressed patients. Indeed, in a complement to this study, I asked people to 'think aloud' while completing the BDI – it turned out that respondents rejected the BDI, or reformulated its questions to suit their current life relevancies. Not only does the BDI offer a particular space in which the depressed self can be expressed, but, crucially, it is a text with which those who are requested to complete it engage in an interaction (Galasiński, 2008).

But one could argue that, social and discursive critiques notwithstanding, the BDI and other such measures simply work and do offer insight into patients' condition and recovery. After all, people have different scores during and after therapy – indeed, improving BDI scores are taken to be evidence of therapy's effectiveness (e.g. Grant *et al.*, 2004). So, the argument might continue, people might not exactly know what the author meant, still they are able to fill in the scale consistently and one is able to have insight into their depression.

Yet, such an argument self-perpetuates the perspective. In the textbook on cognitive-behavioural therapy (ibid.), the BDI is positioned not only as measurement of the therapy's success but also an indication of the areas upon which the therapist might want to focus. In this way, the therapist focuses upon the depression the BDI contributed to constructing. But the crucial problem is that the argument takes an ever-innocent view of the 'professional' patient who somehow knows what to do. He/she knows what is involved and plays along so that the doctor can have the data they need, ensuring smooth functioning in medical discourses. The cross-instrument correlation often given in evidence would result not so much from the instruments' ability to gauge experience, but, rather, from the instruments' roots in the same dominant psychiatric discourse in which the patient is also submerged. Indeed, Kleinman (1987) points out that instruments' consistency does not translate into identification of patient's distress. Moreover, the main weakness of studies such as that of Santor and Coyne (2001) is that while they test the validity of diagnostic instruments they uncritically remain within the constraints of the dominant discourse of psychiatry (see also e.g. Lloyd-Williams *et al.*, 2004; Parker *et al.*, 2001; Rogers *et al.*, 2005; Steer *et al.*, 1999). Finally, knowing what might be at stake – especially in a psychiatrist's surgery – the patient cooperates more or less willingly trying to give the 'right' answers. Incidentally, such cooperation is not very difficult in the case of the BDI – it is extremely easy to realise after reading the first couple of items that there is a pattern to how the scoring is made and one can give answers without even reading the items (see also Dahlstrom *et al.*, 1990).

The model of quantifying the experience of mental illness necessarily underscores the dominance of medical discourse. The patient's experience cannot surface as he/she plays the game, getting more 'professional' every time he/she is asked to complete a questionnaire. Regardless of the theoretical standpoint, whether assuming that experience is primarily discursive or that there is a depression to be discovered behind the words, the situation is hardly useful. By having to respond to instrument items, the patients cannot access their depression. As Edgar (2005) points out, diagnostic instruments impose themselves and their institutionally sanctioned goals upon the patient, inhibiting, at the same time, the possibility of the patient's reflection upon his/her illness and its meaning. Completing a questionnaire is an interaction in which the patients cannot find their voice and offer a story of suffering rather than a measurement of madness (Kangas, 2001), with the potential diagnosis being institutionalised and non-negotiable, thus adding to the trauma of being a psychiatric patient (Sayre, 2000; also Phillips, 2003; Ucok, 2005). The situation is exacerbated by the fact that psychological and psychiatric testing does not account for the power relations involved in the activity. It is crucial to understand that completing the BDI, and indeed other such instruments, is a socially situated, context-dependent activity with a particular configuration of power relations, particularly relevant in the context of a psychiatric examination. Patients are not empowered to challenge the test itself; they are to get on with the task – their cooperation more than likely to be obtained.

Finally, the BDI cannot be seen outside its anchorage in the dominant discourse of psychiatry and clinical psychology. It works within the parameters of such discourse, and so it successfully measures something because it corresponds with the rules of what constitutes such measurement. And while it might identify the major depressive episode (DSM, 296.2-3) or its non-US equivalent the depressive episode (ICD F32-33), it is unlikely to pin down the experience of what we call 'depression'.

Conclusions

In this chapter, I have taken a look at two instances of institutional discourse of depression: one of the psychiatric 'bibles' – the World Health Organisation's classification of mental and behavioural disorders – and a self-assessment scale probing into severity of depression's symptoms. I have shown that, underpinned by a particular ideological and linguistic perspective, they construct a particular version of both depression and psychiatry. The most crucial aspect of the discourses I have analysed is the underlying assumption that psychiatric symptoms can somehow be 'read off' what the patient says. While the ICD objectivises the symptoms into the easily accessible objects, the BDI decontextualises the experiences. Moreover, the BDI is underpinned by a tacit assumption that the response can be transformed into symptoms of depression, which, in turn, have a reference to what the patient actually experiences. The assumption is at the very least problematic.

But I am not merely talking about the often explored question of medicalisation of patients' experiences (Cassell, 2004; Mishler *et al.*, 1981; also Foucault, 1977) through which patients are transformed into objects of interest to medicine. The problem concerns the issue of signs and symptoms in medicine. As Atkinson (1997) describes – while a sign can be objectively observed by an independent observer – the symptoms are subjectively reported by the patient. In the discourses I have analysed, there are I think two process going on. On the one hand, the process of implicit transformation of symptoms into signs, and on the other, an implicit hierarchisation of symptoms.

Now, psychiatry has a significant problem as there are no available signs with which to diagnose depression. In an authoritative review of diagnosis of depression, Stefanis and Stefanis (2002) note that there are no common causes of depression, nor are there any biological markers, making the diagnosis lacking in solid scientific foundation. What is available, continue the authors, is a judgement-based assessment of symptoms reported by the patient (sometimes also by his/her family, one might add). Boyle (2002), offering a comprehensive critique of psychiatry's research and practices into schizophrenia, reports that psychiatric research and classification is quite lax in how it treats the fundamental differences between signs and symptoms, focusing on the latter as the 'objective' basis of diagnosis and nosology.

Even though the ICD DCR is quite clear in speaking only of symptoms in the case of the diagnostic criteria for the depressive episode, they are constructed as, first, objective things, second, independent of the patient's experience and, third, subject to the clinician's judgement. The ICD transforms the subjective symptoms, the dilemmatic, sometimes confused, into clearly defined categories which can be accessed by the clinician. The BDI goes even further. It makes a claim that it can gauge the severity of symptoms, as if the severity was somehow independent of the patient and the level of distress he/she experiences in a particular configuration of context he/she find him/herself in. The scale provides the clinician with an 'objective' and, obviously, numerical value of symptoms which can be easily harvested by the instrument, as if the experiences of depression were a matter of simple questions and even simpler answers to them.

Furthermore, both texts I analysed assume the diagnostician's superiority with regard to the patient's experience (cf. Kraus, 2003). Indeed, Verhaeghe (2004: 197) proposes that the goal of the first consultation is to 'extract whatever symptoms are present'. The statement is quite extraordinary, as it assumes that 'vague complaints' (ibid.) with which the patient comes are not really a proper thing for the clinician to focus upon. It is only through this process of extraction, it seems, that we get to something a clinician can actually work on. Incidentally, the word *extract* suggests that the patient's experience actually hinders the emergence of the symptoms, as if they were trapped there, and some force were needed to get them out. The patient's experience is the problem; it is only after one drains it out through the clinician's sieve that one can get to the 'real problem'. A comment by Kendell (2002) that one cannot contradict a patient who consistently denies being sad sounds almost defiant here.

Not only does it mean that the complexity of the patient's experience of psychological distress is radically reduced to whatever is stipulated by psychiatric classification and testing, but it also means that the patient has no say in how they see, assess, experience what makes them suffer. In this way, finally, the two documents are not only invested with the power and authority of institutional discourse of psychiatry, but also give that power to the clinician. It is the clinician, and in the case of the Polish text, shall I say, the clinician's boss, who knows better. End of matter.

In the next chapter I shall start focusing upon the experience of depression. Thus, I shall begin analysing the data I collected in the interviews with men diagnosed with the depressive episode. The next eight chapters are devoted to exploring the experiences of those who are said to be in depression.

3
The Experience of Autonomy (of Depression)

Introduction

In the previous chapter, I discussed the dominant psychiatric discourses of depression. I showed that the illness, whether one believes in its existence or not, is constructed by the discourses of those who treat it. The illness is transformed into a disease, a standardised version of what people apparently feel when they are very sad. I have repeatedly pointed out that the dominant discourses of psychiatry ignore the individual perspective of the sufferer trying to construct it in objective and measurable terms.

In this chapter, I am beginning to focus on the experiences of those whom I interviewed. I shall explore here how my informants spoke of depression. One of the most noticeable aspects of the stories I heard during the interviews was that depression is autonomous of the people who suffer from it. It exists in its own right, unfettered by those who are ill and trying to cope with it. There were two strategies with which depression's autonomy was constructed. By far dominant were constructions of depression in agentive terms. The illness was constructed as an actor, a discourse participant (Halliday, 1994) which acted in its own right, engaging in activities which influenced others. The other was positioning depression as a condition, a state of mind over which, however, the person had no influence at all.

Agentivity of depression

Speaking of depression, my informants constructed it mainly as an independent entity which had some profound influence upon them. This entity made them do things, or, more often, prevented them from doing them. Although in some cases they represented depression as ill-ness/disease (Polish does not have a commonly used distinction between illness and disease), more often the illness was anthropomorphised, invested with human features, as if it could take purposeful action based on strategic decisions. In their accounts of the agentive depression, the informants invariably positioned themselves as its objects, targets of actions they could just about only endure.

Before I discuss extracts from my corpus, I would like to make a couple of points on the presentation of the data. The extracts I quote below are translations of interviews which I conducted in Polish. I have done my best not only to render the content of what my informants said, but also I have tried to show how they said it. As expected of any language user, also my informants did not necessarily use grammatical, 'proper' Polish, whatever such terms may refer to, my attempts to convey this sometimes resulted in extracts put in disjointed, or in 'bad English'. Quite obviously a lot has been lost in translation. My analyses, however, are based on the Polish originals.

I have also chosen to represent my informants with fictional initials, rather than fictional first names as often is the practice in the liter-ature. This is because I was not on first-name basis with them (the default address form for adults in Polish is the polite form *pan/pani*, the equivalent of German *Sie* or Spanish *Usted*), and also because I have an impression that referring to informants, adult people, only by first names (fictional or not) is slightly patronising and to a certain extent at least puts them in a position of lower or inferior status, something my informants, and probably most other people with mental illness, have to struggle with daily.

Moreover, throughout the book, I have also chosen to refer to my informants as patients. I realise that this is not an 'innocent' choice: there is a large literature on stigmatisation of mental health users (for reviews see Hayward and Bright, 1997; Rüsch *et al.*, 2005), their social and political isolation (Erdner *et al.*, 2005; Kelly, 2006) and particularly the role of labelling in stigmatisation (Corrigan *et al.*, 2005). Indeed a number of studies were carried out into the very use of the expression 'mental patient', finding negative associations invoked by it (Johannsen, 1969; Rabkin, 1972). Also, I am mindful of Speed's (2006) analysis of self-labelling on the spectrum of patients–consumers–survivors, pointing out that it might reflect the position between passive acceptance and active resistance to the mental health system.

Still, I have made my choice precisely because my informants used the word to refer to themselves and it is their right. Also, I think that

Speed's (2006) argument is somewhat tendentious in that he does not consider the possibility that accepting one's patienthood might be part of accepting one's illness (Davidson, 2003; Morse and Johnson, 1991b) and part of a route towards recovery. It might also be part of 'coming out' and challenging the stigma (Corrigan and Matthews, 2003). Moreover, I reject the argument that uniform resistance towards psychiatric services is universally good or desirable. It can in fact be counterproductive.

Consider now the following extracts.

Extract 1[1]

AZ: What is depression for me? Depression unsettles me simply, it is a disorder which unsettles me from the material [unclear]. I don't know what to do at all [...]

Extract 2

BC: Depression takes away the possibility of logical thinking, of assessment of situations.

DG: I see.

BC: It takes away the possibility of taking decisions, about yourself, it takes away very important things, I think, reason to live, it simply takes away the joy of life. It takes away, one can't enjoy anything, one can't give life meaning.

Extract 3

DG: [...] what is depression for you?

CW: It's the greatest burden in life. I mean for me it's a giant problem, it caused to a great extent the break-up of my first marriage. Now, I am on the home straight for the break-up of the second one. It caused, I don't want to blame everything on depression, but it did contribute significantly the break-up of my other relationships.

In all three extracts depression is positioned as an unfettered agent in actions that had direct impact upon the informants. Whether it unsettles the informant, takes away logical thinking or causes a marriage to fail, depression is the 'something' that actually did do these things. There is some variation, however, as to the directness of the object of the illness's actions. Linguistically, the most direct construction is that in Extract 1. Agentivity is built with the most direct form of the agent (depression) doing something (unsettling) to an object (the informant). AZ explicitly positions himself as the object of (his) depression's actions. In the other two extracts, depression's actions are not positioned as targeting the informants. While in Extract 2 depression is constructed to take away the possibility of thinking or taking decisions, the impact upon the informant is only implied; similarly, in Extract 3, depression's impact is upon the informant's marriage, rather than himself.

In the following extract the informant stresses depression's independence of any implicit activities that might be taken in order to fight it:

Extract 4

> DE: With this illness it's such a strange phenomenon that this illness over these three years has like wound itself up. I can't see the moment, perhaps my therapies were not led right or were too late, I can't see the moment when this illness would have started to withdraw.

Despite the medicalised view of depression (it is an illness) which, one would suspect, should lead to a more clear construction of the condition as prone to medical intervention, nothing of the sort happens. Not only does depression wind itself up (this is a translation of the Polish reflexive voice, in English rendered by pronouns ending in *–self*; the verb indicates depression's ability to rise, increase on its own accord), but it also has the power to withdraw. There is an interesting hiatus between the content and the form in the extract. Judging by the content of what the informant says, he clearly positions depression as treatable, but the therapies he refers to, it could be argued, were simply ineffective. Had they been effective, he would have recovered, and the depression would have been got rid of. But linguistically, it is depression which is represented as having the power to rise or withdraw, independently of any treatment the informant might have had. Interestingly, he himself is reduced to the role of an observer of the process of depression's actions or, indeed, the treatment's efficacy. The extract is consistent with constructions throughout the corpus in which the speakers showed themselves as having no impact upon their illness. I shall comment on this at the end of the chapter.

Representing depression in agentive terms is typical throughout the corpus. It is constructed as capable of taking actions, impacting the lives of the informants. But the linguistically 'canonical' model of agentivity was not the only way in which the informants constructed depression's actions. Consider the following two extracts in which on the one hand depression is talked of in terms of its symptoms, and, on the other, the impact is constructed in negative terms.

Extract 5

DG: What does it mean that you are ill of this kind of illness?

EU: A reappearing cycle of various symptoms which escalate and which, by intensifying, do not let me control my own behaviour, my own, I don't know, way of thinking, which incapacitate me in a sense.

Extract 6

FH: A strange illness that doesn't put you in bed. [. . .] what can I say, an illness that to a lesser or greater degree does not let us find ourselves in the surrounding reality.

In Extract 5 the informant introduces a more deeply medicalised view of depression than the one offered by the interviewer. Instead of focusing on the illness, he prefers to speak of its symptoms, although the shift does not change the fact that the symptoms are still constructed as agents. This time it is the symptoms that incapacitate the informant. The informant not only ascribes agency to the symptoms directly, but also positions himself as the object of their actions.

Extracts 5 and 6 share another feature. Both informants construct the depression's influence in negative terms. Depression prevents them from doing things. It is interesting as the informants are put in a position of 'agency', except it is negated, never fulfilled and linguistically only implied. Yet, one could argue that such a position at least shows a certain potential for agency, one blocked by the illness; still, potentially, the informants do see themselves as agents. In such accounts, even though depression wins, the informants are not merely objects, they are failed agents. Although it is difficult to speculate about the therapeutic import of such constructions, it seems significant that some informants chose to position themselves in this way. I shall explore the action potential in the corpus as well constructions of the informants in terms of failed agency in Chapter 5.

Depression's grip upon those suffering from it was also shown in the unusual extracts where the informants did actually position themselves in terms of agency. Consider the following:

Extract 7

> DG: What would have to happen for you to say 'I am healthy'.
>
> GT: I would have to recover from this depression fully, which is unrealistic, because I come back here. I receive treatment, I undergo treatment, because I know that the longer I don't treat this, the greater low I will fall into, problems. Well, I wish it had not happened to me, it hadn't happened to me the first time and those relapses, but I have no influence over it.

Extract 8

> HI: It's not just a simple cut, or a flu which will pass in a week, a month and so on. Or even as with a broken arm, let it take half a year. It will heal. This has lasted quite long. In my case I have been trying to get better since 1999. Better or worse, I have been fighting this illness. But it's been hard all the time, all the time I feel like something weighed me down, always with a burden.

In Extract 7, the informant's relapses into illness are explicitly, at the level of the content of what he said, shown as something he has no influence over. In fact it is so much that he stopped believing in full recovery. In Extract 8, the fight against the illness is unsuccessful (although my informants did speak of fighting, this is the only time in the corpus when the informant explicitly positioned himself as an agent in an action whose object was depression), and he still lives with the weight on him.

But, very unusually for my informants, both informants ascribe agency to themselves in the context of speaking about depression (obviously, in other contexts, e.g. describing their everyday life, the men I interviewed did it frequently). Yet for GT (7) agency is parallel to that of depression, one does not concern the other. His agency is that of going to the out-patient clinic in a hospital. He constructs himself as an object of the treatment he undergoes. He uses quite a formal and marked term for receiving treatment (*poddać się leczeniu*, lit. 'to submit, subject oneself to treatment') instead of the default one *leczyć się* (to receive treatment, lit. 'to treat oneself'; the verb is in reflexive voice). Both phrases can be used agentively, yet the former's agency is defeated by its content – it is an agency of becoming an object of someone else's actions; the other phrase, alternatively, preserves the speaker's agency in receiving treatment. GT's agency is reduced to that of going to hospital, it has nothing to do with depression.

HI (8) is the only informant who positions himself in terms of agency with regard to depression. But this agency is undermined in two ways. First, although he chooses the default form of referring to receiving treatment, he undermines it by introducing it by 'try'. So he does not really get treatment, his agency is limited to trying only. As the fight against depression is more than likely to be linked with his treatment, one cannot but see the trying as encompassing also the fighting. Second, the fight is undermined also immediately after, almost in the same breath he shows its futility. The expression 'all the time' suggests that he has not made any incursions into the illness, his fight did not produce any effects.

The dominant strategy of constructing depression was to show it as independent of the speakers or any treatment, an entity having significant impact upon their lives. Yet, at times, the men also constructed their illness as a condition.

Independent states of mind

In contrast to the agentive depression, in some narratives depression was also constructed in terms of psychological states, as a state of mind or consciousness; sometimes a particular state of being. What is most interesting in these constructions is that these states are also positioned as independent of anyone who might have them. Consider the following examples:

Extract 9

DG: What is depression for you?

EU: Generally speaking [unclear] let's call it, say, something which should not exist for me. [unclear] it is at least for me simply a consciousness, being in a consciousness in which only the worst things come.

Extract 10

DG: [...] what is depression for you?

JS: It is a state of inability to do anything practically. Lasting for a longer period of time, not a short breakdown, but something that lasts day in day out, and day in day out if you have not seen a specialist, as I had such periods of time, it was getting worse and worse, but thanks to medication, and conversation, therapy I went to, this state was getting better.

In Extract 9, EU is explicitly introducing his own perspective in viewing depression, yet the illness is not associated with an ill person. The 'being in a consciousness' is not attributed to himself, or any other hypothetical person. Similarly, the state of inability JS refers to in Extract 10 is also positioned in separation from anyone, including the informant himself. The extract is particularly interesting as the informant does implicitly introduce himself as an ill person, yet it has no explicit link to the state of inability he spoke about a moment before. He also prefers speaking of periods of time when it was getting worse, a euphemistic way of speaking of one's illness. It is only then that he refers to 'this state' that was getting better for him. Implicitly, one can surmise that he refers back to the state of inability he mentions at the beginning of the fragment; explicitly, however, depression, or indeed, the state of inability, is not something that affects him directly. We can see a similar situation in the following two extracts in which depression, constructed impersonally, is juxtaposed with the informants' personal experiences.

Extract 11

KL: This is the worst in my opinion, as you asked what depression means for me, it is losing faith in oneself. I used to believe in myself, so I was able to do many things. Now I stopped believing and all I thought I had been able to do and I could do still, stops being, there is no answer now, there is no success factor.

Extract 12

DG: [. . .] how would you describe depression, what is it for you?

MR: I say depression is, you know, something like a feeling of inability, nightmarish inability, it's such a constant, I have a feeling of lethargy.

Interestingly, KL in (11) linguistically contrasts the period of depression with his experiences before depression. Thus, while depression is represented impersonally, as losing faith in oneself, the reference to himself before the illness is somewhat agentive: he believed in himself, he was able to do many things. The contrast, incidentally, goes on all the way till the implied beginning of depression. It does not cross over though. Depression is represented as impersonal, unassociated with any particular person. In a less pronounced way, MR in (12) also builds a contrast between depression as a nightmarish inability and his own feeling lethargic. The change is not only lexical, it also suggests a change in the degree of the feeling: feeling lethargic seems nowhere near as severe as the 'nightmarish inability'. Also here, however, depression is not predicated upon anyone.

I have, however, found one extract in the corpus in which the two constructions of depression, that of a psychological state, and that investing it with agency, were united in a single account.

Extract 13

> EU: It does not reach me. Reach? It does not convince me that it could pass, that it's not as bad as I think, that there are exits out of it and that it can be solved. I feel powerlessness, hopelessness. Hopelessness of the situation. And it is getting tighter. It's getting tighter, because add this feeling that one has a noose on the neck which, in the case of any action, particularly an action which might even have a positive basis, but doesn't come off. It causes that the noose gets tighter and one escapes into some motionlessness, so one doesn't try anything, because one is scared that this noose will get even tighter. [...] one loses control over one's thoughts, that one is unable, that it is getting deeper, that it is paralysing, that it can enslave you.

This time the informant shows the psychological state, feeling of powerlessness, inability, hopelessness, as applying to him, but then he shifts the account and shows it in agentive terms. Depression as a state of mind not only can 'tighten the noose on the neck', it also paralyses and enslaves the person suffering.

The direct ascription of a depressive mental state to the informant is immediately countered with an account of an onslaught of the illness on the informant. It is not just an innocent state of mind, it is, rather, something that attacks. The vivid metaphor of a noose tightening on the neck brings all sorts of imagery of executions, where powerless people can only wait for the hangman to do his job. But there is another noteworthy aspect of the account. The moment the informant starts talking about depression's onslaught, he shifts from a direct reference to himself to a more distanced account of his experience. He prefers to refer to 'one' (EU uses *człowiek*, lit. 'human being', which is used as an impersonal reference to oneself or others). His personal experience is diluted in the impersonal account of the escape into motionlessness. Similarly, in the last move of the extract, it is again 'one' who is enslaved, rather than the informant. I shall explore distancing strategies in detail in Chapter 4.

I see this shift as significant and I interpret it in terms of a tension between accounts of depression and the informants' masculinity; for it suggests a struggle between the incapacitating experience of an illness which at least implicitly attacks the very core of what is perceived as masculinity. This narrative, together with many others I shall explore throughout this book, is a way of coping with powerlessness, something which is socially unacceptable for a man.

Conclusions

In this chapter I have shown how the men I interviewed positioned depression as an independent actor capable of actions impacting them and their lives. Not only had they no influence over the illness, but they also represented themselves as having little influence over their treatment. The independence of depression is preserved also in the case of the much frequent constructions of the illness as a mental state.

Now, even though constructions of depression's agency were ubiquitous, there were considerably fewer constructions in which the informants positioned themselves as direct objects of its actions. Rather, such passiveness was implied or, as in the last of the extracts I showed, distanced from. I see this as the interviewed men's struggle to negotiate their masculinity in view of the illness that overpowers them. It is important to realise that the men I interviewed were at their most powerless, and on a number of levels. Most obviously, they were men receiving psychiatric treatment with all the negative connotations this entails (e.g. Angermeyer and Dietrich, 2006; Angermeyer and Matschinger, 1999; Jorm *et al.*, 2000a). They were men receiving treatment for depression – an illness perhaps less stigmatising than schizophrenia (Angermeyer and Matschinger, 2003; Jorm *et al.*, 2000b) but one which is associated with women. They were powerless in their inability to shake off their illness, and finally, and very importantly for them, they were stripped off just about the most important attributes of masculinity in that most of them did not work and had to rely on their families for support, while those who still had paid employment were threatened by dismissal (I take up the work stories from the corpus in Chapter 9).

I will show this powerlessness throughout the book, but let me offer one final example in which the speaking man positions himself on his own in his understanding and fight against his illness.

Extract 14

> NP: Depression is like alcoholism, there are no cured alcoholics, there are only those who don't drink. At any moment there can be a relapse, just as at any moment an alcoholic can reach for a glass, I think, this is my opinion, but it does not mean that doctors might be in opposition, that depression can get you at any time.

NP is conjuring imagery of a hunt – depression is out to get him and he is not safe. In the original he uses the verb *dopaść*, which I have translated here as 'get'. But *dopaść* suggests more violence and malice. Someone doing it is not only catching, but does it by pouncing, having actively been looking for the prey. And indeed, even though distancing himself (note the use of the impersonal 'you'), it is the informant who is the prey. And while an alcoholic is constructed as someone who gets his drink, at least linguistically being able to decide what to do, in the case of depression, he is only an object of depression's hunt.

This chapter is the beginning of laying out the social landscape of depression as experienced by men who are not only very powerless but also try to preserve at least some pretences of partaking in the dominant model of masculinity. The pretences of agency I referred to above coupled with only occasional positioning of themselves as objects of depression's actions are manifestations of that struggle. I think this is also why depression is constructed as an independent entity. As much as it is invested with the capacity to act, discursively it is also separate from those who are ill with it. Depression's independence serves the goal of positioning oneself outside it, the goal of preserving the pretence of the masculinity untouched by the stigmatising illness.

Such considerations inevitably lead to the issue of gender in psychiatry. It seems crucial to ask of the extent to which men (and indeed women) are offered mental health care with an understanding not only of the fact that they are gendered beings, but of the fact that they construct a particular view of their experiences. For men, at least according to the data I collected, it is a view that rejects depression. One of the questions I immediately posed for myself is, how do you treat an illness that 'one does not have', rather than 'I have'. If depression is always outside, if it has a life of its own, if it is the cunning hunter, can it actually be successfully treated? To put it differently, is NP in Extract 14 convinced of incurability of depression because of the hunting imagery, or is the imagery only incidental? I shall not be able to offer a good answer to the question, yet the question seems an important one. Moreover, to what extent should the treatment have something to do with masculinity? Should it attempt to 'rescue' him?

It would be very easy to deal with the issue by making it a symptom. People in depression have it like that, they speak of depression in a particular way. I do not think that my describing the discourse of depression as a symptom is the way forward. It does not lead to a diagnosis thereof, this is not the way depressed people, or men, speak *because* they are in depression. It has not got the same status as, say, the so-called Beck's cognitive triad, the postulate that people in depression think negatively about themselves, their experiences and their future, which results in depression (Beck, 1976; Beck *et al.*, 1979), which again is largely based, incidentally, on the researchers' interpretations of what the patients say or do while completing psychiatric instruments. Indeed, it is perhaps noteworthy that Blatt (2004), while criticising Beck's, proposes his own triad (dependency, self-criticism, efficacy).

In contrast, these discursive patterns can be explained by the informants' submergence in the society in which they live: in the dominant gender model, and more specifically, the dominant model of masculinity. Such discourse is a way of social coping with a particular predicament by particular people. But what is the impact of a socially situated discourse of depression upon the nosology and, even more importantly, upon the diagnosis of depression? If the way people speak of depression is also social, how can one make a judgement as to when the 'private' experience starts? How can one distil the 'real' symptoms? There is, after all, an argument that since I interviewed patients already receiving treatment, mostly suffering from the recurring depressive episode, they didn't speak as 'one' speaks, but, rather, as a patient speaks. Since it is difficult to ascertain the sources of the discourse, and they are likely to be multiple – from those in the public domain, through medical ones, to those on the ward or in the family – it cannot be seen only as medicalised. In other words, with its roots in the dominant model of masculinity and social stigmatisation of mental illnesses, the discourse of depression I have described above is partly based on how the society at large constructs mental illnesses and their relationship with gender.

Furthermore, I have shown above that it is through the linguistic form that one can fully understand and grasp what the patients say. If this is the case, what is the significance of this fact for the diagnostic and other practices of psychiatry or clinical psychology? Does it matter how the patient says what they say? Is it merely an academic exercise to show that there are patterns in patients' narratives, or can the diagnostician (provided they are suitably trained) make sense of them? I am unlikely to give definite answers to such questions; yet, I have no doubt that it is important to pose them. If socialness of depression can be shown and argued also at the level of the discursive form, as I hope to do in this book, the questions of how to translate it into clinical practice are of utmost significance both to those who suffer psychological distress and to those whose task is to help them. I hope to be able to begin to answer the questions over the course of this book.

However, by suggesting that there is a discourse of depression, I am not trying to suggest that depression does not exist. It does, or at least there are people who find it necessary to avail themselves of psychiatric help; they are people who feel powerless, distressed or perhaps sad in the extreme. As one leaflet I picked up, while sitting in the office of a con-sultant psychiatrist, said, people in depression are so sad that if one can imagine the saddest they have ever been, multiply it by a hundred and it will not come even close to how sad a person suffering from depres-sion is. Their distress is as real as can be and no amount of discourse analysis is going to deconstruct it. In contrast to the anti-psychiatric movement, I think that it is psychiatry in alliance with psychology and psychotherapy that is, for the most part, the most useful and productive site where such distress can be dealt with. It does not mean, however, that nothing can be made better and that linguistics cannot play a use-ful part. And I have no doubt that understanding the social dimension of depression, its construction by those who suffer from it, could be an important part of improving the lot of those who are at their most vulnerable.

This chapter ends the first part of this book, the part that dealt with depression in its own right. I showed what the dominant view of depression is: it is the view of psychiatry. I also showed that psychiatry constructs depression in a particular way. Regardless of the particular theoretical or 'atheoretical' (as the authors of diagnostic manuals would have us believe) take on depression, the illness is constructed by the discourses of those who describe it as a disease, those who attempt to dia-gnose it by the various instruments or those who describe it in academic discourse. In this chapter, I have shown the discourse of experience of depression. I showed that my informants constructed depression mostly agentively, as an entity acting in its own right and through these actions influencing the informants as well as their lives. Even the less frequent constructions in terms of psychological states positioned depression on its own, unrelated to any person who might have those states.

This chapter has also started the main focus of the book: the exploration of how men diagnosed with depression, and receiving treatment for it, speak of their experiences. The next part will explore the constructions of the self in relation to the illness. I am interested in how the men I interviewed constructed themselves, or their selves, in relation to their illness. I shall begin, in Chapter 4, by showing that the predominant way in which they did was by distancing themselves from the illness. It turned out that the self is never actually explicitly ill.

4
At Arm's Length.
The Not-So-Depressed Self

Introduction

This chapter starts my explorations of how the 'self' is positioned in men's accounts of depression. I am going to explore the relationship between the self and the illness, as well as its constructed place in the informants' biography and everyday life. I shall examine to what extent depression was 'espoused' by the self, that is to say how directly my informants constructed themselves as depressed, or in depression.

To a considerable extent I shall be reporting my astonishment with the data. In contrast to my expectations, depression was actually never fully ascribed to the self. The interviewed men invariably distanced themselves from the illness, never directly constructing themselves as depressed. All this despite the fact that all of them had been receiving treatment for depression for considerable amounts of time and that they all had accepted their diagnosis and the fact that they were ill. Yet, at the level of the linguistic form, they actually rejected depression. Thus, I shall begin by discussing the concept of distancing and then move to review the distancing strategies used in the narratives. I shall finish by trying to make sense of these results in terms of the dominant model of masculinity.

Distancing from depression

As I have just said, one of the most noticeable features of the corpus under consideration here is that a vast preponderance of men's accounts of depression was done by means of what could be termed distancing. The speaking men avoided constructing themselves as ill. I realise that it is difficult to describe a 'canonical' way in which people speak of their illness. To make things more difficult, the social scientific literature on illness experience is rather unhelpful here. Researchers so far have focused upon the narrative structures of the narrated experience. There are a number of accounts, from a broadly social scientific (e.g. Greenlagh and Hurwitz, 1998; Hurwitz *et al.*, 2004; Mattingly, 1998; also Charmaz, 1999; Murray, 2000) to more discourse and language based (Chatwin, 2006; Gwyn, 2002), which describe how people talk about their illness. None of these studies takes up the issue of the most basic structure of 'illness talk': how does one actually say 'I am ill'? Simple as such a statement may be, it could be seen as a yardstick of direct ascription of illness.

Needless to say, I am far from claiming that this is the only way of directly speaking of one's illness. One can, of course, imagine a number of other ways: 'I am depressed', 'I suffer from depression', 'I have depression' and probably quite a few others. It seems to me, however, that all these alternatives, as well as the likely others, have two features in common. First, they explicitly refer to who is ill (i.e. such a statement would be a self-reference); second, they actually do explicitly refer to the speaker in terms of illness. The reverse is true of distancing. Thus, I shall assume here that discourses distancing the self from illness are those in which either the self or depression (or indeed both) are not explicit. Thus, distancing strategies are about 'dissolution of ownership' (Bavelas *et al.*, 1990) of the illness.

So, distancing strategies consist in making non-direct reference to who is ill and what he/she is ill with, regardless of whether it is a medical term or not. But in contrast to such discourses as those of emotions and strategies distancing from emotions, which I explored elsewhere (Galasiński, 2004), there is at least one more aspect of 'illness talk' which I think is important to point to. I think that in order for such talk to be direct, non-distanced, the perspective adopted in it must be that of 'experience', the perspective of the person who is actually ill. All those narratives in which the perspective is different are, I shall argue, also indicative of distancing. I am not proposing, however, that the perspective must be that of the patient (Parsons, 1951; also Freund *et al.*, 2003; Williams, 2005), but, rather, that of someone who experiences illness. For saying: 'I am ill' is quite different from saying 'I think I am ill', 'I realise I am ill' and the like. Such constructions shift the position of the speaker from the 'experiencer' to that of an observer. In the latter cases, the speaker takes different rights and duties, a different 'position' (Harré and Slocum, 2003) through which we might expect a different account of the illness.

Now, there is a possible discussion as to the spectrum of directness of illness reference with or without the medical label. Is there a significant analytic mileage to be gained from assuming that someone saying 'I am depressed' is less direct than someone who says 'I have depression'? I tend to think there is not. More importantly, I think that in order to introduce a gradation of directness based on the type of label, one would need to begin the considerations with the actual medical term. Yet, no one speaks of suffering from 'depressive episodes', but of depression. If one rejects the medical term as most direct, terms such as 'depressed' must be seen as equally direct. Moreover, it is difficult to assume that in the context of an interview in which the experience of depression was to be talked about, words such as 'depressed' might not be a direct reference to the illness. Finally, it is probably analytically more fruitful to explore those discourses in which illness is not labelled at all.

I have found all three possible distancing strategies. I shall start with that of making non-explicit references to the self. I shall then show how the informants distanced themselves by adopting different positions from that of the experiencer. Finally, I shall show a few instances in which the informants undermined the illness itself.

Unspecified ill men

The most frequent distancing strategy in the corpus was that of avoiding ascribing depression to the self directly, and only implying self-reference. This is quite significant even though the implications did not make the meaning of self-reference uncertain in some significant way – the statements were quite easily interpretable as referring to the speakers. Let me first show three extracts in which the speakers distance themselves from their depression, the extracts show a complete deletion of the speaker's self from the linguistic form of what they said. Consider the following:

Extract 1

EU: At the beginning, there was the stage that I was able to overcome it, say, in a way, put more effort into engaging into work. But if it didn't produce results relatively quickly, there appeared a sort of internal anxiety. Insomnia was the first effect. Beforehand I didn't pay any attention to it. Now, after another episode I know how it progresses. And later there would come this total incapacitation, I wasn't able to do anything. Locking myself at home, wanting to be at home in bed only. Lack of appetite, difficulty in eating.

Extract 2

FH: I am waiting, very often I am waiting for the evening because this means going to bed and I manage to sleep well so, sleeping is this, like cutting off from these problems, these thoughts. Thoughts circling in the head, generally these more destructive. They are not nice [...] I mean they are thoughts of the kind, perhaps I expressed it wrong, they are not so destructive now, strictly, I mean so destroying, they are more like suspension. What now?

Extract 3

KL: This the question of the problems at home that appear, the question of problem in life that appear and a certain moment they begin to create a mountain, too far to jump off, isn't it? And too low to simply go down. That's how it appears. And later you don't notice that you are by the abyss and now the question. I think I will shoot myself in the head. A statement. And simply, then a problem starts, because people around say, it's impossible to live with you.

In all three extracts there is no hint of the person suffering from the problems mentioned, whether its sleeplessness in (1), destructive thoughts in (2) or the mountain of problems in (3) – they are independent of the people speaking. But it is Extract 1 which makes the point of distancing in the corpus particularly forcefully. The speaker alternates between direct reference to himself and complete backgrounding of the self, that is to say removing the self-reference from explicit discourse (see also van Leeuwen, 1996). Thus while anxiety and sleeplessness (they 'appeared', or 'were there') were not attributed to anyone, EU's attempts to fight them do explicitly refer to him. Even the will to spend time in bed at home is not attributed to anyone. The informant makes only one direct reference to himself with regard to how he experienced depression when he declares he was not able to do anything (in Polish rendered by a verb *potrafić*, with the speaker taking the position of an agent). But I think it is precisely negation that allows the direct reference. Negation constructs the informant as a 'failed doer', someone who constructs themselves in terms of actions, yet these actions are only an aspiration, rather than reality. I shall explore this in some detail in Chapters 5 and 9.

Such shifts between direct self-reference and self-backgrounding also occur in Extract 2. This time, however, the informant speaks of himself directly when he refers to waiting for the relief of the evening (he is an actor of the process of waiting), yet again, the experience of depression, the destructive thoughts, are not attributed to anyone. They are constructed in separation of anyone who might actually think them. Finally, there is also a direct reference to the speaker's possible suicidal thought in Extract 3. Note, however, that he makes the reference in a dramatised way, it is not him speaking here and now. Rather, it is a hypothetical quotation of what he might say to a question that might arise. The direct reference is, actually, an enactment of what might happen, rather than an actual reference to thoughts of suicide and thus experiences of depression. These are invariably distanced from.

The three extracts show the most frequent pattern of distancing consisting of making an implicit self-reference: by means of backgrounding the self, removing it from what is explicitly said. In the following extracts, the distancing is different. It is done through recasting of individual experience. Witness the following:

Extract 4

NP: And this is depression for me, apart from this, perhaps it is also a state of mind.

DG: Could you say more about it?

NP: Well, I don't know for sure whether this state of mind results from this, bad functioning of neurons, or some other things. I don't know, God's intervention, or something like that.

DG: And what is this state of mind in depression?

NP: This state of mind is the way I feel, perhaps not physically, that I feel like doing nothing, but that some powerlessness envelops you.

Extract 5

EU: I feel powerlessness, hopelessness. Hopelessness of the situation. And it is getting tighter. It's getting tighter, because add this feeling that one has a noose on the neck which, in the case of any action, particularly an action which might even have a positive basis, but doesn't come off. It causes that the noose gets tighter and one escapes into some motionlessness, so one doesn't try anything, because one is scared that this noose will get even tighter. [...] one loses control over one's thoughts, that one is unable, that it is getting deeper, that it is paralysing, that it can enslave you.

The two speakers use the same linguistic form to refer to themselves in a distancing way. What I have translated using the impersonal 'you' is rendered by the Polish *człowiek* (literally 'human being', 'man'). Apart from removing the direct reference to the speaker and thus achieving distance, the phrase also recasts the individual experience as more general. Thus, the two fragments position the informants' experiences as what happens to all people in the situation. The powerlessness the speaker might feel does not result from his own individual weakness, rather it is something 'normal'. This is the way things happen, we seem to be told, a natural course of events.

It is interesting to note that also in Extract 5 there is a shift from direct reference to the speaker to the impersonal one. This time, however, the shift is parallel to the increasing strength of the experiences. From powerlessness which is directly ascribed to the speaker, the narrative moves to the feeling of the noose on the neck. The speaker seems to make a judgement as to what is an acceptable level of depression he can ascribe to himself. In both cases, the speakers use the impersonal form in constructions in which they are either explicitly objects of depression's actions (see the previous chapter), or implicitly so, as in Extract 5 in which escape results from the noose of depression tightening on the neck.

These attempts to recast the experience as a more general one, the experience 'one has', is even clearer when speakers decide to position themselves more explicitly within a group of people:

Extract 6

KL: The worst in depression is that we don't get out. That we can't deal with something. Here is the problem. If we know that we used to be able to deal with something. If we know that we used to know it, we used to do it as a matter of course, just like with this eyesight, isn't it? We used to see normally and suddenly something gets darker. We can't deal with something. This is depression for me.

Extract 7

DG: When you heard that you had depression, what did it mean to you?

FH: A strange illness that doesn't put you in bed. [...] what can I say, an illness that to a lesser or greater degree does not let us find ourselves in the surrounding reality.

In Extract 6, by using 'we', the speaker explicitly positions himself as part of a larger group of people. As in the previous extracts, this not only serves the purpose of diluting his individual ownership of depression, distancing himself from it, but also, importantly, tames the experience by showing it as partaken of by a larger group of people. Interestingly, the speaker in Extract 7 also shifts references to 'self', except this time it is a shift between no reference himself (the reference to the illness which is not putting [anyone] to bed cannot easily be seen as a distanced reference to himself) and the reference in terms of the first person plural ('we').

Now, particularly Extract 7 could be seen in terms of the informant's face concerns. What is an acceptable level of depressive symptoms which can be ascribed to oneself? Moreover, disorientation in the world, stereotypically, an un-masculine thing to have, is perhaps better swallowed when shown in a group of like men. It is easier to show oneself as suffering from something in tandem with a number of others. At the same time, of course, the reference dissolves a direct link between the speaker and his depression. What FH is doing is attempting to preserve his 'positive face' (Brown and Levinson, 1987; also Goffman, 1959); that is, oversimplifying, the positive image one has and others have of oneself.

Outsider's perspective

Another distancing strategy used by my informants was the adoption of what I would call an 'outsider's perspective' upon their experiences. In other words, they shed the position of someone who experiences certain problems and adopts one of an observer. The observer position had two manifestations. On the one hand, the speakers spoke of themselves, taking a calm, rational discourse of self-observation; on the other hand, they explicitly took the perspective of other people observing them. In this way the point of view upon depression was located outside the speaker, distancing depression from the speaker even further.

Consider first the extracts in which the speaker adopts the position of a self-observer.

Extract 8

> DG: I understand that the decision to get treatment, the first one, was not your decision?
>
> NP: It was partly my decision because I knew [...], I noticed those symptoms, I noticed because I saw myself, that I am weak, tired, that I sweat and so on, that I can't sleep. These are obvious symptoms.

Extract 9

GT: After my father's death, I was under great pressure, psychologically and physically, I simply could not cope with it all. So I could see that I was not in control of myself. Of all the matters. And that I was giving in at times, I realised that I would not be able to go through it all on my own.

Extract 10

DG: When did you learn you were ill with depression?

GT: I mean I noticed it seeing myself that there was something with me, with my nerves, because there were moments that I simply started to shake. I was irritable. Everything irritated me. Sometimes I ran away from things. I just withdrew. I didn't want to speak to anyone. So they were these symptoms for me that I don't control my nerves and there is something with me.

In all three extracts depression is not introduced as the speaker's experience, but as the result of a rational observation of themselves. The rationality of the observation is particularly clear in the case of Extract 8 in which NP not only introduces his experiences by means of knowing and noticing, but he constructs them as symptoms. The introduction of medical discourse (theoretically, it is doctors who see symptoms, patients are supposed to have experiences) shifts the speaker's discourse even further into the realm of rationality, presumably in even starker contrast to the stereotypical image of mentally ill and depressed people unable to hold a rational thought. But this rationalisation of the accounts goes even further, I think. By identifying one's illness, and especially one of a mental kind, one takes some control over it. Thus, while GT in (10) might be saying he was losing control over his nerves, he still was able to observe it, and thus exercise some control over himself and his capacity to assess reality. This is precisely why I am thinking of such strategies as distancing. By choosing to take the position of an observer, the speakers detach themselves from their experiences, positioning themselves in a bird's-eye view situation. This detachment allows them the distance from their illness.

But I would like to show this strategy as somewhat more complex and argue that it is not only through clauses referring to mental processes

(Halliday, 1994), seeing, thinking, knowing and so on, that speakers introduced distancing in their accounts. Consider the following extract in which the speaker introduces his experiences of depression through an account of his abilities:

Extract 11

> WT: And at the moment I go, I can go to the gym and sit in the car with my bag for an hour and I can't convince myself, my thoughts fight each other, so I won't go in and I go back home because you have to undress there and push too much of it. I hate, I detest that state.

Instead of talking about problems with getting into the gym, WT prefers to shift the perspective onto a more general view of himself. He takes the perspective of someone stepping back and making an assessment of what he is capable of. Furthermore, the generality of the construction removes the focus from the individual visit to the gym, or even the practice of going there, and puts it onto the level of ability with regard to that practice. Note also, incidentally, that the perspective is introduced after a repair – he starts by talking of the practice of going to the gym, and decides to change it onto the more general perspective of potential. The extract here shows the ability of the informant to take an external look at himself, to assess his ability or lack of it (he speaks of being unable to go to the gym). Linguistically, the form offers a more detached view of the illness and thus implies some control over it.

Consider the following extracts in which the speakers look at their experiences through the eyes of other people:

Extract 12

> NP: As regards the first depressive episode, the first signals came to me from my family. More exactly it was my family, my mother, brother, employees even. I became silent, gloomy. Head in the sand. Tired, constantly the somatic symptoms presented themselves, like sweating, I could not get to the first floor without resting on the landing. This kind of phenomena. [. . .] more signals reached me for example, I began to stutter, stammer. That I look bad, don't laugh at all at parties, I sit somewhere aside instead of partying with others. So I realised that I was suitable for the clinic where I called, persuaded by my mother the first time, and later of my own accord.

Extract 13

DG: It might be a difficult question [...] how did depression contribute to your marriage breaking up?

CW: Generally it's the problem of sex. Because all this medication I take now in large quantities causes a major decrease in libido. And it's a problem with a man who is constantly sad and constantly has a lot of problems. It's difficult to bear it. I do realise it.

Extract 14

AZ: Well, my family are fed up with me. If only I could calm down, if only I could stop bothering them. Because I simply need help from someone. Right? So someone could give me a pill or something so something, but one simply, I start crying. I am pestering in general, for my family, I'm making their life difficult and that's it (...).

Despite the similarities, there are some interesting differences between the three fragments. Extract 12 is closest to the rational discourse I discussed above. The informant uses others' perspective as a way of 'diagnosing' that something is wrong with him. But what he constructs as 'first signals' is the beginning of a process which has its resolution in his decision to seek medical help. NP positions others as 'helpers' in his own assessment of himself, his behaviour and emotional states. Indeed, the story of the symptoms perceived by others ends in the informant's assurance that he realised that he needed psychiatric care; and after his mother's advice, he went to see a psychiatrist of his own accord. The rationality of the account is rendered not only by its medicalisation, culminating in the reference to somatic symptoms, but also by the reference to 'signals reaching him from outside'. The speaker uses a formal register, one located somewhere between a scientific and bureaucratic discourse, connoting impersonality and a cold view of the world. It is almost as if he were talking about data he was receiving. In this way the speaker presents a story of depression which is both detached from emotional experiences and constructs him as capable of assessing himself as well as taking seriously the assessment of others.

Extract 13 is somewhat different in that it could be argued to have two distancing mechanisms. The initial problem of sex is not ascribed to anyone, while the lowering of libido is not ascribed to the informant either. The account bears the hallmarks of a leaflet citing the side effects of anti-depressant medication and the only clue that the account might be about him is that he actually does take the medication. But then

CW shifts the perspective onto one which is implied to be his wife's and combining it with the impersonal 'man' to convey it. One could say this is a case of double distancing as it both removes the informant from the illness and shows it more as the wife's problem, rather than a 'real' one. The informant's account is extremely face-threatening (i.e. one which puts his (positive) face at much risk, Brown and Levinson, 1987). The story of his lowered libido, implicitly put from the perspective of his dissatisfied wife, is a direct threat to the informant's masculinity. To put it bluntly, a grown-up man's admission that he is unable to perform sexually questions the very core of his stereotypical masculinity. I have little doubt that the double strategy of distancing is used by the informant precisely because of the extreme face-threat of the situation. The distancing is an attempt to save CW's manhood and masculinity.

The outside perspective in Extract 14 takes what is happening in the previous one even further. Depression is shown as, primarily, a problem for the family, rather than a 'real' one and is contrasted with that of the informant's. While they are fed up, he needs help. Depression is not only shown through the family's eyes, but it is also rejected by them (I shall discuss it in detail in Chapter 10), and, quite poignantly, the rejection seems to be accepted by AZ himself. Note also that while the contrast of the perspectives removes the speaker from depression, his own statement of needing help is made in very ambiguous terms. The informant does not specify why he needs help, or what kind of help he needs. He simply does need help. While it might be argued that given the context of the interview and its topic, AZ might have decided not to have mentioned depression explicitly, admittedly, however, his ambiguity could also be seen as distancing from depression itself.

On not being ill at all – the depression's perspective

But I would like to discuss one final extract. It harks back directly to the previous chapter in which I argued that the constructions of autonomous depression can be seen in terms of the informants' wish to preserve their masculinity and personhood, more generally. The extract below is precisely showing depression as autonomous, and the person ill with it as the object of the illness' actions. Witness the following:

Extract 15

DG: What does it mean that you are ill of this kind of illness?

EU: A reappearing cycle of various symptoms which escalate and which, by intensifying, do not let me control my own behaviour, my own, I don't know, way of thinking, which incapacitate me in a sense.

The construction of the informant as the object of depression's actions is done both in the form and in the content of what he said. In form, depression is put in the position of the agent in constructions of allowing, incapacitating (even though mitigated by 'in a sense'), while it has a life of its own, in its escalating and increasing. In content, the speaker talks about incapacitating, that is lack of control over his/her actions.

The construction of the self as the target of depression can, in my view, be also seen as distancing strategy. For if the 'default' way of speaking about illness is to ascribe illness to the person who is ill, as in 'I am ill', 'I have depression' and so on, the change of the agentive structure is quite significant. Not only is the illness autonomous, as I demonstrated in Chapter 3, but the self is actually not ill. Thus, if being ill is primarily a relational process (Halliday, 1994), a process of 'being something' (once again, I am not proposing that this is the only or the canonical way of speaking of illness, rather it is typical, exactly as in the United Kingdom one would speak of 'having a cold', or 'having a bit of a virus', or simply 'having a flu'), it requires forms of ascribing an illness to the ill person. The systematic representation of depression as an agent must be seen as marked and the markedness consists precisely in removing the illness from the ill person. The relationship constructed in such forms is perhaps that of a struggle, or some other action, but not that of being ill.

What I am proposing therefore is that there is a close link between representations of depression as an autonomous entity and representations of the self in illness. These constructions have one overarching goal – to detach the illness from the ill self. As in the previous chapter I see this in terms of both the preservation of masculinity and, at a more basic level, the personhood of the ill person.

Depression undermined

The least frequent in the narratives of the men I interviewed was the strategy which distanced them from the illness itself. This is probably to do with the fact that, as I said earlier, the context of the interview was a hospital in which the informants were receiving treatment for diagnosed depression. The distancing itself was also at its weakest, mostly done in tandem with the other strategies. Still, there were a number of instances in which my informants talked about themselves directly in the context of their depression, but the illness itself was undermined, problematised, distanced from. Witness the following extracts.

Extract 16

KL: I mean the problem of depression appears a bit later I think. Instead [unclear] it is a fairly complex problem because I acted in distress. I was in this pseudo-depression right? Which could be said because I became closed, but I was very aggressive with it, and I acted very much to the detriment not only of myself but all those around me. Simply. So it was such aggression with depression of a kind.

Extract 17

DG: When did you learn you were ill with depression?

GT: I mean I noticed it seeing myself that there was something with me, with my nerves, because there were moments that I simply started to shake. I was irritable. Everything irritated me. Sometimes I ran away from things. I just withdrew. I didn't want to speak to anyone. So they were these symptoms for me that I don't control my nerves and there is something with me.

Extract 18

GT: What is depression for me? It is a psychological low of a kind. In which I see the absurdity of life. Unwillingness to live. Everything irritates me. I would like to be on my own. To isolate myself. Perhaps even to commit suicide. Just to be left alone.

All three informants take a different approach to undermining their condition. KL in (16) shows the 'medical' complexity of his condition, presenting it as not sufficiently 'depressive' or pure. It is underscored by the labelling of his illness as pseudo-depression. The undermining goes further in his use of the pronoun *taka* (here: 'of a kind') at the end of the fragment. It is not a 'real' depression, it is only attached to aggression which in itself is 'of a kind'. The speaker in Extract 17, on the other hand, prefers to be indeterminate about what it was that was happening to him. Even though he exemplifies what kind of things made him think that something was wrong, these are explicitly positioned as symptoms of the never identified 'something with the nerves'. Note also that he also uses the temporal frame to show that the symptoms might not be as severe as one might think. While there were only moments when he shook, the other events – which he represents as symptoms – happened only sometimes. And it is the indeterminacy of what might be thought of as symptoms which is at the core of the distancing in Extract 18. Also here the pronoun *taki* ('of a kind') is used, but it introduces even more uncertainty when combined with *pewnie* (an adverb which is used to introduce uncertainty into what is being said, I am translating it here as 'I guess'). But the uncertainty is not merely an indication that the speaker is not sure of what is happening to him, rather, it indicates that he is not sure that he can actually use the expression *psychiczny dołek* ('psychological low'). The term itself is in fact quite mild and normally used when people are simply in a low mood and certainly would not normally be seen as pathological.

The final extract I would like to discuss here is perhaps less clear, still it shows an attempt to construct depression as a mild, gradual condition, which eventually is decided upon by the person himself.

Extract 19

> DE: So it started, this illness of mine. I drove my car to get work, I functioned normally, but I started to withdraw from those duties at work and at home and that was it. It came by itself, the thought, it was such an intensification of this pain, of it all, of this inability to be normal that one had to appear, no one advised me.

From the indeterminate reference to 'this illness of mine' (in itself a distancing strategy), the speaker shows his path from the gradual onset to the decision to get medical help. The informant's decision to label what had been happening to him as illness is quite unique in the corpus and in contrast to representations of depression as autonomous. Moreover, DE shows himself as responsible for withdrawing himself from his duties. But it is the brief account of the decision to get help which is I think the most interesting here. It seems that when it comes to receiving psychiatric treatment, the undermining of the illness is not enough. And this is indeed the moment when he shifts from a direct reference to himself to a very distanced one. Not only does he use the word *człowiek* (here 'one') to refer to himself, a strategy to ambiguate who actually is ill, but he also never actually explicitly says where he decided to 'appear', backgrounding in this way the possible reference to the psychiatric clinic. The verb 'appear' is interesting in its own right as it does not imply agency, a decision. Save for things supernatural, appearing refers to being perceived rather than to a decision to 'beam down' somewhere.

Conclusions

In this chapter I asked the question of how the men I interviewed discursively constructed their selves in relation to their depression. The answer was quite surprising. Despite that all the men who talked to me were diagnosed with depression, accepted it, received treatment for the illness, in some cases for many years, for which they came voluntarily with a stronger or weaker conviction that it was working, their narratives invariably constructed a problematic relationship for the self and depression. The self was never directly in depression, it was always outside it. The speakers achieved it by using three distancing strategies. They ambiguated the self which was completely deleted from the structure of what they said, or backgrounded in some other ways, for example by the use of the impersonal forms or the use of 'we'. Second, they took an outside perspective on depression. It manifested itself by adopting either a 'rational', external observer's look at the illness or the view of others. The third distancing strategy was that of undermining, belittling the illness itself. The informants represented their depression as not a real one.

I think these discourses have roots both in the local level of interaction and in the macro-level of gender ideologies. Let me briefly explore particularly the former. Although it has been established that patients tend to be reluctant to disclose emotional distress (Cape, 2001; Cape and McCullough, 1999; Kadam *et al.*, 2001; Prior *et al.*, 2003), face concerns are rarely taken up by researchers. Pollock (2007) proposed that it is face concerns that influence patients' willingness to disclose distress in order to present themselves as 'good', that is uncomplaining and stoic, patients (see also Salmon and Manyande, 1996; Werner *et al.*, 2004). What I would like to suggest, however, is that it is not only the disclosure of emotional distress or mental illness that is at issue. It is also the question of *how* it will be presented.

The accounts I presented above are not suggestive of concealment of depression or more generally distress, but, rather, of mitigating it. Now, mitigating devices are normally described as those expressions which are used to soften the intention behind an unwelcome action (Ng and Bradac, 1993; also Brown and Levinson, 1987; Galasiński, 2000). Mey (2001) proposes a more helpful definition here, saying that mitigation devices take the edge off 'face-threats'. As the informants are required to 'open up' and speak of distress in a non-intimate situation, the distancing strategies help them negotiate this requirement, precisely taking the edge off the face threat. The informants are able to do both: to speak of their psychiatric illness but in a way which is safer. Particularly this kind of argument shows the acute need of more discourse analytic studies of the discourses of mental illness, for it is through the analysis of the discursive form that one can achieve a deeper understanding of the relationship between the patient's face and his (or her) psychological distress and ways in which it is negotiated and discursively constructed.

The macro-level roots of the distancing strategies are to do with the gender context of my informants' illness. The dominant model of masculinity (I discuss it in some detail in Chapter 8) requires men to be strong, emotionally detached, rational, while illness, and depression in particular, makes them anything but. The strategies the men used allow them to recover and preserve some of the masculinity that can be seen to have been lost through depression. But the three strategies achieve it differently. Those focusing on the self and the illness simply remove the self from the realm of depression – the illness is constructed as inapplicable to the particular individual. In this sense, undermining of depression also has a similar effect. The outside perspective achieves distancing by changing the discourse of illness into a discourse of rationality, particularly by taking the position of an observer and locating the speaker in the rational discourse a man is stereotypically expected to have.

The question that arises here is that of the relationship between depression and gender. I shall be discussing it throughout this book; here, however, I would like to signpost one particular issue. Gender and its expectations not only seem to underpin men's discourses of the self, but, importantly, they are also a source of suffering. If indeed it is the case that the distancing strategies are in part a result of the dominant discourses of masculinity, then they can be seen as the men's constant aspiration to partake of those discourses. And as they are unable to, what is left is only a symbolic action concealing the fact. This is the first time that we encounter the double bind of men's depression. Not only do my informants suffer from depression, but they also suffer from the fact that they are men in depression.

Yet, choosing to interpret the discourses above in terms of the dominant model of masculinity, I was careful to note that it is one of their roots. It would be quite simplistic to propose that it is only gender in which the men's narratives are submerged. There is little doubt that there must be a number of other discursive resources the men fall back upon. The distancing strategies can also be seen in terms of avoidance of stigmatisation related to mental illness. As people who are mentally ill are socially rejected and distanced from (Angermeyer and Matschinger, 1997, 2004; Link et al., 1999; Socall and Holtgraves, 1993), distancing strategies can very easily be seen as means to avoid stigmatisation. If it is not me who is ill, if I can display 'rational judgement', if I am not ill of a 'real depression', perhaps I might escape one of the multitude of negative labels related to mental illness.

There is of course no 'right' answer to what is *the* discursive resource my informants drew upon. Most likely, it was all three resources at the same time, together with some I am unaware of. What I am proposing, however, is that those which are to do with masculinity and with stigma are *likely* to be the dominant ones. In Chapter 5, I continue exploring the relationship between self and depression. I shall be focusing on how the men I interviewed talk about their everyday life and how depression features in it. I shall show that the discourses used in the accounts of daily life are anchored in the same predominant theme of removing depression from the masculine self.

5
Life Illness. Depression and the Accounts of Everyday Life

Introduction

In the previous chapter I explored the relationship between the discursively constructed self and depression men suffer from. It turned out that the self is situated outside the illness. Whether the self was backgrounded, or the speaker took the position of an observer or, finally, undermined the illness itself, depression was always detached from, never experienced directly in, the men's narratives. With some reservations, I located the roots of these constructions in gender ideologies, which lay out a host of expectations of what it means to be a man. Being depressed is not one of these. In this chapter I am continuing the exploration of the discourse of the depressed self.

Now, another expectation I had with regard to the data I was collecting was that the narratives of my informants would be constructed predominantly in terms of how they feel, their psychological or emotional states. This expectation too turned out to be wrong. The narratives of the 'depressed self' were predominantly told in terms of actions. In this chapter I shall take the following route. I shall first discuss the action-orientedness in constructions of self. I shall point out that this also locates the illness in life, so to say, rather than in the self. Finally, I shall juxtapose these constructions with the narratives of the life without depression and show that the implicit normality of life without depression is the primary ideology permeating the men's discourses.

Depressed actions

One of the most striking features of the corpus is that when speaking of depression, the interviewed men constructed themselves predominantly in terms of actions. They spoke of doing rather than being. Moreover, even in cases when agency is linguistically limited and is mediated by, say, a state, there is a strong tendency in the narratives to construct the self in action terms. Consider the following examples first:

Extract 1

JS: If I work, I try to fight the depressive state, but it looks like that I go to work and immediately after coming from work I go to bed. I cover myself with a blanket and even if I have something to do for the next day I tell myself that I will do it in an hour or two and I struggle till the morning. And that's the way it looks. Usually I don't do what I have to do and I go to work again and obviously if I don't do what I had to do, for example preparing for a lesson, then the lesson goes worse and automatically the pupils start behaving worse and I stop managing with them and everything winds up so, day in day out and it's getting worse and worse. That's the way it happens.

Extract 2

BC: My day is mainly, mainly anxiety. I mean I get up in the morning with the anxiety that I have to go out. I wake up in the morning and I look at the watch, a moment more, a moment more. Then I get dressed. My wife gives me a lift to the [theatre name]. From the theatre I go on foot or I take a bus with my daughter who goes to school. I live outside [city]. With anxiety I go to therapy. That I won't manage, won't cope. But then the therapy passes. There is this anxiety all the time. Headache. I mean not so much a headache but a terrible tension and the anxiety. I don't know what I am supposed to do. And later I either arrange to meet my wife, usually, so far she has picked me up from here, because it's the first week I have been coming here. Today it's the fourth time I am here. So my wife has so far picked me up. Today, I spend the night at my mom's and I have to get there by bus, so it scares me a little. Generally these means, for 25 years I have driven a car, so these means of transportation, at the moment I have to use them and they are a problem for me, a big challenge. And there is this hopelessness that at the moment I don't know this therapy helps me a lot, that it must chance. Chemistry in the head which simply, this way of thinking, like yesterday, that it all looked different.

The extent to which depression for the two informants is constructed in terms of actions is quite striking. The two men are not unfettered in their actions, there might be limitations, difficulties, still depression for the two informants means doing things, albeit in a particular way. Sometimes it might mean not doing what is planned (as in Extract 1), still both informants construct themselves predominantly in terms of material processes (on types of process, see Halliday, 1994); that is, they do, lie down, go, dress and the like. This is complemented by behavioural processes: they spend the night, cope, tire and so on; also here the action-orientedness is quite clear. In contrast to the constructions I shall show below, the ones above are also striking in that the speakers construct themselves as actors, doers. In their narratives, depression might limit the action, make it more problematic, yet, it does not take away the ability to act.

The question I asked myself when I was reading the data was that of the source of this action orientation. There is of course the relatively easy answer of the dominant model of masculinity – a man is expected to do rather than to be, and the action orientation is an attempt to preserve this aspect of masculinity. I thought perhaps even a depressed man must still do things in order to partake of the masculinity he stands to lose. But then, I think the reasons for the action orientation are deeper than that. Let me first show the following two extracts in which the action orientation of my informants' discourse continues even if their actions are not framed by the speakers' agency. Witness the following extracts:

Extract 3

> GT: When I am in depression, unfortunately I wake up at night, between two and three in the morning. Coffee. A cigarette, I have those thoughts, idiotic, even suicidal. Sometimes. I find it difficult to get going in the morning. Get dressed, wash, shave. I walk the dog and I have such a day, I lie a lot. I can't do anything. Despite that I have a lot to do, because there is always something to do at home, I can't concentrate. I push away these various matters, issues. It's worse then. It's worse so I doze through, skive the entire day, then I wake up in the night, coffee, cigarette till tiredness.

Extract 4

> AZ: What is depression for me? Depression unsettles me simply, it is a disorder which unsettles me from the material [unclear]. I don't know what to do at all, I don't know what to do, how to organise work for myself. Certain things which were obvious for me, to do things,

improve lighting, if something went out, or to repair a socket, now it takes the significance of hard work with which I shall not manage, because I have no idea how to do it, while beforehand I would do it, I enjoyed it.

In both extracts the informants introduce action through mental processes, what they can or cannot do, what they do or do know how to do, what they find difficult or push away. The action orientation is mediated through the informants' abilities and inabilities. But apart from the mere focus on doing, I think what they are also constructing is a social expectation that they would do all these things. Note that both men refer to those mundane jobs about the house, which are, traditionally, jobs for a man. And, traditionally, to my eternal frustration, jobs that not only every man should be able to do, but quite a lot of men actually are. The action-orientedness turns out to be pressure to perform also.

This is in line with the point made by New (2001), who pointed out that the area of work (as in military service or criminal justice) is a site of systematic inequality suffered by men. The life as the two informants (both university graduates) know it is that they are supposed to be able to repair a socket or improve the lighting. And if they cannot, they are probably lesser men. For both men, depression means at least to an extent their inability to perform the 'manly' tasks. It might also be about how they feel; yet, it is actions and the inability to perform them that grinds them down further.

There is of course a marked difference between the first two extracts I quoted (1 and 2) and the two above. While in the former the men constructed themselves as doers, here, at first sight, the men construct as not doing things. But I think the four extracts are stemming from the same source. The speakers in Extracts 3 and 4 do not so much *not* do – I would describe them as 'failed doers'. They are expected to do and they accept that 'duty'. It is just that they are unable to perform it and become more depressed. In this way, here the dominant model of masculinity can also be seen as a source of suffering. Once again, my informants suffer from depression not only as human beings, but also because they are men. It is their masculinity which is an additional source of distress.

The pressure to perform that is placed by social expectations of men is perhaps best rendered by the following extract:

Extract 5

BC: At the moment I can see a wall, I mean I can't see any perspective, any possibility of snapping out this. If thoughts start running along such existential tracks, I mean, because I am unable to function simply, then simply I am almost [unclear] unable to function. I am unable to earn, keep my family, I am unable, perhaps I shall be, I don't know, there are already such thoughts I simply don't know what will become of me, because even in order to beg, in order to be a beggar, you have to show some initiative, cunningness. Yet, one cannot imagine this worst existence because it also requires some skills, cunningness. Instead in this state I have no such skills. I am unable and what's worst, it's hard after coming back from a depressive state to believe that it will change.

BC's problem is subsumed by the word *funkcjonować* ('to function', 'to operate'), one which carries with it connotations of normality, of meeting social expectations, although perhaps not exceeding them; it is often collocated with *normalnie* ('normally'). The verb encapsulates the entirety of actions that are 'normally' performed by a person, in this case a man. Depression for BC is precisely the inability to operate normally, not to do all those things. It is complemented by his inability to earn money and to provide for his family. But the expectation to act is manifest also in the latter part of the extract. Note that BC is speaking of his lack of initiative. Not having the initiative even to be a beggar is represented as disqualifying him, and also as distressing.

Yet, the expectation to do things is not only related to masculinity, though. It is also related to fatherhood. Depression is not only about performing as a man (or a handyman), but also as a father:

Extract 6

EU: There comes for example a wave of powerlessness that I simply, either I will force myself at the particular moment, I can't leave a six-month child to lie on its own, a soiled nappy, hungry, crying, so, I grit my teeth and I try to take it positively, that I have someone to do it for. But sometimes, the little one's asleep, I have something planned, to do something at home and I land in bed, not being able to, and I lose track of time. I want, I would like for example, I would like for example to rest, say, 10–15 minutes, an hour comes out of this, the child won't wake up, for example. And I have very bad feelings that I have wasted the time. That I have not used the time for a rest. Let's say I feel worse than before.

The action-orientedness of what EU said is mediated through his volitional states, his ability or inability to force himself to do things. Crucially here, it is not only the inability to do things which is depressing for EU here, it is also the fact that he does not perform well enough. The distress comes from wasting time, as if the man's time is precious and not to be wasted. But there is another point I would like to make. In a rare study on fatherhood and mental illness, Williams (2007) notes fathers' solitary discourses of coping with their conditions and their attempts not to disclose them. I think EU's account ties into such discourses. Forcing himself to tend to his baby, and we almost hear the gritting of his teeth, I think EU also is trying to show himself as a responsible father who can take care of his child. As in Williams' study, there is no attempt to seek help, but rather attempts to contain his feelings combined with a rational account of what was going on.

The discourse of the depressed self of the men I interviewed is strongly action-oriented. It not only means that the narratives I collected positioned the speakers as actors, however limited – the most typical account was that of inability to do things – it also means the positioning of the speakers as 'failed doers', those who are expected to do things, who want to do things, but are unable to.

Life hurts

But it is not only the pressures of what it means to be a 'real' man which are important here. What is also significant is the more general location of the narratives in the realm of, shall I say, life, rather than self. In other words, by focusing on actions, whether actual or failed, the speaking men focus upon their lives, rather than their selves and their psychological or emotional states. Let me exemplify it a little further.

Extract 7

> FH: [speaking of his job as a design engineer] I could sit and some, well, I don't know how to solve this, it kind of seems, but I don't know how to draw these lines, which ways, how to solve this problem, so it's solved properly till the end. Because a little fragment here, but what next? Because it's related to designing something which must have a beginning which always makes for a problem, so there must be an end, one which makes the problem stop being a problem, but gets a full solution in its entirety. And to the extent that I could sit in the office for the entire night, sit with a drawing, smoke a pack of cigarettes and not really solve the problem.

Extract 8

BC: The thinking kind of gets twisted round this existence and one is afraid of pain. One is afraid of suffering. Afraid of cold, afraid of hunger, afraid of everything. There is such fear. Despite that one stops watching TV or read, because everything is associated that I would definitely not manage in such a situation, that the world requires fighting. That it requires an action, and one is not capable of any action. Despite the comfortable conditions that I have, because my [business] partner takes care of the company, my wife takes care of me [unclear], I see it as one total great disaster. That it will all end tragically for me, for my family. Except that here is the main stress, because in illness one thinks mainly about oneself, simply because one suffers. So I think about the family, how the children will manage, how my wife will manage with it all. But mainly I simply can't see the possibility of managing myself.

Extract 7 is relatively straightforward in the context of this discussion. The speaker, a design engineer, shows himself unable to do his work, agonising over problems he is no longer able to solve. Depression encroaches on life and takes away the ability to get on with it. But Extract 8 is more interesting in this respect. The speaker starts in the way I expected most of the narratives would he focuses on problems of existence, his fears, anxieties. But this focus on himself is very quickly changed into a story of how he and his family cope with life. It is a story about the brutal world with which he cannot cope despite his work, his business being taken care of by his business partner and his wife. Even the explicit declaration of the focus upon himself is quickly changed into that upon his family and their ability to manage in life.

But it is not only professional or 'financial' life which is at stake in the men's narratives. The men talked also about their ability to partake of and cope with the mundane. Witness the following extracts:

Extract 9

EU: The situation when she is the person bringing money home, when I am afraid to go to a shop. I am afraid to do the shopping because I don't know what to buy, when I can't decide, when I am at the mercy of social security officials, or in the tax office, wherever I am, such an inhumane approach to you. One is treated like a crook, like a tramp. It makes me feel incapacitated.

Extract 10

> DE: A certain distance has arisen between me and [my family] but more because I am unable, shall I say, to function normally, I mean I am unable to perform the duties of a husband and wife, phew, husband, father [laughs] so this is why this distance arises, right? I am on the margin, I prefer to shut myself in a room, or lie down and do nothing.

Both speakers cannot participate in everyday life of their families as they cannot fulfil the expected duties of a family member. Once again depression is not so much what is inside (the sadness or whatever else) but it is about exclusion from 'normal' life. Interestingly, however, the problem is not only the speakers' as both informants show it as a problem for others. And while EU in (9) shows the negative attitude of the officials in the social security or tax offices, DE in (10) shows his family as having a problem with his withdrawal. The distance between him and the family results from his inability to perform his 'normal' duties of a husband or a father as he prefers withdrawing from life. Interestingly, the informant seems to accept the family's rejection by using *przecież*, a word notoriously difficult to translate into English, which I rendered here as 'after all', through which it is the family's version of the story which is given the status of validity.

This feeling of surrender that can be sensed in Extract 10 was relatively rare. The informants preferred either talking simply in terms of inability, as in (9) – with the struggle perhaps culturally implied in the accounts – or to show their struggle, be it as in (7), when as much as the attempts to solve the problems were futile, they were also long and hard made. Consider another example in which the informant is trying very hard to show himself as useful (a trait I will explore more in Part 3 of the book when I talk explicitly about the relationship between depression and masculinity):

Extract 11

> FH: I try to help with something for the dinner. Or I wash up. As I said to the ladies here, I say that the dishwasher has a night off and I prefer to wash up than to make the load and turn it on. I like keeping myself busy with something.

The speaker undermines his actions right from the start. He talks about trying to help out with dinner, rather than just helping, and the help is reduced to doing 'something'. Still he is constructing himself as useful, trying to take part in the daily life of his family. Not only does he joke about it (the dishwasher had a night off), but washes up straight away is his choice. In this way, he also controls part of that life, however minute. The end of the fragment, a statement of liking to do something, offers further evidence to his being able to do something useful and contribute to the family.

The final extract I would like to show here shows that even the more existential narratives still inevitably refer to the world of action:

Extract 12

> WT: For three years, it caught me and something I never had, I always thought about the basic day, a day which exists and I used to pick out optimistic things from life. I mean I have this to do, I have to go there, instead for three years I have been thinking about the entirety of life. About the idiocy of what I did, no pension, no, really, if I sprain a foot and I am unemployed, what have I achieved? At the moment when no one knows me, when it comes to summing up, I can see how shallow everything is, it was not supposed to be like that. It's a waste of time, because one is 41 and as I used to defend the thesis that age is not important, the way one feels is important, more and more often I recall my age and I think that's it. I will not do anything else in life.

For better or worse, WT is taking stock of his active life, an assessment which does not appear to be favourable in his view. And while he does not offer insight into his views on what caused what – is it depression that makes him take stock or whether the assessment is so negative that it is depressing – still it is clear that depression means limitation in his activities. He is not going to do much more in life – depression is putting an end to his activities.

The main point I would like to make in this chapter, one based on the data I collected and thus not aspiring to an acontextual universality, is that in contrast to the diagnostic manuals and, probably, psychiatric practice, depression, at least that suffered by men, might not be about depressed mood, or perhaps, to put myself on a safer ground, it is not primarily about depressed mood. In the narratives of the men I interviewed, depression is about the ability to cope with life, to face and manage what life throws at the person. To put it differently, depression is about the ability to meet the society's expectations as to what a man is supposed to do in his daily duties. While I shall explore this statement on a number occasions throughout this book, let me offer an extract in which the speaker almost explicitly makes the point I have just made.

Extract 13

> DE: I would harness, harness myself to life again, which was such a positive [laughs] stimulus in life for me.
>
> DG: You miss the harness?
>
> DE: I do. Nothing pulls, I don't know which way, which way to go, and one always went straight, one used to go straight, and now one goes sideways, one leans out too much, doesn't know what to do with oneself. This is the worst, not to know. You come home and you don't know, neither to go out, nor to stay, nor to lie down, sleep, nor to help out with something. You don't know how to organise your life. Which is the worst for me in this depression, this is the worst. I would prefer being pressed more, than be so free.

Putting on the harness of life for the informant means being able to be active. Depression, on the other hand, is the opposite. Depression means he has not got the drive, he is unable to organise his life, take control, be active. The speaker is not interested in enjoyment, in happiness or even lack of sadness. His is interested in a yoke, in a duty one has to cope with, he wants a struggle, something that grinds him down while manages to cope and overcome it. The imagery of the harness is the imagery of a working horse that has to pull a wagon which is so heavy that its back could break. But the wagon starts and the horse wins. This is the life without depression – it is a life in which DE can win against the odds.

The location of depression in life rather than in psychological states is significant as it positions it in terms of being able or unable to deal with the society's expectations upon a man. This, I think, might have significant consequences for understanding the depressive episode as I shall discuss below.

The happy medium?

However, the construction of depression in terms of action and placing it in the realm of professional and everyday life leads to an interesting contradiction in the narratives I collected. When my informants talked about themselves as they were before suffering from depression, or before the current episode, they represented themselves mostly in action terms. Except that for the most part these constructions concerned their work, and it was rendered in terms of excess. They worked too much, they tried too much, and eventually something gave. Obviously, these constructions were not as ubiquitous as those of the activities in depression. The individual contexts of depression weighed very heavily here. For example, I interviewed a man whose child was killed in a road accident. On a different occasion, I interviewed a man who saw his depression very clearly as the result of his wife's marital infidelity. These men would not have spoken about their lack of rest before the illness. Quite interestingly, however, these contexts were still overridden when the men talked about their life while depressed. They still constructed themselves in terms of action and located depression in the realm of life. With this reservation in mind, consider the following two extracts:

Extract 14

> GT: It came from I think that I never took care of myself at work. For several years I didn't know what a holiday was, I never took it. I was always in the middle of production, among people, and dealt with many things. I was a bit of a workaholic. And for the decision whether I would get out after 8 or 10 hours didn't matter. [...] I was always involved in everything, I was managing, always high revs.

Extract 15

> KL: Look, every person, when he worked for a time, should rest, do something else, I don't know, making snowmen, or clay ashtrays. Or perhaps airplane models. Walk the dog, right? Talk to the child. Talk to the wife about topics unrelated to work. Go for a beer with a friend. Or watch a match with a group of friends [...] instead, I forgot about this all. Simply. For me it was going to work, coming back from work, yes, darling we'll go for a walk, right? We came back home, and dad turned the laptop on and worked on. At half past midnight dad finished work and at 9 he was at work, somewhere in Poland.

The two informants construct work as the source of their depression. They worked too much, they were under too much stress, they forgot to rest and relax. What is quite fascinating in these accounts is that it seems that the difference between depression and health is that of the kind of excess. While healthy, the interviewed men constructed themselves in terms of excessive work, forgetting about themselves, not taking the time to rest or relax. Their activities were too intensive, too draining. When depressed, their activities became a problem: they were too slow, too little or did not happen at all. Mental health as implied by the narratives of men diagnosed with depression is that of a lack of a happy medium of activities.

Such a statement is quite significant for an understanding of mental illness as a thoroughly gendered affair. While work and activity are central planks of dominant masculine ideologies, it is difficult not to see the accounts my informants offered in such terms. Now, I do not wish to engage in a discussion on the merits of a biological, psychological or social understanding of depression (for a review see Mann, 1989) and I realise that patients' beliefs about the causes of their illness might not be accurate (e.g. Prior, 2003). And indeed, I do not wish to say that it is gender ideology which is responsible for my informants' depression, as such a statement would be both simplistic and more than likely untrue. Yet, what I shall be arguing is that the discursive construction of the illness might point to a possible direction of where recovery from the illness might be found. Thus, what I am arguing, more generally, is that the narratives of self that are offered by the men I interviewed are underpinned by worldviews which are difficult to ignore in considering men's depression and routes to recovery from it.

Conclusions

In this chapter I was interested in the narrated self being typically constructed in terms of action. The key conclusion of this chapter is that in the narratives of the men diagnosed with depression, the illness is not so much related to low mood or any other psychological or emotional state, but to their inability to cope with life. This is indeed why my informants practically did not speak of sadness, preferring to speak of powerlessness or incapacitation. The core of their depression seems being a 'failed doer'. Let me stress that I am not suggesting that people in depression lack the drive to be active. What I am suggesting is, in contrast to the psychiatric knowledge, that depression is located 'out there' rather than 'in the heads' and that it is coping with the social expectations that is at its core, at least for the men I interviewed. Moreover, my data could be seen as contextualising more a study by Strandmark K (2004), who demonstrated that ill health was seen in terms of powerlessness by her informants. The powerlessness I am talking about here is only indirectly related to one's self-image, as it primarily is located in stories of life, rather than the self.

I would also like to comment on the diagnostic criteria of the depressive episode. First, I reject Stefanis and Stefanis (2002: 9), who point out that 'the depressed mood is always there, it only needs to be elicited' (for a brief critique, see Kendell, 2002). You can only wonder how much elicitation might in fact be needed before the mood is finally elicited. I also realise that one of the two key aspects of the diagnostic criteria of the depressive episode is 'loss of interest or pleasure in activities that are normally pleasurable' (WHO, 1993: 83; with a similar but slightly more elaborate criterion present also in the DSM). My informants were not interested in having fun with their life, or interested in doing things as part of the pleasures of life, however those pleasures are to be understood. They were not talking about their inability to maintain interest in previously enjoyable activities (Stefanis and Stefanis, 2002; see also Zimmerman, 1994 for the line of questioning appropriate in diagnosing major depression, clearly showing the loss of 'fun' the patient might experience in his life). In contrast, my informants wanted to maintain their participation in what they consider 'normal' life. To make the point even in stronger terms, DE in (13) put it in an interesting way: he wanted a harness, with all its negative connotations. There is no wish to be interested, to find pleasure or satisfaction. DE is interested in being able to work hard and then, probably, moan about it. His primary interest, however, is to be able to fulfil the expectations the society placed on men.

There is a reservation to be made here. It is important to note that my argument is not part of the strand of illness experience that deals with meanings of illness, its biographical disruptions, strategies of coping and so on (see Lawton, 2003; Pierret, 2003) or the lay beliefs of illnesses (Prior, 2003). It is based upon ideologies, or world views, accomplished by the lexico-grammatical form. Such a focus also means that the argument I am proposing is not based on what my informants set out to tell, but on how discursively constructed is the reality in which they are submerged.

Now, academics are quite in agreement that paid employment and, more generally, purposeful activity is one of the cores of the dominant masculine ideology (for a more detailed account, see Chapter 9). A study by Willott and Griffin (2004) reports that long-term unemployed men continued to construct their identity around the persona of the breadwinner, although they had no access to the kinds of capital (Bourdieu, 1984) with which to support such constructions. There is no reason to believe that men in depression are somehow exempt from such discourses. Indeed, one could even speculate that because their inability to engage in purposeful activity results from mental illness, the discourses of masculinity apply even more readily (incidentally, patients diagnosed with schizophrenia saw their discharge for hospital predominantly as a possibility of being ordinary – a 'normal' and productive member of the community, Lorencz, 1991). After all, while unemployment might result from all sorts of external economic, social and other configurations, lack of work resulting from depression can very easily be seen as resulting from the man himself. In this way, the inability to satisfy the requirements of the model might be taken as more acute. Furthermore, in view of such evidence, it seems necessary to understand depression in terms of gender and gender ideologies, with implications for psychological and medical practice, as well as a potential changing foci of treatment.

Now, I also realise that the corpus I collected is not representative of a population of depressed people, or even men, and I do not wish to make such claims. It is quite possible that in other such corpora the narrative relevancies might be different, with different foci, emphases and so on. This, however, does not undermine my argument. Rather, it helps to see depression as varied and having various sources of suffering and various paths to recovery. The presence of such varied discourses would show even more strongly that attempts to find one universal 'fit for all' description of depression is implausible. And even assuming that such a description would indeed have some reference in people's experiences, its generality would render it just about useless.

My final comment here is that the argument I presented does not necessarily imply exclusive socialness of depression and the rejection of the biochemical model of depression. My argument is parallel to such discussions. What I am proposing simply is insight into the relevancies of narratives of men's depressed selves. Regardless of whether depression is social in its origin or biochemical (and there is no conclusive evidence either way, NICE, 2004), what seems to be important for the men I interviewed is to be useful. Let me exemplify it further. One of the most poignant and difficult interviews I conducted was with a man whose daughter was killed in a road accident. I heard much about the little girl and the informant's grief after his loss, the grief that, earlier, resulted in an attempted suicide. Still, regardless of this overpowering context, he also, just like others, talked about his inability to find permanent employment, to provide for his wife, who thanks to the informant's support and, later, engaging in campaign work managed to beat her depression. The fact that he was a man and he was expected to work and be the breadwinner was still very much part of his story, regardless of the overwhelming grief for his daughter. I have no doubt, as he too did not, that help also meant being able to become a 'real man'.

Now, as in the previous chapter, I accept that gender is unlikely to be the only discursive resource for the constructions of the self I discussed. One of those outside gender (although clearly still somewhat related to it) is what I would call an expectation of normality, which of course is a notoriously difficult term to pin down (but see A. Phillips, 2005). I see it particularly in the action-orientedness of the narratives I analysed. In her analysis of the discourses of the DSM-IV, Crowe (2000) notes that they are underpinned by a certain notion of normality. According to the *Manual*, normal behaviour has four attributes: productivity, unity, moderation and rationality. Thus, discussing productivity, she notes that when a person fails in their efficiency, goal-directedness or rational sequencing of their actions, they might be suspected of having a mental disorder. Now, as much as I agree with Crowe (2000) that this suggests a neo-liberal underpinning of the DSM, and it seems that this is also the kind of 'normality' that the men interviewed assume in what they said. In other words, in contrast to what Rowe seems to be suggesting, it is not merely an imposed normality: it is actually espoused by the 'person in the street'. My informants do strive towards a goal-directed life, with the time they have on their hands being rationally occupied. Although particularly normality can be seen as gendered, what is seen as normal for a man might be quite different from what is assumed to be normal for a woman; yet, here is probably a common ground in which expectations of both genders overlap. Such discourse is also quite likely to underpin my informants' narratives.

In Chapter 6, I am going to take a look at my informants' biographies and explore how depression features in them. I am interested in how depression is constructed within my informants' life-course.

6
Normal Biographies. Depression and the Life Story

Introduction

In the previous chapter I demonstrated that the men I interviewed consistently constructed themselves in terms of actions, locating depression in the realm of life, rather than the psyche. Depression was about what they could or could not do, rather than about psychological distress. I also showed again the anchorage of these constructions in the dominant ideologies of masculinity, pointing out gendering as an important aspect of what it means to experience depression.

In this chapter I am going to focus on my informants' biographies. Right at the beginning of the interview I asked the informants to tell me 'something' about themselves. Invariably, the informants offered me their brief biography, a sort of 'official self', with the vital statistics of their age, marital and family status, level of education, professional activities and the like. It is this element of the interview I would like to focus upon here.

My argument here is going to be twofold. First, I am going to show that illness is constructed as a 'natural' development in the lives of the informants, rather than as a 'biographical disruption' as often shown in the literature (Bury, 1982). Complementary to that is the construction of depression as a background in all the informants' activities in life.

Autobiography and illness

In contrast to the previous two chapters, I am drawing exclusively upon the initial exchange between me and the informant. Thus, I am interested only in their responses to my initial request that they tell me 'something' about themselves. First, I think that my question explicitly positioned my informants as those required to tell some sort of story of themselves. I positioned them as people with a story of themselves, with a personal identity (Harré and van Langenhove, 1999b,c). While the informants talked about themselves throughout the interview, it was particularly in this fragment of the event that they took on the position of someone setting out to tell a story which 'made them intelligible' (Gergen and Gergen, 1988) within the particular social context. Judging also by the kind of stories they told me, they took the opportunity to construct their 'official self', a biography that provided me with the most crucial elements of their lives. This is a biography of milestones. As Harré and van Langenhove (1999c) put it, they presented me with a number of past events and/or episodes which crucially contributed to who they are.

It is important to realise that autobiographies are not stories which merely develop over time. Autobiographies are, in fact, stories which are malleable, socially situated and fit for the context in which they are told. As Harré puts it, not only is there not a single autobiography which can be told, but the one chosen from the multitude of available stories is a function of the particular context in which it is told (Fischer and Goblirsch, 2007; Harré, 1998, 2005). They are not so much an 'accurate' account of one's life, rather they are an account which is most congruent with the current view of one's self (Barclay and DeCooke, 1988; also Misztal, 2003). Rubin (1988) makes the point that the autobiography is much more a creative process of constructing, rather than merely reproducing (also Brockmeier, 2000). The past is not something fixed and stable, but, rather, it is a resource which is continually framed and reframed from the point of view of the person's current concerns and relevancies (King, 2000; see also Mischler, 2006). Just as identity is now commonly accepted to be changeable rather than fixed (see Barker and Galasiński, 2001), the statement must also apply to the autobiography as the most overt and explicit activity of expressing one's identity.

Now, there is considerable research on how the chronic illness interweaves with the ill person's identity and becomes an inherent part of such identity (Charmaz, 1983; Goffman, 1990; Lupton, 2003). Illness encroaches on all aspect of life and often is perceived as taking over. This is indeed why Herzlich (1973) shows illness as 'occupation' (see also Lutz and Bowers, 2005; also Frank, 1995). One of the most cited pieces of research into experiences of chronic illness is Bury's (1982) study in which he demonstrated that patients with rheumatoid arthritis positioned their illness as a 'biographical disruption' (Bury, 1982, 1991; for a critique see Williams, 2000, though). Bury proposes that with illness there comes the disruption of the taken-for-granted life practices, one's identities as well as of the more general outlook on life. Illness not only becomes a major event in one's life, but it is a fault line through one's biography: life before illness has little to do with that on the other side. Although Bury's findings were contextualised (e.g. Pound *et al.*, 1998; Sanders *et al.*, 2002; Wilson, 2007), the basic conceptual framework has remained.

Research by Charmaz (1983) supports this account in that she speaks of the 'loss of self' engendered by illness, and later on (Charmaz, 1991) she speaks of chronic illness as interruption, constructing it also in terms of a 'turning point' in life (ibid.). It is after this disruption that people are said to live 'disrupted lives' (Becker, 1997), needing a 'narrative reconstruction' (Williams, 1984), a new account of the new relationship of the ill person with the world around them (see also Carricaburu and Pierret, 1995; Corbin and Strauss, 1987). Following Strauss (1992), finally, Karp (1994, 1996) proposes to speak of illness as an identity turning point – the moment in life when we begin to look at ourselves in a new light.

Given the devastating nature of depression and its profound impact upon my informants' masculinity, this is also what I expected to find in the narratives I collected, particularly in my informants' 'official self' stories. In contrast, the biographies of the men I interviewed did not construct depression as a disruption; they did not contrast their ill selves with their healthy ones (as reported in Cheshire and Ziebland, 2005). Depression was represented in two ways. On the one hand it was shown as part of the 'natural' unfolding of life, and on the other, as background to all that was happening in life, a sort of default that one takes into account in life. In this way I shall be attempting to strengthen a significantly underexplored strand of research in which it is the biographical flow which is stressed both in the data and in the account (Faircloth *et al.*, 2004). In line with Faircloth and his associates (ibid.), I shall also make the point of a fuller contextual insight into the understanding of the illness and its position within biography.

Depression as a milestone

The first aspect of my informants' autobiographies I would like to discuss is that they constructed depression as one of the milestones of their life. Information about depression is positioned as equally important as the 'usual' demographics of age or family status or education; it is also given in the same way. There is no drama, no 'disruption', depression is a milestone, much as a doctorate would be. I do not, of course, wish to say or imply that falling ill with depression is an event of the same or comparable magnitude as, say, getting a doctorate. I have no doubt that it is not. The point I am making, however, is that this is how my informants render it. My informants talk about depression in the same way as they talk about other significant events of their lives. Let me explain it with some examples.

Extract 1

EU: I shall be 49 this year, in a few [more than 10] days. I have been married for 12 years. Two children, daughter 11 years old. My son was born in March. He will be 7 months old in a few days. [. . .]. Well, I'm here the second time. These kind of problems have been increasing for 4 years. At various degree of intensity. With different problems. These problems are, symptoms are related to some existential fears. I have always been an independent person. Managing on my own for the most part. But various factors had a tendency that I was losing control. And I got these depressive states.

Extract 2

BC: I am 44 years old. Married. I have three almost adult children. The daughter is 18, in November. One son 21, and 23 years old. They study. I have been leading a company with a partner [female] for 19 years. I am ill with depression. It came out at the age of twenty something with first marital problems. I had a severe depression then for the first time. I was getting out of it for half a year. Then for 15 years there were periods of lower mood, but then except for a brief stay in hospital, one for a week, and a few visits with a doctor, I did not really take up regular therapy. Simply I managed to get out it on my own. Wait it out, get out.

Extract 3

SB: I am a design engineer. For many years I worked in an institute [unclear]. I was an energy systems designer, but I worked in automation in the energy industry. I worked in this institute for many years. It's important because under the auspices of that institute I went to America, which was financed by a UN agency. And my illness started there. And it's important because the fact that I was reading my work only myself started bothering me. So I started working for different companies, first we set up a firm, right? But somehow we couldn't agree. Then I worked for companies, well with foreign capital. Then my work consisted in more and more, sometimes only, foreign travel. Or domestic. Obviously there is also the energy industry in this country.

Particularly Extract 1 is interesting for the discussion here. After listing all the 'important' information, EU moves to depression. But it is constructed almost as an afterthought (the informant introduces the shift in topic by *no i*, which I translated as 'well'), the last piece of information, an addition that should not be forgotten, but is not as relevant as the previously mentioned things. Although he devotes more time to talking about depression (but then, we were talking in hospital, and he was asked to speak to me because of his depression!), depression is not something overwhelming, it is not *the* major event of his life. Interestingly, the direct reference to depression comes right at the end of the extract and is also introduced as an addition by means of the 'and'. Once again, the importance of the illness is played down.

In a similar vein, BC in Extract 2 in one breath tells me about his family and moves to depression. His way of constructing it is also notable. He speaks of his depression using the verb *ujawniać* ('come out', 'come to light', 'appear'), as if it had always been with him, it simply came to light at a particular juncture. Incidentally, this construction opens two lines of exploration: first, the construction of life junctures and significant life events; and second , the existence of depression throughout life. Thus, depression for BC is something latent in his life, something that he might not have realised, but it was there. In consequence he shows depression not so much as an illness, with a beginning (and possibly an end), but, rather, as the way he is. In contrast, SB in (3) shows depression as an illness whose beginning coincided with an important event in his life. Yet, as in (1), depression here is a footnote, albeit important enough to note it. Having mentioned depression, almost to fulfil the duty of the biographer's accuracy, the informant moves on to talk about the more important things. There is no disruption, no drama, no major event. Life goes on, except that it goes on with depression.

That said, informants in Extracts 1 and 2 do construct moments when depression stops being a mere signpost, a default aspect of their life. It happens when their condition turns more acute and they have to do more about it, seek residential treatment for example. Bury's (1982) biographical disruption is transformed from a major disruption of life to a localised one. The informants talk about a disruption of life in the sense that its more or less uninhibited development meets an obstacle and they have to devote themselves to removing that particular obstacle. Severe depression meant that life was going off tracks and had to be put back on tracks in order to go on as smoothly as one would expect.

The informant below, however, goes even further in constructing the no-drama depression. For him, the illness happens when the conditions are right:

Extract 4

> KL: I am 40, so it's hard to tell. This is the period when you either achieve successes or you have depression. This is my view. [...] coming back to professional matters, because this is a very important area for me, each success wound me up. Say, each success would me up and each success, I think I forgot about myself very often at that moment, because I forgot, I always thought for someone. I always thought about managing, I always thought of delegating activities, right? And I used to forget about something like rest. One, I simply used to forget. I had to, I travelled very much and I used to work very hard, 16, even 18 hours a day, and it had its effect, that I really did forget about myself.

At the beginning of the extract, the informant constructs depression as something natural, linking it to what is normally referred to as middle age. The simplicity of the construction 'no success – major depression' positions depression as a natural life development. Incidentally, this lay view of the association of middle age with depression is one which is often found in the literature. There seems to be a consensus that the middle years are associated with depression, anxiety, desperation, both in lay accounts (e.g. Hepworth and Featherstone, 1982, 1998) and academic analyses (Oleś, 2000; for a critique see Benson, 1997).

So, depression in middle years simply happens, it is a natural and unremarkable aspect of life. Once again, there is nothing to be particularly surprised with. This view continues a moment later in the interview when the informant shows his gruelling schedule in which he 'forgot about himself'. For KL, depression is a natural consequence of his behaviour. Note that it is quite clear that depression did disrupt the speaker's professional life, still he does not construct it like that. Depression for him is a stage that follows from what he did before. In this way, his biography, at least as he constructs it at the beginning of the interview, is quite smooth. Illness simply happened. There is almost a feeling of 'it serves me right' attitude. He forgot about himself, about resting, so he had to suffer the consequences.

Depression as a background

The construction of depression as unremarkable is complemented by a number of informants who positioned it as a background to their life stories. Admittedly, it was a background which was notable enough to be spoken about, yet it was no more than that. Thus, in some contrast to the stories I have just analysed, the informants below do not talk about depression at the same level as other events of their life. Rather they position it as the omnipresent context in which life unfolds. Consider what three of my informants had to say:

Extract 5

> AZ: So, I am 55 years old. I have university education, I am a veterinary doctor. Maybe it was an unfortunate coincidence for me, the choice of my profession, may depression inducing, but what shall I do. I worked for 25 years in the profession, despite my depression.

Extract 6

> RP: So, I am 51 years old, I was born in [place name]. And for ten years I have lived, I moved 10 years ago here to [place name]. I got married and that's why among others I live here. My education is A-levels in car mechanics. I don't work anymore and I am on incapacity benefit because of my illness.

Extract 7

> JS: I mean I am divorced right now, last week. As it happens I have a seven-year-old daughter. I am a maths teacher. And at the moment I am on sick leave. My contract ends just now at the end of June. So I shall be looking for a job, after this contract ends. A different job, I don't know whether in the teaching profession or not. This depression certainly, it causes that if you go through this state, working at school further deepens it, I can do the job only when I feel well. And when I feel unwell, unfortunately I go on sick leave and obviously the employer doesn't like this kind of thing.

Extract 5 stands out in the three I am quoting here. Depression is constructed as a context which hinders life. The informant's activities, his career, happens despite depression. This is in contrast to Extract 6 in which depression is the cause of the informant's being on incapacity benefit, an account probably closest to constructing a disruption due to the illness. Still, both mention depression as a sort of explanation of what happens, even though in different ways. Both use the illness context as a *mis en scene* for their professional activities. One as a positive aspect of himself – he had worked so long despite the illness – the other as an explanation for why he is on incapacity benefit. It is important to note that RP does not construct depression as the cause of his being out of work. This is only implied as the illness is responsible for his being on incapacity benefit. Thus, the informant does not work because he is on benefit – I think, this is more an attempt to justify his work idleness, rather than construct disruption. The third example is somewhat more complex, but also here the informant positions his teaching career in relation to the illness context within which he has to operate. Depression is not merely mentioned, as in (5) and (6), still it is only used as a means to account for what is happening in his professional life. It not only explains the sick leave he is currently on, but is also responsible for the problems he is encountering.

In all three cases, the informants do not position depression as a force in its own right. It is not even a milestone, not a contributing aspect to their identity. Rather it is reduced to the part of the story which explains what happens in their lives. To put it more generally, there is a shift in the narrative role of depression. In the examples in the previous section, depression was part of the story of the self. It was, as Harré and van Langenhove (1999c) put it, one of the past events or episodes which contributed to the biography of the person, on a par with other major aspects of one's biography. Here it changed: depression is no longer part of the story. Rather it is the part that enriches the complexity of the story; it provides texture and allows us to understand the person who is telling us the story better.

Importantly for my discussion here, in neither case is depression shown as in one way or another an event obliterating life or biography. Depression is something that one lives with and only occasionally has to put life on track again, only in the case of flare-ups. Quite surprisingly, the biographies of the people I interviewed – with all the negative connotations of receiving psychiatric treatment, of having being diagnosed with mental illness – are quite smooth. They are biographies preserving normality. I shall explore it further in the conclusions.

Life's not so little disruptions

But there were three autobiographies in my corpus which were far from suggesting smoothness of life. In fact, as will be clear in Extract 8 below, for one of my informants, life simply fell apart. Still, it is notable from the point of view of the discussion here that it is very clear that depression is once again positioned as a logical outcome of what happens. It is not depression which is a problem, it is life, life which becomes too much to take. Consider first an extract from the most dramatic interview I carried out.

Extract 8

> OC. As any person, I have worked. I was brought up in an orphanage. [...] there were bad times, there were good times. Marriage. Child. This is in brief. I had an only child, I lost her. At first I felt well, then I broke down.

I have already mentioned this interview on a couple of occasions earlier. Before I offer some analysis, I would like to contextualise the extract with some more information I gathered outside the interview, as the case became quite well known in the city where the informant lived. OC's daughter was killed while crossing a street on a zebra crossing, and the speeding driver was under the influence of alcohol. To make things worse, the perpetrator was never punished for reasons which are unclear, the justice system did not offer the closure the parents so craved for. The event resulted in the child's mother's depression. Her husband, my informant, became a full-time carer, which resulted in the loss of his successful business, which in the process led to considerable financial difficulties. The difficulties in turn were made worse by the fact that he had not been able to find and keep employment. As with all other interviewees the fact that OC could not support his wife financially was a source of considerable distress. Intensive psychotherapy, the support from OC and turning to active campaigning for justice resulted in his wife's recovery. That coincided with the diagnosis of my informant's depression, as well as, not much later, his suicide attempt.

As I said at the outset of the book, I have a political project in this work. I want to show men at their weakest. But this informant offers me the possibility of showing the caring masculinity, masculinity that was able to hang on, because the man was needed to care. Only when dismissed from his duty by the circumstances (I am choosing the phrase on purpose as I do want to construct what happened in stereotypical masculine terms, but in no way do I intend to suggest that it was a dismissal by the grieving mother, OC's wife) did he allow himself to crack up. The pressure to be the breadwinner only added to his distress.

As might be expected, it is the dramatic events of his daughter's death that are constructed as the major disruption of life. Depression is almost a 'natural' consequence of what happened. It is life that became disruptive, too much to handle. The autobiography, however brief, still does not position depression as an event in its own right. It is associated with what happened, it is a consequence. In this way, as above, depression becomes something natural, a background rather than a contributor to the informant's biography.

The two remaining extracts show other and less dramatic events, as in the case of (10), that are constructed as disruptive:

Extract 9

GT: Well, my name is [. . .]. I was born [place name] on [date]. I went to technical high school then university. After university I started working, I was finishing university during the martial law, in '82. so it was hard here in Poland. I studied tourism, so it was all shut down, all foreign travel. So I started working along the lines of my vocational training. Printing, in a printing house. [. . .] I reached the position of the production manager. Everything went very well, I did not have any health complaints, psychological. Perhaps tiredness, such weariness, because it's the people and the production, it is a burden after a whole day. But in 2000 I had a few problems and I crashed. My father committed suicide. My mom got depression after the event. My mom's sister died, so for me many such events accumulated. My in-laws died and I had a low and I could not see a way out. I lost my job. I undertook a suicide attempt, but I was rescued. And at present I am receiving treatment and I am on incapacity benefit.

Extract 10

NM: I am a locksmith, vocational training. I am married. Except that the children are now independent. I am on my own with my wife. What else, I lost my job. I mean I didn't lose it because I was sacked, but because my company was closed. And I think this what it is associated with. This depression of mine. Or perhaps it was a bit earlier, because when I worked, I already had lack of concentration, and I was irritated. Stressed. And when I am irritated and stressed, I can't concentrate on work at all. And I had a problem with it, a huge one. After the company's dissolution, I was on unemployment benefit for half a year, then I went to work for a private company. I worked for two years for a private company. On a building site. I mean it was a renovating-building firm. You had to do everything, as a locksmith, I worked as a carpenter, anything. There I go an even worse depression.

While GT in Extract 9 shows very dramatic events as the source of his depression (particularly the suicide of his father, with whom, as transpired during the interview, he was very close), in Extract 10 it is the job loss, qualified by the implied pressure at work, which led to stress and the informant's inability of cope with what life throws at him. In both cases, however, depression again is a result, a consequence, rather than an event in its own right. Depression has not got a place in the informants' autobiographies.

Autobiographies of depression

In the final section of this chapter I would like to present three more extracts. They were distinctly different from the rest of the autobiographies I collected. Consider the following:

Extract 11

FH: I was born, since I am here. I lived and didn't suspect that this type of illness would get me. It never crossed my mind. But it got me earlier, I had the first episode in '92, then in '95 it was a beginning when I got it that something was wrong and I jumped for out-patient help and it was possible to cut it short. Now, this year, it's the third time.

Extract 12

HI: I am almost 44 years old. My psychiatric problems started in '99. It was a rise in tension at work, nervous background. And this is when it started. My first contact with a psychiatrist whom I didn't particularly want to see, because why did it happen to me? To all, but not to me. Why me? In time, however, I did allow the thought that I must see a psychiatrist and I went the first time. I told her about all my problems and she said that my fainting was not cardiological, but nervous. And that's how it started, the lady decided it was neurotic depression.

Extract 13

CW: [informant's name], I have been ill with depression for 11 years, my condition has been getting worse year on year. What else?

DG: Whatever you want. It's meant to be your interview [. . .]

CW: OK. In my life I used run a firm. Now it is really managed by my parents. Married once, divorced, second time, now married, three children. That's it.

The autobiographies in (11) and (12) are quite astonishing. The informants focus on just about one event: depression. In (11) the basic information about being born is given jocularly, probably to emphasise the importance of depression. The informant was born and then, bang!, depression. Similarly in Extract 12 the informant seems to want to give only his most basic demographic – his age. But then there is only depression, his autobiography consists only of having a problem with mental illness. We could say that the medicalisation (using medical terms in contexts in which one would not normally expect it, Ballard and Elston, 2005) of their experience is extreme. There is nothing more but their illness. Finally, Extract 13 that starts with depression straight away – there is nothing else, but depression. Only when prompted does the informant give the basic information about himself – still, admittedly, it is hardly a fulsome biography.

So, how can we account for these narratives? First, there is probably the inevitable conclusion that being ill has completely taken over the informants' 'official' story of the self. The extracts show a complete shift of the life story onto the illness, or, better put, the history of the illness. The self is completely submerged in the illness. Yet it not the sort of shift that is described by Charmaz (1983). Her informants talked explicitly about living a restricted life, social isolation, discrediting definitions of self and becoming a burden. In one way or another, the loss of self was something that the informants constructed in their narratives. Nothing of the sort happens here. The three informants show depression as the most important aspect of their official story, yet there is still a smoothness of their biography. There is still hardly any drama, although admittedly, Extract 11 is the most 'violent' in constructing depression as it got the informant and he threw himself for help.

But, secondly, what of the medicalisation? One could simply see it as a particular social configuration of relevancies in a particular context. Given the context of the interview, the informant's story is perhaps at its most tellable. If tellability is not defined in aesthetic terms, but more to the point, as Georgakopoulou (2006) argues, in terms of effectiveness, appropriateness or consequentiality for the interaction that ensues, then the informants' stories are extremely tellable: I came to hear about their depression, straight away I got a story about their depression. There is a 'but' here, though. It is that these heavily medicalised life stories are not only in contrast with all the other stories I collected, but also with the practice of telling a life story, or whatever it means to tell 'something' about themselves. One does not introduce oneself by talking about one's illness and one's illness only. So, while I am not certain what the signi-ficance of such medicalisation might be, it is probably quite important that it occurred at the particular juncture of the interview. Medicalisa-tion of one's experience is probably inevitable in lay discourse, not only because doctors speak like that to us, in interviews and on other occa-sions, but also because, especially in psychiatry, medical and scientific discourse is the dominant one in which to see illness, and the medical perspective is the dominant one in which to make sense of the illness. Yet, there is probably a significant difference between medicalisation of one's discourse on depression and one's official story about oneself. A fuller explanation must be deferred till more research has been done.

Conclusions

The discussion in this chapter concerned the issue of how depression is positioned in the brief autobiographies at the beginning of the interview. I have found two main constructions in the corpus. First, depression was represented as a milestone, on a par with others in the informants' biographies. Thus, as the informants talked about their families, their education, they also talked about their depression. Second, depression was constructed as life's background, a context in which things happened in their life. In addition, I also showed constructions of inevitability of depression – it was a logical consequence after certain significant events in life.

There is a reservation to be made here. My comments here are based solely upon a particular fragment of the interviews – the informants' autobiography. As such, the points I make are limited. Although in other parts of the corpus, I did not find much evidence of constructing depres-sion as disruptive of life, it does not mean that such representations are completely absent. But this does not undermine the argument as made of a particular context and communicative genre. While it might be the case that constructions of the biographical disruption of the illness can be observed in men's narratives of depression, they cannot in their stories of the 'official self'. It is significant as the informants choose to demedicalise and 'tame' depression in their stories which are to show their life trajectory. Depression is backgrounded where it matters the most, it seems, where the men had an explicit chance to account for themselves.

Now, the association of depression with disruptive events, or life events, is well known. It was introduced in the classical study by Brown and Harris (1978, also 1989), who explored the link between depression and life events, which they define as in one way or another disruptive, eliciting change to the established routine. There is a clear parallel between what I have shown here and their research (and others following in their footsteps, e.g. Clark and Watson, 1988; Nazroo *et al.*, 1997; Puskar *et al.*, 1999). However, there is also a significant difference. What I am suggesting is that 'life events' are a lived category in terms of which people see their depression. In contrast, the study by Brown and Harris (1978), despite some claims to the contrary, created an analytical category within which to assess people's experiences. Even though they explicitly say that they are not so much interested in the kinds of events that precipitate in depression but in people's emotional reaction to them (ibid.: 5) and indeed this is why they eschew giving a rigid definition of a life event (p. 66), they are interested in creating a model of the relationship between life events and experience without taking a closer look at the actual story behind it, not only the social context in which the story-teller finds him/herself, but also the one they construct with their narrative (a shortcoming the authors actually acknowledge to an extent in the conclusions to their study).

The shift between the analytic and lived category is significant not only because it gives voice to those who actually suffer (see Kangas, 2001), but also because it focuses attention on the actual configurations of the human experience. In this sense, my argument is similar to that by Kangas (2001), who, in a rare and interesting study of experiences of depression, reports that in interviews depressed people did construct depression as resulting from life events. Yet the focus of this chapter is different. I am interested in autobiography and the position of depression within it. Narrowing down the base of my data, I am attempting to achieve insight into the relationship between depression and the lived 'official story' of the self. The 'experiential coherence' (Blaxter, 1993) achieved by my informants is at the level of the officially 'inhabited identity' (Blommaert *et al.*, 2005). Moreover, by focusing only on men's narratives, I am also attempting to put the autobiography and its relationship with depression in terms of dominant gender ideologies.

Now, with the above reservation and the likely contextual nature of the constructions of biographical disruptions in mind, an obvious question that can be asked here is that of why I did not find much evidence of disruptiveness of depression. After all, depression is a serious chronic illness with which people have to live sometimes for years. Lupton's (2003) reminder that serious illness and disability can even redefine such 'mundane' activities as washing oneself cannot easily be brushed aside. Yet, there is very little evidence in the corpus I have collected of the sort of disruption suggested in other illnesses.

My study, however, is not aimed at disputing the findings of research I quoted above, but to show its potential complexity. There might be two reasons for this. First, in contrast to somatic illnesses and physical disability, depression does not limit life in an obvious, or default way. In contrast to a heart attack sufferer, a person suffering from depression does not have to lie in bed, does not have to rest and avoid physically exerting themselves. The limitations of mental illness are different and I think my study shows it here. The disruption might be more nuanced, more negotiated than that of some somatic illness or a crippling disability (see Smith and Sparkes, 2004). The problem of being unable to conform to social expectations is not only more contextual, but it is also much less visible than, say, having to use a wheelchair. The second, and perhaps more significant, reason might be the data I am focusing upon. It would seem then that the 'official self' cannot be limited by an illness, and depression cannot be seen as an event which is so disruptive as to interfere with a life story. Positioned in this way, the data I have discussed can be seen on a scale. The stories placing depression on a par with other life events acknowledge its contribution to the self's official story, those constructing it as background do not even do that. In this context, my earlier postulate for more research into contextuality of biographical disruption is not merely one of more intellectual understanding, but also a call for more insight into ill people's ability (or indeed inability) to accept their illness and its consequences for therapeutic processes.

Finally, I see the position of depression in the brief autobiographies as an attempt to preserve normality. If normality can be understood in terms of what happens 'normally', usually as the default, a contrast to abnormality (see Canguilhem, 2000; Verhaeghe, 2004), then this is precisely the men I interviewed tried to achieve. They were born, they had families, they had education and careers and they had depression. Allowing the construction of depression as a 'biographical disruption' would make their biographies, their lives, abnormal. Instead, they showed themselves as 'normal people'. Striving to be 'normal', whatever that might actually mean, is likely to be one of the most crucial concerns in public or semi-public contexts. The beginning of the interview, a crucial juncture at which to present oneself, must be underpinned by the drive to appear as normal as possible, with as normal a life as possible.

I would like to finish the point about normality by showing one last extract, in which normality, in a very positive sense (on normality as a self-presentation tactic, see Galasiński, 1992), seems to be precisely the underlying theme of what the informant had to say:

Extract 14

> DE: I am 48 years old. A wife, three children, house, car, in principle all a man this age should have, I have. I got it by working hard. And one would think that it's live and never die. Yet, something stood in my way and I found myself here.

'All that a man should have at this age' is precisely the reference to normality I am discussing here, and even though this normality is disrupted by the 'something' that stood in his way (rather than by depression), the informant's life is normal, and it was achieved through hard work, just as is expected of a man. Interestingly, the informant is not so much positioning himself in terms of success, rather, importantly, precisely in terms of what is *normally* expected.

My informants' narratives are once again an attempt to 'tame' depression. To show it as something that had not got much to do with them, and if it did, it did not affect them to the extent that would warrant concern, let alone the label of abnormality. It also shows the uneasiness with which one, especially a man, thinks of his mental illness such as depression. Chapter 7 is the last one in which I shall be discussing the relationship between self and depression. I shall show the constructions of depression as inevitable, not as illness, but as something that simply was there. It is yet another way men show they are not really ill.

7
The Timeless Self. The Inevitability of Depression

True selves

In the previous chapter I explored the brief autobiographies which my informants were asked to make at the beginning of the interview. I demonstrated that, contrary to expectations, the informants constructed their lives as smooth, unfettered by depression. The illness was represented either as a life milestone, on a par with other life events, or as a background to life. I interpreted these findings in terms of the informants' attempts to show themselves and their lives as 'normal'.

In this chapter I am ending the exploration of how the depressed self was constructed in the corpus. Throughout the interviews, my informants occasionally constructed their 'selves' as timeless. They spoke of their 'true' nature, what they are like 'deep down'. What is interesting in these constructions is that they were invariably linked to depression. There are two ways in which the informants represented themselves. On the one hand, they ascribed some timeless characteristics to themselves, and on the other, they spoke of being moulded in childhood, mostly due to their upbringing, in a particular way. Both ways were done at similar levels of genericness and non-changeability.

Before I present the data, I would like to make a couple of theoretical points, though. Taking the constructionist and anti-essentialist view of self and identity, I assume that there is no such thing as a 'true' self. In fact, I assume that there is no self outside discourse and that self and its identity are a discursive product (e.g. Harré, 1998; Harré and Gillett, 1994; also Barker and Galasiński, 2001; Benwell and Stokoe, 2006; Hall and du Gay, 1996; for a useful review, see Joseph, 2004). But having this analytical concept does not preclude people from creating narratives of their 'real selves' and in fact, van Langenhove and Harré (1993) posit that the anti-essentialist understanding of self and identity is in contrast to folk theories and common belief.

The cultural repertoire of the Western world holds that we have a true self, an identity which we possess and which can become known to us. Identity is thought to be a universal and timeless core, an 'essence' of the self that is expressed as representations recognisable by ourselves and others. It is this whole self that is healthy, while a divided one is sick, as Porter (1997) puts it (on the changing nature of the modern self, see Gergen, 1991, 2000; Rose, 1996, though). That is, identity is an essence signified through signs of taste, beliefs, attitudes and life-styles. In his review of the commonsensical Western notion of the self, Sadler (2007: 114) characterises it by agency, the sense of being 'a purposive actor'; identity which distinguishes one from others; life trajectory, 'a sense of purpose and future'; history, a sense of having one's individual past; and perspective which reflects one's unique point of view and experience.

Even though academics agree that there are no transcendental or ahistorical elements to what it is to be a human being and that the very notion of what it is to be a person is cultural and consequently variable across time and space (Flax, 1993; Parker, 1992), this is in contrast to what we as non-academics think. The individualism and self-centredness of Western societies was aptly summarised in a much quoted extract from Geertz, who suggests that

> The Western conception of the person as a bounded, unique, more or less integrated motivational and cognitive universe, a dynamic center of awareness, emotion, judgement and action organized into a distinctive whole and set contrastively against a social and natural background is, however incorrigible it may seem to us, a rather peculiar idea within the context of the world's cultures (Geertz, 1979: 229).

For Elias (1978, 1982), the Western 'I' is a self-aware object, a modern conception which emerged out of science and the 'Age of Reason' (also Rose, 1997). It was at this point in time that the more obvious group- and moral-based identities of the Middle Ages began to be surpassed by considerations of the self as possessing reason, knowledge and an inner world. Increasingly, the predominance of external, abstract regulatory rules of governance backed up by punishment gave way to a reliance on the 'internalization' of morality and the rules that regulate conduct. Giddens (1991), in turn, explores the notion of developing the self-narrative as part of the notion of 'life politics'. As social agents have to make increasingly difficult life choices, for example relating to the role of ecology, globalisation or food in their lives, the issue of 'how to live' and in effect who I am not only is difficult, but it becomes crucial to answer it in an attempt to create a coherent story of myself. These choices are integrated into the 'reflexive project of self' by the need to produce and sustain 'coherent, yet continuously revised biographical narratives' (Giddens, 1991: 5). This coherent narrative in turn is characterised by the 'ontological security', the confidence that the world and the self are as they appear to be (Giddens, 1984; for a critique, see Shilling, 2003). Illness, as a new and potentially disruptive force to such narratives, becomes an important context in which to maintain a coherent and socially acceptable narrative of self.

Carbaugh (1999) notes that not only each interaction presupposes forms of action and identity, but also suggests a cultural premise which assumes that a person has one 'self'. From this, an idea that this one self, responsible for the person's uniqueness, is the 'true one' is only logical. In this sense also, one can lose one's self in illness, as Sabat and Harré (1999) demonstrate in the case of persons suffering from Alzheimer's disease and Heifner (1997) shows in the case of men's depression (see also Rogers *et al.*, 2001), while Cheshire and Ziebland (2005) show on the basis of their data that the 'real' self that was constructed is unaffected by illness.

The final point to be made here is Rose's (1989) proposal that an act of confession (whether private or institutionalised) is particularly instrumental in creating a sense of self. And so, the interview I carried out seems to have been an ideal opportunity for inspecting the self. But the interview became part of the larger psychiatric context that is designed to offer instruments within which to find and assess 'normality', which in turn frames the inspection of the self (Rose, 1990). The process of forging the sense of self, as Burr and Butt (2000) say, happens within the processes of disciplining, normalising and confessing.

The timeless self

By far the most frequent construction of self 'as it is' was in terms of the attribution of various characteristics to it. In some cases these attributes 'spoke for themselves', in some cases the informants made an explicit link between them and their illness. But what was particularly fascinating was that in a few cases, the source of such constructions was represented to be a clinician, mostly a psychiatrist. Moreover, some informants made a direct link between 'the way they are' and their responsibility for depression.

Consider first three typical instances in which informants construct themselves in acontextual, generic terms.

Extract 1

JS: If this is the reason that the big stress causes depression in me, then obviously the organism is in stress the entire life and simply one will have to react immediately to this stress. As I said, I am going to see the specialist and try not to take on too much.

Extract 2

NP: I have never spoken to anyone about it [referring to his suicide attempt].

DG: Why not?

NP: I don't know, I don't talk much usually, I am withdrawn, closed up and I don't easily open up. I am learning this at the moment really.

Extract 3

EU: I feel different. I mean, simply, I feel different. I feel peculiar, a peculiar individual who exists on strange rules.

DG: What does it mean?

EU: I avoid social life. I have few acquaintances. Practically no friends. I rarely keep in touch. In principle, I am most pleased when I am with my wife and with my children. With my child beforehand, now with my children. And everything goes according to plan, that is to say we have time for a stroll, for play, we are happy with our child's success at school. [...] I can't dance. I don't like parties where there is, so, to a certain degree, for my entire life there has been this thing. It's probably a way out. A consequence of my upbringing, at home.

I am unhappy with it, because, I am unhappy with it. But it's difficult to change. Particularly in circumstances when it's hard. When I feel unwell. When there are financial problems.

As I am given accounts of what the informants are like, all three show themselves in a-contextualised, general terms. Although only JS in (1) makes an explicit link between the way he is, or, to be exact, the way he/his body handles stress and depression, the other informants' negative evaluation of what they are like is an important clue as to their assessment. In Extract 2, the informant positions the way he is in contrast to what he strives for; in Extract 3, EU is explicit about his peculiarity and the strange principles he lives by, emphasised by the claim that he feels badly about it. However, given the context of the interview, I would argue that the rejection of what the informants are like positions these attributes in a relationship with depression. First, they both focus on attributes which are associated with major depression, and, of course, as long-term ill they are more than likely to know that. Second, in the case of NP in (2), learning to change the way he is, is shown as part of his activities in hospital and thus as part of the therapeutic process. It is notable that he seems to set up a context in which he simply talks about his proclivity towards silence, yet it is clearly positioned as a problem that he is attempting to manage. In the case of (3), finally, the link with depression is made explicit by the reference to periods of feeling ill. To add to the pathology of his 'strangeness', EU blames it on his upbringing (I shall take it up below).

Both NP and EU assume that change is possible, even though it is as elusive as ever. In (2) the informant is learning to change, a process which is unfinished, and in (3) the informant chooses to stress the difficulty of changing himself, especially that he had been like that all his life. As they are just about the only references to change in the corpus, I think of them more as embedded within the medical and therapeutic discourse, especially in the case of (2) where the change is put clearly in the context of the hospital, rather than the informant's life.

Some informants chose to position their timeless selves more clearly on a temporal line and represented it explicitly as originating in their childhood. Witness the following extracts:

Extract 4

BC: [...] now from the perspective of time, I can see that these symptoms were there in my youth [unclear], perhaps even in my childhood.

For example, the school stage was marked with such rises and falls. I could not, I had problems with [unclear] and then I managed very well.

Extract 5

DG: What do you think where did [your depression] come from?

RP: I mean certainly all these, from the accident and the failure, where else? From my childhood. I have always been a closed person, shy. I was different from my peers, I was always the smallest and so on, so I had some complexes already then, right?

Extract 6

DG: And could you tell me why do you think you have fallen ill.

AZ: I was a sensitive child. It was not taken into consideration, I am from a village. A farm boy. It was not taken into consideration and no one took it into consideration that I simply would not cope with certain life difficulties. Like building a house or something. Although without building a house, I also was in depression. So, for example, when I worked, my work gave me satisfaction, although it did keep me in a certain tension. And that was bad. I mean it gave me satisfaction, I found it difficult, but in 14 years of work there were no major failures. For me to feel depressed or in anxiety or something. I had such stages when I did something wrong, because it's never that you always do things well, right? One has such feeling of guilt, fear that nothing worked out for him.

DG: So, if I understand well, you see.

AZ: The cause in that I was a delicate, sensitive child, with a very unstable nervous system. I should not even have got married.

That all three informants answer the question of the causes of their depression in social terms is probably not particularly surprising. What is interesting, however, is that they explicitly locate the causes of their illness in themselves (although the informant in (5) does put himself as the cause on a par with an accident he had had which spurred the current episode). Moreover, references to childhood seem to be an attempt to show deeper roots of depression in the self than in the case of the informants I quoted in Extracts 1–3. They allow the speakers not only to show the long-term aspect of their depression-related attributes, but also, potentially, imply their inborn character. They did not get it a few years earlier , rather it is a sort of a trait in their character that spans decades. The self cannot be truer than that, also it cannot be more timeless for that matter.

Note also that apart from Extract 1, which puts depression in an agentive construction, this time as caused by the stress, all informants choose to construct themselves in terms of attributes. They refer to themselves using relational processes ('I am ... ;' or 'I have....' Halliday, 1994). In this way, they construct traits, characteristics, positioning them as much more timeless than, say, practices. In fact only one informant chose to describe himself in terms of a practice. However, he uses it to imply the way he was and the sadness he felt:

Extract 7

MR: So at a certain moment I was competing with my father, you know I earned more money than he as a young man, except that I did not experience this joy. I won an all-Poland competition as one, two hundred people competed, I was the best and to an extent there was no joy. There was this constant feeling of sadness. I felt great in autumn, I like going to the seaside a lot. After the season I went to [place] or to [place] and the September this was my season of the year. Wonderful, I felt wonderfully, I chose loneliness and silence. And, let me go back to depression, depression for me is the inability to take any decision. Not because you don't want to, but it is this state, I try to do something, I know I should and I don't know how [whispers]. I think, shit, I think I have gone mad. I don't know [...]

Now, I think that the significance of constructions of the causes of depression in terms of the timeless self is in using them as an attempt to 'de-medicalise' it. For if it stems from the way I am, it cannot be a proper illness. Moreover, if all starts in childhood, it not only suggests the true long-term self, but it also removes the possibility of ever actually falling ill. I could speculate that this is indeed why only one informant mentioned chemical imbalances in constructing themselves or indeed depression itself. It might have been too indicative of an illness.

There are, however, a number of fragments in which the informants explicitly invoke the medical perspective. Consider the following extracts:

Extract 8

DG: Do you think you can speak about one cause why you fell ill?

HF: I think I have a very sensitive and delicate and weak psyche. And for example, a doctor once told me that I can't hold anything, I have to tell everything. You have a very weak psyche.

DG: Do you agree with it?

HF: Yes yes yes yes.

Extract 9

DE: I just would like to point out that in me it's not such a pure depression. I have anxieties in this depression, and some other phenomena which my doctor who has treated me for three years, perhaps two years, he gave up and said, look, I gave you so many of these pills and so many ways I started that I don't know how to treat you anymore. So it's not so pure in me, but it is certainly depression because there are these symptoms, right? But there is much, this personality I have, unstable and perhaps at this moment I don't know, it's difficult, but I would like to point out that it's not such a pure depression, because there are more of these issues. This is all I would say [laughs] about my life path, but it's not too interesting.

The medical perspective is invoked to show psychological weakness, as in (8), and the complexity of the problems, as in (9), one that included problems with personality as well the general inability to treat the informant successfully. I would argue, however, that the medicalisation is not so much employed to show the medical nature of depression, but, rather, to support the informants' claims about themselves. It is particularly clear in Extract 8, where the claims to psychological weakness are followed by 'evidence' (introduced by 'for example') from the informant's doctor. The medicalisation of the self in what the informant said in (9) is more implicit. The reference to the physician's inability to treat him is complemented by reference to his 'unstable personality', whatever that might actually mean. Thus, indirectly, the informant gets his medical 'certificate' of being difficult, while showing himself as problematic. The medicalisation is invoked not so much to show depression, but to show that it is he himself which is the problem. Similarly,

I think, in the following two extracts the informants are also drawing upon medical/scientific discourses in order to construct their selves. The use of 'damaged psyche' and particularly 'eugenics' (the informant probably means 'genetics') shifts the discourse from that of lived experience to that of medicine/sciences. Consider the following:

Extract 10

GT: I receive treatment, I undergo treatment, because I know that the longer I don't treat this, the greater low I will fall into, problems. Well, I wish it had never happened to me, that it hadn't happened to me the first time and those relapses, but I have no influence over it. It's beyond me. It's a damaged psyche and it simply cannot be cured.

Extract 11

BC: As I told you, for me the basic thing is eugenics. I have predispositions after my father. And for me it was a trauma, emotional, [unclear] my wife betrayed me and then my world collapsed. I thought it was the end of the world. A disaster and all. And that coincided with my predisposition and it caused the first major depressive episode.

In sum, after proposing that the construction of the timeless self serves 'de-medicalisation' of depression, I have also argued that when medical discourse is invoked medicalisation it centres around the 'self', rather than the illness. Medical 'evidence' is used as support for the claim that the informant's self is problematic, strange in a stable, rather non-changeable, way.

Messed up selves

The other strategy of constructing the timeless self was to show it as negatively influenced by the informants' upbringing. Just as above, these 'messed up' selves are as stable and central to who the informants are. Witness the following extracts:

Extract 12

CW: The problem is in my childhood. This is where the problem is. On the one hand the doctors in the [name] hospital, when I was there after a suicide attempt, described my personality as schizoid. On the other hand in gestalt it was determined: a pure psychopath [unclear]. if there is a bit of this, a bit that is for me, that results from this story, for many years I had no one close. My parents abandoned me when I was a month old. I mean they took me to my grandparents. I returned to my parents when I began school. And later a whole lot of fighting between my parents. In pulling me like a ball, to one side or the other. I think this is where the cause is, this is where there is one piece. And the other piece is that probably it is innate. Yet looking with my eyes at my father, I also think he was ill. Except then one did not treat this, no one knew about it.

Extract 13

SB: I used to be quite a forward-going man, although, you need to [unclear], I once asked the doctor here what significance it has, I was brought up in a [place name] home as a boy with complexes. I had to struggle with it for many years. To stop having complexes and start having successes, manage a group. These were long years of struggle and I kind of defeated them. But I think not completely because at the moment it comes out.

Extract 14

MR: I did think about where whence the illness. I'll tell you, not without reluctance, I agree that this illness must have appeared in childhood, because it was like classical. I was raised without a father.

I have decided to put Extract 12 in this section because it not only has explicit reference to the informant's upbringing, but is also the most explicit and fulsome account of the medicalised self, the upbringing, the inborn characteristics and the depression. CW starts by identifying the cause of his problems – no qualifications, no hesitation: childhood. And then he offers his 'credentials' – a summary of what he is: schizoid personality, underpinned by another quite menacing 'diagnosis', this time from gestalt psychotherapy. And it is these 'credentials', admittedly, quite difficult to argue against, that form the platform from which he begins his account of why he is the way he is. There is a clear shift between the description of himself and the explanation for it. The expression 'if there is a bit of this, a bit that is for me, that results from this story' serves as a frame between the two kinds of stories. In the 'explanation' part of the story, the informant persistently constructs himself as the target of his parents' actions – they are the agents in processes in which he is constructed as object. Not only was he abandoned, driven away to his grandparents, but then he was dragged across in a tug-of-war kind of struggle between his parents. As if this was not enough, CW finishes his account with a statement of his inborn predispositions for depression.

As I said, the account has just about all the elements I mentioned throughout the chapter. However, in contrast to others, he does mention depression in medical terms. Interestingly, though, it is done in reference to his father, rather than himself. I have little doubt that the account leads inevitably to the conclusion that as he is the way he is, it is only natural that he suffers from depression, and depression is also an illness. But medicalisation serves another purpose here, I think. As much as it is a means of putting the description of the self on a 'firmer' ground, it is also a means of implicitly distancing from the description. The informant sees his diagnoses as a perspective in which to frame his experience, still CW also notes his distance from them. His words 'if there is a bit of this, a bit that is for me, that results from this story' indicate that as much as he might accept the diagnosis, it is not something he has internalised. There are only bits which are relevant to him. I think the informant suggests his location in a different perspective, in a world without diagnoses, for him they are not necessarily fully relevant. This distance is underpinned by the fact that the informant introduces the diagnosis through the medical perspective. It is unequivocally constructed as 'their' diagnosis, rather than his. Incidentally, given such a diagnostic history, it is probably quite fortunate that the informant shows at least some distance to it.

Before I move to the other extracts, let me finish with a comment on the damning account of psychiatric and psychotherapeutic diagnosis. As much as he distances himself from fully espousing the diagnosis, he is also unable to challenge it. The distance does not introduce the possibility that the diagnosis might actually be wrong. For CW there is no hesitation, the diagnosis simply makes a summary of what the informant is like. It is the basis upon which he sees himself and attempts to square himself into the pronouncements. Stigmatising as it is, the label of schizoid personality pales in the face of that of 'psychopath'. The distance he introduces seems to save him from a complete condemnation of himself.

Moreover, the diagnosis is not only a label summarising the entirety of what the informant is, it is also taken as a true piece of information that is supposed to be lived around. Despite the distance, CW starts his reasoning assuming the truthfulness of the diagnostic verdicts. Note the direction of reasoning in what he said. Logically, he should start with the way he is, with his childhood, his *illness* and all that should lead him to the diagnosis. He does it the other way round. The labels become the evidence (indeed, just as in other extracts above), the truth and life must be matched accordingly. The diagnoses offer an explanatory framework in which to see his life. Now, I am not claiming of course that this is what either diagnosis said, that it was given in this crude and summarising way, still, this is what the informant, and patient, remembers from it, this is how he experienced it. Regardless of what was actually said, the result is quite frightening.

Although I have found stories of the diagnosis in the corpus, I have found none so clearly positioned as the frame for the account of the self. Even if such a diagnosis is completely atypical and it is an exception rather than a rule, still, it is significant that this is how the informant sees his diagnoses. Of course taking into account a large body of research suggesting the dominance of medical discourse in medicine and, specifically, in psychiatry (e.g. Kleinman, 1988a; also Filc, 2004; Lacasse and Gomory, 2003), CW's words are not particularly shocking. They merely show how what is only one particular discourse on psychological distress becomes part of an individual account of distress, one which not only is taken to be true, but also which provides a framework in which to see life experience. It is, however, particularly invidious precisely because of the ongoing discussions in psychiatry about the nature of mental illness (e.g. Bolton and Hill, 2003; Thomas and Bracken, 2005), the process and accuracy of psychiatric diagnosis and its stigmatisation.

Now, the other two extracts I quoted above also show upbringing as a cause for what the informants are like and that this had had a direct link with their illness. Unusually, SB in (13) assumes the possibility of change of what he is like, and just as he is saying that he has won, he actually undermines it. The defeating of his complexes is qualified with the word *niby* which I rendered by the English 'kind of', but it is, in fact, more negative. While 'kind of' is a hedge which qualifies the predicate, *niby* questions it. The Polish original suggests that he did not prevail in the struggle, that the victory is an illusion only. The illusion is underscored by the explicit repudiation of the success. The changeability is undermined at practically the moment it is assumed.

The final extract I would like to present here is the least explicit of those I have quoted so far. It is quite a poignant account in which the informant both implies what he is like and speaks of his toxic father and dramatic childhood:

Extract 15

DG: What would have to happen for you to say 'I am healthy'.

KL: As far as I am concerned, I need success. I know it's the little steps again, which one must make. But just simply I need success. And this will let me live normally. I need stability, stability that would ensure that I can live normally. Never in my entire 40-year life. Because depression is not that it comes from somewhere. And that's it. No. It is the period of, say, 20, 30 years. Sometimes the entire life. That's my view. And everything has been a struggle for me. I envy people for whom it has been easy. Perhaps not easy, no. Those who simply do something and achieve success, not even success, they live normally. Simply. I want to live normally. I don't want to have a past where my father beat me with, I don't know, a cable, right? I don't want to have a past when. No. I would like to forget about the past, simply, about all that was. Perhaps that's the way.

'I don't want to have a past where my father beat me, I don't know, with a cable'. These dramatic words just about summarise KL's account of his depression and his, shall I say, scarred self. But when I came to this extract first, I assumed that the informant was talking about a professional success (this is presumably my own masculine bias – if a man talks about success, he must mean work!). But I think that the success he dreams of is the 'normal', stable life. A life that would be a contrast to the current one and particularly his childhood, in contrast to the life that resulted in depression. But where is the self in this account? I think that the self is implied in the needs KL expresses. He not only needs his success, but also the peace and quiet in his life, something that he did not get in childhood, and did not get as an adult. This is the dramatic background that haunts him and not only makes him what he is, but also spawns depression. But as much as he wishes he didn't have a life as he had, he constructs it as grinding him down into the illness.

Conclusions

In this chapter I have discussed my informants' constructions of their 'timeless selves'. I have shown that on occasions, and particularly in answers to questions on the causes of depression, my informants constructed, more or less explicitly, their selves in generic terms. They showed what they are 'really' like, be it by ascribing certain attributes to themselves, or by showing some significant life events as responsible. It is this 'real' nature that was responsible for depression. I have interpreted these constructions as the informants' wish to de-medicalise depression, to construct it not as a 'real' illness. After all, if it results from the way one is, there is no 'falling ill', it is simply a logical outcome of what the informants are like. Put like this, incidentally, there is a clear relationship between this naturalness and the naturalness of depression within the informants' autobiographies that I spoke of in the previous chapter.

Both aspects of the corpus can be seen as a means of taming depression, stripping its dramatic character, while leading to its normalisation. I do realise, however, that my interpretation might seem to run counter to the extracts I quoted – after all the speakers constructed themselves in quite negative terms. Still, I would argue that, socially, it is less undesirable to be strange or withdrawn than be ill with a mental illness, including depression. Note the final extract in which the rejection of the illness is quite explicit.

Extract 16

> SB: With me, there were three relapses. In the meantime I was active. I travelled abroad. I worked in Germany. But how they can stress you, big time. And as a project manager at various levels, sometimes quite responsible, I don't know what it was, I was promoted a few times to a manager and a few times in my life I gave it up. I don't know whether it was some predispositions of mine. Of personality I think more than those of illness. Because it was much earlier than this illness appeared.

SB attempts to weigh the influence of his characterological predispositions as opposed to those illness-like. What sways him towards the former is the longitude of the character. The illness that he somewhat grudgingly accepts is only something that comes later on. What is also striking is that he chooses the strategy I described in Chapter 3, in which depression is constructed as autonomous. He didn't become ill, the illness appeared. Thus, while he quite readily accepts his characterological problems, illness is something to be distanced from.

What I have described here is not only a complement to the previous chapter in which depression was a natural event in the informants' biographies, it is also a complement, and a counterpoint to my initial argument about constructions of depression (Chapter 3) and the relationship between the self and depression (Chapter 4). I could say that while illness should ideally be outside the self, if it cannot be and it does have to be associated with it, the self will be distanced from it, or, as here, it cannot be a 'real' illness, one you can fall ill with.

In this part of the book I have explored the uneasy relationship between depression and those who suffer from it. I have shown that my informants have struggled to keep it at arm's length. I have argued that a significant part of this uneasy relationship are the expectations of the dominant model of masculinity, one which expects men to be active. This is indeed why I have demonstrated that depression is predominantly located within the realm of life, rather than the psyche, and it is the inability to act which is its core for the informants, rather than the depressed mood, as modern psychiatry would have it.

With Chapter 8, in which I shall explore the relationship between depression and masculinity, and show the extent to which masculinity is under threat from depression, I am starting the final part of the book. I shall now be exploring my informants as speaking men. Thus, I shall start with the relationship between depression and masculinity, I shall then move to consider the place of work in the narratives of depressed men and their difficult relationship with their families.

8
Lesser Men. Depression and the Model of Masculinity

Introduction

In the previous chapter I ended the part of the book devoted to the constructed relationship between self and depression. I have shown that this relationship is uneasy, with the self never fully espousing depression, or depression as an illness. I have also interpreted the uneasiness with which the self relates to depression in terms of the dominant model of masculinity. And it is masculinity that I shall be primarily concerned with in this and the following two chapters. Exploring the relationship between depression and masculinity, I shall show my informants as men positioning themselves with regard to their illness and their illness with regard to them.

In this chapter I shall show that depression is constructed as inherently interlinked with the informants' masculinity as well as, more generally, with the model itself. The illness is invariably constructed as an assault on masculinity – the social expectations of what it means to be a man, what a man does (or should do), his role at work, in the family and so on. There are two ways in which depression is constructed to be linked to masculinity. On the one hand, it undermines masculinity, depressed men are not men, or at the very least are lesser men. On the other hand, depression disturbs masculinity, it makes it impossible to execute it. Before I discuss it on data, I would like to remind readers where I stand with regard to what masculinity is.

Men and masculinity

I view masculinity in two dimensions. On the one hand, it is to do with the locally negotiated identities, always provisional, always in a state of flux. It is men's performance of being a man, always done anew, always in a particular local context. It is the 'repetition with a difference' (Lloyd, 1999). I think women cannot perform masculinity in this sense, inasmuch as men cannot perform femininity. On the other hand, masculinity is a social construct, a gender ideology, a society's way of associating certain practices with gender. Here masculinity can be seen as a configuration of social practices, but these practices are not there to be read off what men say or do, they are mediated by the society's ideological constructs. This is not to say that we, as analysts, shall not be able to observe certain patterns in constructions of identities, we shall precisely because of the men's submergence in ideologies and the society's narratives of what it means to be a man. In their local negotiation of identities, men of course make use of such discourses, practices which they associate with masculinity – this is indeed why we normally would expect men to be, say, dressed in a particular way. But my argument is that while people speak 'the way one speaks', that people dress 'the way one dresses', it does not mean that such practices are linked to masculinity in some sort of essential way.

Let me now briefly explore the issue of the dominant model of masculinity. In his analysis of masculinity and emotions, Jansz (2000) proposes that contemporary masculinity can be seen in terms of four attributes: autonomy, achievement, aggression and stoicism. Jansz' formulation, despite the claims to the contrary, leads to the inevitable essentialising of masculinity. Furthermore, there is little controversy in the literature that one cannot speak of masculinity in separation from such other identity categories as historical location, age and physique, sexual orientation, education, status and lifestyle, geography, ethnicity, religion and beliefs, class and occupation, culture and subculture (Beynon, 2002). Elsewhere (Galasiński, 2004) I have argued that such categories as disability, personal experience, illness, trauma, accidents, political system, military system, imprisonment also interact with masculinity, problematising it and offering new ideologies and contexts for lived experience.

However, Jansz' model of masculinity is useful as a description of the dominant model of masculinity. This is in fact the model that is not only anchored in the stereotypical images of men, but also in the academic descriptions of what Connell calls 'hegemonic masculinity' (Connell, 1995), common in cultural studies and social theory critiques of men and masculinity, represented most acutely by Seidler (1989, 1994; see also my critique of such studies in Galasiński, 2004). Men, according to Jansz (2000), are characterised by

Autonomy: A man stands alone, bears the tribulations of life with stiff upper lip and does not admit his dependence on others.

Achievement: A man is achieving in work and play in order to be able to provide bread for his loved one and family.

Aggression: A man is tough, and acts aggressively if the circumstances require so.

Stoicism: A man does not share his pain, does not grieve openly and avoids strong, dependent and warm feelings.

I shall assume here that men's explicit or implicit references to such aspects of behaviour or practice are related to the dominant model of masculinity. I do realise that without an explicit reference to men or masculinity, one cannot be certain that it is the model of masculinity that is at stake in the narrative (Schegloff, 1997; but see also Kitzinger, 2000; Stokoe and Smithson, 2001; Wetherell, 1998). However, the informants' narratives cannot be analysed outside the social context of both the socialisation and the continuing submergence in the ideologies of masculinity. It is therefore likely that references to achievement, toughness, taking care of one's family are anchored in discourses of masculinity rather than any other.

Saying this, I am implying that I shall mostly be operating at the level of gender ideology. I shall be interested in how the dominant model of masculinity is translated and incorporated into the informants' narratives. But this does not mean that I shall automatically be analysing my informants' narratives as those in which they speak *as* men and indeed there is no easy way to make such a judgement without reservations. Indeed, I shall assume that there are no systematic discursive markers of identities (see Cameron, 1997, 1998; Johnson, 1997; Ochs, 1992; for a review see Galasiński, 2004). Rather, the analyst is faced with the necessity of arguing for the 'discourse of belonging' locally, in reference to the particular context of interaction. And what counts as orientation to masculinity in one context does not necessarily count as such in another, with speakers drawing upon different resources, often contradictory, to construct themselves as 'being' or 'belonging' (also Meinhof and Galasiński, 2005).

Lesser men

The most dramatic construction of depression's relationship with masculinity is positioning it as undermining it completely. Depressed men are not men enough, they are not 'real men'. Depression takes away the informants' participation in the model of masculinity. By implication, therefore, the illness situates men in depression outside the bipolar world of gender: if people are either men or women, my interviewees are outside the dichotomy. It goes without saying that the stigmatisation of such exclusion is extreme. Consider first a number of extracts in which the relationship between depression and masculinity is made explicitly and is applicable to the speaker himself:

Extract 1

AZ: With men it's a bit, so that a woman is more like, I mean there are mostly women on the ward, right? And I have always seen that. Women have their nervous system more prone to depression. And men simply, I mean that I am not a man. It insults me a bit. Do you understand? But I don't care, as long as I am healthy.

Extract 2

DG: And why do men mask it?

GT: I don't know, perhaps certain masculinity will be hurt if it's revealed, maybe it simply is not becoming for it to be [...]. That's what I think. Hurting of masculinity. Simply, if I admit to it, I am no longer a lad, people think differently, and take it. Men also have different consciousness. To be honest, not everywhere, I don't always speak of it. But it doesn't mean that I my masculinity is hurt. I simply don't talk for other reasons, in order not to be discriminated in the society. Our work environment, or something. But I believe that men do think about it. God forbid I don't try to observe the doctors or something, but I see myself that men have inferiority complexes.

Both informants see their depression at the background of men in depression in general. Thus the dramatic 'I am not a man' is not AZ's own assessment of his experience, but rather is a translation of how men who are depressed are seen socially. And the directness of the formulation leaves no doubt as to how immediately applicable is the social aspect of men's depression. Similarly in (2), admitting to depression leads to undermining masculinity. The informant uses the word *chłop*, which I translated here as 'lad', yet the translation does not fully render the connotations of the Polish word. While the 'Jack the lad' kind of connotations are less pronounced, *chłop* connotes more the physical side of masculinity, its crudeness. The word epitomises the dominant model of masculinity. Depression does not allow the informant to partake of masculinity, and certainly not its core. But while AZ is talking about depression undermining masculinity more generally, GT refers to admitting to depression – in order to preserve masculinity, he must conceal it.

As could be expected, neither informant accepts the social judgement of masculinity being undermined by depression. The issue is face threatening in the extreme and the informants must negotiate it with care. This is indeed why the distance from the perceptions is rendered by the explicit pronouncements that they are touched by them. Also, the level of disjointedness in what they say (especially in Extract 1) suggests that the issues are very far from being resolved in their own narratives. In other words, the informants have not yet got anything that resembles a coherent story in which to talk about it.

But while GT, even though he disagrees with social perceptions, accepts them and simply acts accordingly, AZ takes a more cavalier attitude. He shows himself as above the concern. By expressing his lack of care, he attempts to defy the rule, but at the same time, I think, he also attempts to reaffirm his masculinity. It is perhaps only someone strong enough who could be beyond caring. At the same time if it is something one does not pay any attention to, all the more it is not something that can be seen as true. In this way, any potential implication that the link between depression and masculinity might apply to them is repudiated before it is actually made.

Note also that the informant in the next extract not only confirms the social lack of acceptance for men's depression, yet he only offers a very generalised comment on it:

Extract 3

> KL: No, depression in men, no way. It doesn't apply [laughs]. Let's forget it. It's simply like when depression appears in men, it's like in this joke: a woman has a period once a month, and a man daily in such a situation. Simply, if depression in a man, it means he has a period every day. So no, no. that's my view. A man should not have depression.

The speaker's choice not to adopt his own perspective and to speak generally allows him to move to safer ground and thus the opportunity not to have to take a stance. What the informant said sounds almost as if the problem of depression did not apply to him and he was taking the position of a social observer. Extract 3 is also the strongest in constructing the society's rejection of male depression. Not only does the informant augment his statement by introducing colloquiality ('Let's forget it'), but there is no trace of any attempt to qualify what he says. But it is precisely the distancing, and thus not invoking the informant's own perspective, that allows for such an unequivocal statement on the rejection of male depression.

Now, apart from such direct formulations, a number of informants constructed depression's destructive influence more implicitly. Witness the following extracts:

Extract 4

> EU: My business partner, it hurt very very much. My business partner at work, when I tried to plod on more or less, in order not to be immobile, my business partner belittled it completely, laughing: just take half a bottle, it will go away.

Extract 5

> WT: I always thought I would achieve great things. At the moment when my wife begins to support me for three months, I use her money, I start realising that I prefer to borrow from a buddy than take from her account. So this is not a normal situation. Mother of God, is this the way it's going to be? I am a guy without balls and suddenly there is panic, interwoven with fright.

Extract 4 is typical of a host of extracts in which depression is greeted with the 'get a grip' advice, to which my informants normally reacted with irritation (I shall discuss this kind of advice in Chapter 10). But this extract was different in the sense that it was implicitly gendered. Although it has been changing, masculinity in Poland has always been associated with drinking, and, normally, heavy drinking. This 'analgesic' in the form of a bottle of vodka (normally half a litre) is what EU refers to here. If you have a problem, you have a few shots of vodka and your problems go away. This 'masculine' way of dealing with depression is suggested to the informant who, of course, rejects it as belittling his condition. However, it can also be argued that if the informant rejects this universal and masculine 'therapy' he is not enough of a man. A real man would get drunk and his depression would be gone. Especially that the hangover the following morning would prevent him from thinking about anything else but the headache. WT in Extract 5, on the other hand, stops being a real man when he needs to get money from his wife. While he explicitly positions himself as a 'man without balls', the link with depression is only implied. But as much he is not a real man, the reason why he is not stems from the fact that he is not able to execute the duties placed upon him by the society. This was a typical way in which depression was shown to have impacted upon masculinity.

Men who don't perform

Masculinity was of often associated with duties men have. Depression in turn was what made it impossible to perform these duties, thus undermining the informant's masculinity. There were two spheres in which the lack of performance was represented. On the one hand, and more often, the informants spoke about their duties to support their families financially, and on the other, they spoke of family life and their duties as husbands and fathers.

Failed breadwinners

Witness first three extracts in which the informants position themselves explicitly as those who fail in providing for their families:

Extract 6

DG: And depression in men?

BC: It's particularly difficult because usually it's the man who bears the duty of fighting for the family, or defending the family or providing for the family. Thus, this burden makes it more difficult. Whether one feels such a weakness, one thinks, really, that, I think that I am the weakest man in the world, that I am unable to do anything in depression.

Extract 7

JS: I think that for [people] depression is such a condition that is caused by the ill person themselves, and they simply give in and they are ill because if they got a grip they would be healthy.

DG: And depression in men?

JS: I think it's more [unclear] because it is that the man should provide for the family, and depression makes it hard.

Extract 8

EU: My sister [unclear], she is 36 years old and she loves me very much and to a great extent she took over the role of the parents. Mom. She feels responsible, although that drags me down that she feels responsible for me, that she worries. But [unclear] because I am a man, that I am older, that life is hard for her too. And she can do it.

In all three extracts there is an explicit link between the masculine duty, providing for the family, and depression's power to make it impossible to fulfil it. But in (7) the informant also talks about public attitudes towards depression. And while they are negative, they are more so towards men's depression, as it is the man who carries the burden of being the breadwinner. Indeed, in a qualitative study of men earning less than their wives, Ryba (2003; also Waddington *et al.*, 1998) discusses strategies in which men positioned their wives' earning and work as less important than theirs, a result of an accident, rather than women's competence or success. However sexist one might judge such opinions to be, and however discriminating they might be for women, it is precisely the dominant model of masculinity that is responsible not only for the sexism, but also for more suffering of the men I spoke to. This is the model that gives them the power, if you like, but is also their undoing.

Thus, Extracts 6 and 7 show the men's 'double jeopardy' in depression, which I have already referred to earlier in the book. Men suffer from depression, but they also suffer from depression because they are men. Depression is not only an assault on the person and their 'normal' life, it is also an assault on masculinity. Illness experience does not merely become a 'resource' in the construction of identity, but even more significantly, it can be seen as reconfiguring identity resources completely and making masculinity a particularly problematic one. I shall take up the argument below.

Failed family men

As I said above, my informants constructed themselves as failures in their family life too. Their inability to fulfil the duties of husbands and fathers undermined them and their masculinity. Consider the following:

Extract 9

> DE: A certain distance has arisen between me and [my family] but more because I am unable, shall I say, to function normally, I mean I am unable to perform the duties of a husband and wife, phew, husband, father [laughs] so this is why this distance arises, right? I am on the margin, I prefer to shut myself in a room, or lie down and do nothing.

Extract 10

> DG: It might be a difficult question [...] how did depression contribute to your marriage breaking up?

> CW: Generally it's the problem of sex. Because all this medication I take now in large quantities causes a major decrease in libido. And it's a problem with a man who is constantly sad and constantly has a lot problems. It's difficult to bear it. I do realise it.

Both men show themselves as problems. They are a far cry from being strong and autonomous, they on the margins of the family (see Chapter 10). Both informants show themselves as unable to do what is expected of them, be it the general duties (whatever they might actually be) or perform sexually. What is striking in these two fragments, however, is that neither shows himself as attempting to oppose it. Both seem to accept that they deserve what they get for the failure. Thus DE in (9) is simply confirming his marginality within his family (and imposed by his family) by withdrawing even further. Incidentally, one could see the lapse in DE's narrative (accidentally calling himself a wife) as indicative of the strength of the family unity in his family narrative, one which is undermined by the story of his illness, though. The self-exclusion of CW in (10) goes even further. Even though the problem is his inability to perform sexually, the informant seems to accept and justify the 'problem' by suggesting that he is just one big problem, not only in sex terms. He takes the perspective of the family (or perhaps of his wife) and undermines himself as a valid husband. Thus, the undermining of the informant in his masculine role seems to be justified by the informant himself!

Note that the latter part of Extract 10 constructs the informant in lay rather than medical terms. He shows himself as sad and with many problems, although it is more complex and I shall return to it in Chapter 10. It is as if the problem is in him, not the illness. Similarly in the next extract, the informant shows himself as a failed father, and also he shows himself as the problem, the failure is in him, not the illness.

Extract 11

> ST: On Saturdays I go to visit my children. I leave there miserable, broken down, not fit to live. On Sundays I still go through it emotionally and I still feel like doing nothing after a Saturday like that.
>
> DG: And could you say why you leave miserable and broken down after visiting your children?
>
> ST: I mean, because I think I have wasted not only my life but also my children's life. They haven't got a normal family, like they should have.

This is not a story about illness, it is about wasted lives of the informant and his children. Once again, it is he who is the problem, it is he who is not an adequate father. Depression seems to have nothing to do with it. He constructs himself as an agent of the process of wasting, it is his action that wasted those lives. Implicitly, I think what he says is anchored in the dominant gender ideology – as much as he is the failed father, he is also man enough to take the blame and the illness, it seems, is hardly an excuse.

Men like women

In the final section of this chapter I would like to present a few extracts in which my informants explicitly juxtapose men's and women's depression. It is significant, however, that any such comparison was invariably a result of my questions and was never volunteered by the informants. So, towards the end of the interview I asked two questions concerning the informants' views on depression in men and women. One was about who, men or women, is more likely nowadays to fall ill with depression, the other was about social perceptions of depression in men and women.

Most of my informants told me that women are more prone to depression. They based their judgements on a number of reasons. There were the sexist remarks about the female psyche being weaker, there was evidence from the hospital or the clinic (there were by far more women hospitalised or in the queue in the out-patient clinic), finally, some quoted epidemiological evidence. Quite clearly, the remarks about women's weakness are anchored in ideologies of a patriarchal society, underpinned by the traditional gender dynamics – they are a way of stereotyping women negatively. However, the point I am trying to make is that as much as they target women negatively, they also have a double edge in that they are a source of suffering for the men also. For, if women are weaker, more prone to depression, how come men can also be depressed? The dominant model of masculinity, one which no doubt oppresses women, is also oppressive of men. One could say, in fact, that the dominant model works quite well for the men who barely need it, as they fulfil it so well. The moment a man falls out of the 'groove', the model turns against him and shows him as even more powerless than he might be (see also Paechter, 2003).

This argument is not merely an academic one, it is also based on explicit accounts of my informants. I have already indicated, in the case of Extracts 6 and 7 above, the implicit reference to the fact that the position outside the dominant model of masculinity is a source of suffering. In the following extract, the informant explicitly situates masculinity as a problem in depression:

Extract 12

EU: For a woman, it is easier to admit to it. Perhaps also easier to come out of depression than for a man. Because a man has double problems. Usually he bottles it up and doesn't show that something like that is happening.

Masculinity is a hindrance, as men bottle up their problems. But I do not think it is this inability to speak of one's emotions that the informant refers to here. Rather, I would argue, it is the society's sanction on men speaking of their depression that is the cause of the bottling up, exactly as in the next extract:

Extract 13

DG: [...] what do people think of depression?

WT: I think that, as the sources inform, it is more and more widespread, the situation in which we live, yet, despite that, people know very little about depression, usually they rather laugh at it rather than take it seriously.

DG: And depression in men?

WT: The funnier it is. Depression in men. Women, women always were described and talked about, while male depression not at all. And perhaps this is why, perhaps it's shameful, because people are ashamed, men are ashamed to talk about it. It's something that cannot apply to men. And, sadly, perhaps this is the funniest.

The sanction is so strong that the informant chooses to speak of the shame of depression. It is quite fascinating to see that the contrast between men and women is that between levels of laughability and men's depression no doubt must be funnier. While women are somehow excused, there is no excuse for men. The extract also completes the undermining of masculinity. It is both from within, the men I interviewed construct themselves as failed men, and also from outside, the society is constructed to take away the 'privilege' of being a man. It could be said, finally, that the discourse of 'the master of the universe', as Faludi (2000) puts it, is as much empowering (and discriminating of the women) as it is disempowering. As much as women do not fit in, men in depression do not fit in even more.

Conclusions

In this chapter I showed that depression is constructed as inherently interlinked with informants' masculinity as well as, more generally, with the dominant model of masculinity. The illness is invariably constructed as an assault on masculinity – the social expectations of what it means to be a man, what a man does (or should do), his role at work, in the family and so on. There were two ways in which this assault was constructed. First, my informants showed themselves as lesser men, or not men at all. Second, depression hindered masculinity. It didn't allow men to perform masculine duties.

Now, I would like to come back to the issue I flagged up during the discussion and explore some more the issue of the relationship between identity, masculinity and depression. As I said above, illness experience does not merely become a 'resource' in the construction of identity, its relationship with identity discourses is more complex. It can be seen as reconfiguring identity resources completely and making masculinity a particularly problematic one.

What I would like to argue is that depression as an identity resource introduces a conflict in the possibility of accessing the dominant model of masculinity as such a resource. So, the problem is not so much that depression 'articulates' (Hall, 1990, 1992, 1996) with masculinity in that

it offers a way to construct an ill or depressed masculinity, a locally negotiated identity which has no anchoring in the dominant ideologies which
underpin such identities. There is no evidence of such masculinity being
constructed in the corpus I collected. I agree with Charmaz (1983) that
depression, like other illnesses, does not provide those ill with positive
images upon which to build the new self.

Depression undermines the dominant model of masculinity to the
extent that a positive 'articulation' is impossible. Depressed men are
not men, rather than men who are depressed. The clash between the
metanarratives of mental illness and depression and the dominant masculinity is too great to be squared in a locally negotiated identity. The
flip side of it is that any such masculinity would simply be too distant
from what is accepted socially, as well as from what the men accepted for
themselves. In that sense, Charmaz' (1983) point about the self can be
applied to the corpus. My informants are unable to position their selves
within the model they used in their self-narratives.

However, the problem is that this relationship with the dominant
model of masculinity is always an ambition and aspiration. It never ends
and it continues to be a reference point for the men in depression. In
that sense, there is no loss of self (ibid.). The 'real man' is ever present
in the stories of my informants. More than likely it results from the fact
that giving up on the 'real masculinity' is ideologically impossible. For
the opposition is not that between ill and healthy, or perhaps even an
ill man and a healthy man, it is between no-man and a man. A lesser
man and a real man. This is precisely why depression can be seen as
devastating for men suffering from the illness.

Incidentally, also Emslie and her colleagues (2006) point out 'hegemonic masculinity' as the frame of reference in men's accounts they
analysed, one which was found to be an unattainable goal. What they
did also find, however, was that some informants were able to find themselves within the model; for example, by constructing decisions to take
medication as indicative of re-establishing control. Still, across the British
and Polish sample, it seems, the dominant masculine ideology is a major
frame of reference for the identity work of men in depression. One can
only speculate on the differences between the data; even though they
were minor, they were significant. It would seem that it is the differences in gender dynamics and politics in the two countries, with Britain
further away from a rigidly patriarchal view on gender relations.

Furthermore, the constant struggle for masculinity contributes a new
aspect into identity discourses of the men in depression. It introduces
failure. So, if being a real man is ever present as a potential identity

resource, ever unattainable in the local context, inevitably, identity becomes ridden by failure. Again, men in depression are failed, rather than ill. And this struggle to maintain masculinity can be seen in the final extract I would like to present here:

Extract 14

> KL: I mean you have helped me in a sense because I was able to describe certain things for myself here, but it's not that. I realised that a conversation with another person doesn't hurt. You know, it's like I see my doctor and I won't tell her that, simply because I thought it hurt, that one should not say it, right? So, that's why I am saying that you have helped me. Because a couple of guys sat down and talked about a thing, it seemed, in a way shameful in our society.

The repositioning of the interview in terms of a conversation between two guys shows, I think, the struggle to maintain masculinity in the context of the interaction. The informant rejects the possibility of talking to his female doctor, a conversation with her would be a source of pain. Immediately after that, he constructs the interview (never before referring to it in this way) as a conversation between 'two guys'. The use of the word *facet* ('guy', 'bloke') suggests a certain bonding, a rapport based on masculinity. But it also introduces a hint of toughness, 'real manhood', it's a conversation between two persons who are not afraid of topics, who can face whatever comes their way. And indeed, the embarrassing nature of the illness that was the subject of the conversation is introduced by 'seemed', not only a verb referring to a mental process undermining the objectiveness of the state of affairs, but which was put in the past tense, as if even the appearances of shame pertain to the past. All that is said in the context of the informant's statement that the conversation helped him, a statement quite interesting for the social anchoring of research and its ethics.

This account, based on the argument throughout the chapter, shows illness quite backgrounded. Depression reconfigures access to identity resources, disenabling some and introducing others. Thus, rather than a resource *per se*, depression becomes a platform, a frame in which identity construction is done, without actually interacting with it. If this is the case, we must see depression in men as particularly pernicious. It becomes an invisible context, a background in which masculinity crumbles away. Depression does not introduce illness into masculinity, but, rather, excludes the man from masculinity. In this way, it does not so much erase the former identity, it introduces a new one, with the other being an ever-unreachable aspiration.

In this chapter I have begun considerations of the constructions of masculinity in the narratives of men in depression. In Chapter 9, I shall be exploring how the men I spoke to position themselves and their illness with regard to work and paid employment as one of the central planks of masculinity.

9
Men's Imperatives. Men, Depression and Work

Men and work

In the previous chapter I began considering the constructed relationship between depression and masculinity. I showed that depression is constructed as undermining the informants as men. I further argued that the illness reconfigures the identity resources available to the ill men, introducing failure as one of them. I argued that masculinity is not so much erased from the men's identities, but it becomes an ever-unachievable goal. Here I shall focus on how my informants positioned themselves and their illness with regard to work and paid employment. By way of reminder, in Chapter 5 I argued that in the narratives of the men diagnosed with depression, the illness is not so much related to low mood, but, rather, to their inability to cope with life. The interviewees did not speak about sadness, preferring to talk about powerlessness or incapacitation. The core of depression seems being a 'failed doer'.

I linked this finding with the fact that the dominant model of masculinity espouses work, including, crucially, paid work, as a central element of masculinity. Indeed, there is agreement in the literature that work is at the core of the dominant gender ideology (for an overview, see Collinson and Hearn, 2005). Unemployment is a major assault on one of the foundations of men's identities or masculinity in general (Brittan, 1989; Morgan, 1992; Willis, 2000; Willott and Griffin, 1996, 1997, 2004). Masculinity has always been associated with paid employment, men were supposed to provide for themselves and their families (Mattinson, 1988); in fact providing for the family is part of the success of what it is to be a man (Hood, 1993; Nonn, 2001; see also contributions to Hood, 1993). Unemployed men feel disempowered, useless, emasculated, their self-esteem is shattered (Beynon, 2002; Brittan, 1989), with the ultimate humiliation constituted by being supported by one's wife (Kelvin and Jarrett, 1985). On top of that, male unemployment is a source of social stigmatisation (Lee and Owens, 2002; Smith, 1998).

Moreover, there is some evidence of a relationship between unemployment and mental health (for a review, see Farr, 1987; also Grove *et al.*, 2005). The ESEMeD /MHEDEA 2000 Investigators (2004; also Farr, 1987; Tausig, 1999) report a correlation between unemployment and an increased risk of any mental disorder in general, and particularly mood and alcohol disorders, and that correlation is reported to be stronger in men, particularly for depressive disorders (Timms, 1998; see also Gary, 1985). Moreover, unemployment is said to be a significant suicide or suicide ideation risk (Kessler *et al.*, 1987; Levine, 2005, for problematisation of the link see Beautrais *et al.*, 1998). The relationship between unemployment and depression is also noted in studies of experiences of mental illness and particularly depression. Joblessness was reported as one of the reasons given for depression by people suffering from depression (Lewis, 1995; Kangas, 2001).

Willott and Griffin (1997) offer ethnographic evidence to Brittan's (1989) claim that unemployed men need to come to terms with their uselessness. Their study of working-class masculinities shows the unemployed's discourse as constructing them as 'idle scroungers', falling back on the welfare system, rather than paying their way. Unemployed men in that study are consumers who cannot consume – particularly beer in their pub. They are breadwinners without the bread (see also contributions to Gaillie *et al.*, 1994). But unemployment is not only about masculinity for masculinity's sake. Unemployed men need to deal also with masculinity in relation to their partners or wives. Willis (2000) posits that unemployment means shedding the traditional dignity masculinity was invested with on account of a job. This, continues Willis, might have dramatic consequences for working-class women who might be asked to respect the man for what he is, rather than for what he does, while the men will continue working on their biceps' definitions and the visibility of their six-packs (Willis, 2000). There is also the reverse side of the gender relations coin. Pyke (1996) shows that the masculine power of the 'unsuccessful' man may shift to the resentful wife, the less-earning, let alone unemployed, men can very easily be blamed for not caring enough. This is the case of the Mr Phillips character from John Lanchester's novel *Mr Phillips*, who, having lost work, still keeps up appearances, gets up, dresses up and leaves for work (just like another character in the hugely popular British film *The Full Monty*). How can a man tell his wife that he is not working? Be it as it may, Jones (1991) proposes that it is men's job-lessness, rather than being in employment, that challenges the structure of family relationships.

In her account of modern masculinity, a radical feminist author pro-poses a view sympathetic to men. Men have been stiffed – the society has removed the very plank upon which masculinity has been hinged: employment. Comparing women's 'problem-with-no-name' (Faludi, 2000: 15) with men's predicament, she suggests that while women organ-ised themselves into more or less informal support networks, because of the 'master of the universe' kind of masculinity, men get more and more isolated. Isolation also means that there is no real replacement for paid employment. And if the six-pack is not an option, loss of employment is a hole that just about cannot be filled in a man's life.

What is quite interesting in the narratives of the men I interviewed, however, is that the explicit centrality of work is only part of the pic-ture constructed by the interviewed men, as it is, at least at face value, constructed in rather ambiguous terms. On the one hand, work leads to depression, as it is responsible for the stress which cannot be handled by the informants, but, on the other hand, lack of work, unemployment (and especially losing one's job) is also conducive to or causes depression. Moreover, work is the goal of recovery. Yet, I shall argue that all these constructions are underpinned by an implicit imperative to work, an assumption that a man must work, an imperative that cannot be opted out from.

Losers

Before I discuss the data I collected, I would like to contextualise my discussion by referring to an extract from an interview with a woman. In a study concerning women's (re-)negotiation of gender roles in post-Communist Poland,[1] when asked about her views on the 'position' of the head of the family, one of the interviewed woman said the following:

> BR: Men . . . were the first to lose their jobs, secondly they are like big children, they have no character at all, they break down completely, it would be best if they were allowed they would hang themselves and the problem would be gone. They weep a lot, they complain much and they do little, but want a lot of fuss around it, big time. They are impractical. I can't see them, maybe in the past, when there were these caves, and he went with the spear and caught the animal, for free, so the woman could hunt it, but now it has got flatter big time. And here life is now a jungle, battle to survive. They just do not fit

in. Maybe they would fit in the jungle, but absolutely not the urban one. Women are more practical and smarter. That's what I have said.

Interviewer: [laughter] and what's it like in your family?

BR: That's what I said, as above, exactly, exactly the same.

What is striking about this statement is not merely the complete reversal of stereotypical masculinity, but also the speaker's total lack of hesitation in making it. The helpless men are juxtaposed with practical women who mange to survive in the urban jungle. Linguistically, they are constructed as agents in activities such as crying, while their bread-winning activities are limited to catching animals long long ago, with connotations of luck, rather than strategy. It is women who are possessed of strategy and skill and thus can be the real hunters. It seems men are not even capable of taking their own lives, waiting for permission which is unlikely to come.

The reason why I am quoting the extract here is the informant's view on the role of paid employment in the lives of men and their families. Not only have the men lost their employment, but, it seems, they have not been able to get it back. This is not merely undermining, it is disqual-ifying in the eyes of the woman. The disqualification is so ultimate that they may well hang themselves. Masculinity is about hacking it, making it in life. Those who cannot make it, men who cry, break down, have no spine, no character, are simply disposable.

One could of course dismiss it as a token-utterance, completely unchar-acteristic of any 'discourse of masculinity' and, indeed, I am not at all suggesting that all women are likely to say similar things. Yet, it is dif-ficult to ignore a clear anchoring of the words in the dominant gender ideology in which men are associated with what they do. Incidentally, in a recent exchange on an Internet forum on the website of the largest-selling Polish daily, *Gazeta Wyborcza*, one of the users asked for advice on how to handle her husband, whom she suspected of showing signs of depression.[2] The initial responses immediately assumed that the man had problems at work and were combined with the advice to 'pack his rags' and kick him out of the house. Only in reaction to this did voices advising support appear.

Work as stress

Work as the cause of depression was constructed in two main ways. On the one hand, the informants talked about their employment as some-thing they could not cope with. On the other, the informants showed themselves as workaholics who, after years of working too much, cracked under pressure.

In the extracts below, showing the former representation, there is a spectrum of agency constructions – from the self positioned as the object to its being positioned as the agent in the relationship with work.

Extract 1

HI: This job influenced me in a discouraging and very bad way. I was once on a black list for dismissal. I took it very badly. But somehow I managed to keep it, but constantly, constant stress, constant work in tension. In addition it was shift work. Unslept nights, all that had an effect on me. And later I found myself where I found myself. And I am in a state in which I am.

Extract 2

AZ: It was not taken into consideration and no one took it into consideration that I simply would not cope with certain life difficulties. Like building a house or something. Although without building a house, I also was in depression. So, for example, when I worked, my work gave me satisfaction, although it did keep me in a certain tension. And that was bad. I mean it gave me satisfaction, I found it difficult, but in 14 years of work there were no major failures. For me to feel depressed or in anxiety or something. I had such stages when I did something wrong, because it's never that you always do things well, right? One has such feeling of guilt, fear that nothing worked out for him.

Oppressiveness of work is not only stated explicitly, but also constructed linguistically. The speakers position themselves as objects of work's actions, whether it is just being influenced, or being kept in a state of tension. They cannot do much to counter what happens to them, and thus they have ended up in depression. These constructions are quite interesting as linguistically they place the responsibility for what happens on work. It is not the depression, nor the informants – the problem is work itself. The next extract deletes the explicit agency of work. Consider the following:

Extract 3

NM: I was on incapacity benefit and I wanted to try whether I was already able to manage at work. And I went to the same employer where I used to work. He took me on and I worked for a month and

I decided that it had not helped. It was like it had been before. [. . .] it was an ordeal for me. Psychologically I was finishing myself. When I came home from work, no eating. When I returned from work I didn't have dinner, I didn't eat, no eating. I was so resigned that I didn't feel like anything. Only after an hour or two, three, I was coming round.

This time the informant chooses to focus on himself more than on work. His job is only implicitly shown as the source of his ordeal. Interestingly, the speaker positions himself as an agent in the situation. It is his responsibility that he was 'finishing himself' although only 'psychologically'. It seems that while his employment was the source of suffering, his responsibility was in remaining in a stressful situation. The problem was with work and once again not in him; his problem, which he rectified, was to give up work again. The shift towards the focus on the self and the self's agency continues in the next extract:

Extract 4

SB: [depression] is a huge burden. It now, when I started having problem with work, it started being a terrible burden. Because it was like a vicious circle. Because I could not get work or I was losing it. Because this illness was in me and sometimes I would come out with something, probably not controlling myself, or I was ill-disposed. And on the other hand, it was hard to get a job, when one could not sell oneself and walked in so miserable.

The extract is different from the previous ones in that SB clearly shows work as his responsibility. It is he who could not get the job or hold it, and he who lost it. But the speaker's agency is not unfettered. The reference to the 'illness in me' constructs him as almost possessed. The illness is separate from him, it is, shall I say, a presence in him, yet one which made him say something, or be ill-disposed. I would like to stress the constructed separation of the illness and the speaker. He does not construct himself as ill, but, rather, under the influence of the illness, much like the influence of alcohol.

Thus, despite the spectrum of constructions of the relationship between work and the informants, the men I spoke to never fully position themselves as those who lost their jobs. They are never uninfluenced either by the job itself or, as in Extract 4, by the 'illness in them'. The main point, however, I would like to make here is that in all four extracts there is an unspoken assumption that men work, men are supposed to have jobs, they are supposed to hold them, and not lose them. They are supposed to be good at them. In Extract 2, the informant is talking about his guilt for being unsuccessful in something, in (4) the informant was not able to sell himself well, in (1) the 'black list' of people to be made redundant that the informant found himself on was taken badly. It can be seen particularly clearly in Extract 3, where the informant, already ill, is not giving up, but is trying to find out whether he was able to work again, as if working were some sort of imperative. He tries it even though it is an ordeal, giving up seems unsayable.

Now, I discussed the following two fragments in Chapter 5, raising the issue of excess work as the cause of depression. But this excess is not so much a decision which the informants make, rather, it is underpinned by a work imperative which drives the men. They cannot but work:

Extract 5

GT: It came from I think that I never took care of myself at work. For several years I didn't know what a holiday was, I never took it. I was always in the middle of production, among people, and dealt with many things. I was a bit of a workaholic. And for the decision whether I would get out after 8 or 10 hours didn't matter. [...] I was always involved in everything, I was managing, always high revs.

Extract 6

KL: Look, every person, when he worked for a time, should rest, do something else, I don't know, making snowmen, or clay ashtrays. Or perhaps airplane models. Walk the dog, right? Talk to the child. Talk to the wife about topics unrelated to work. Go for a beer with a friend. Or watch a match with a group of friends [...] instead, I forgot about this all. Simply. For me it was going to work, coming back from work, yes, darling we'll go for a walk, right? We came back home, and dad turned the laptop on and worked on. At half past midnight dad finished work and at 9 he was at work, somewhere in Poland.

Both speakers show themselves as hard workers who had worked themselves into depression. They worked so hard that something gave and they fell ill. Except what is quite fascinating in these accounts is that there is not a shadow of judgement upon how they worked. Even with hindsight they do not assess their working practices. And while KL could be seen to make such an assessment, in fact he does not so much evaluate his working practices, but states the fact that he did not have a hobby, as one should. A man works, even if it means working himself into illness.

Even with hindsight, there is no assumption that you can actually stop working. You may want to take a hobby, not be a workaholic, but you still work, work, work.

Regardless of the harm paid employment might actually be doing, a man is expected to work. This is indeed why the interviewed men attempted to show themselves as not responsible for the 'problems at work', this is why they did not evaluate their working practices, shifting the problem onto something else. But the imperative of work will be even more clear in the next two sections, where I shall discuss unemployment as the cause of depression, and recovery which quite often was linked to being in employment again.

Life as work

The imperative to work can be seen more clearly in the more positive constructions of paid employment. The informants construct work as the ultimate goal of their lives, whereas their inability is represented as a cause of depression. Recovery, in turn, is being able to go back to work. Witness first two extracts.

Extract 7

FH: The current episode came from that there was supposed to be a downsizing at work. Among others in the department where I worked, in a company where I worked practically from the beginning, because in Germany the company operated for a year when I was employed. It developed quite strongly and, not bragging, I think it was much of my doing, because it was intensive work in this company, 12, 16 hours a day.

Extract 8

DG: [. . .] when did you realise that something was going on?

NM: When I learnt of the company was being dissolved. I worked in that firm for 25 years. 25 year I was associated.

DG: Quite a stretch of time.

NM: A stretch of time. And I had this situation that I could have stayed in the hotel, it was the same company, but unfortunately I didn't, someone else stayed in that position. And it broke me down big time. And I went to that private work [. . .] So I broke down even more there.

There is no hesitation, no qualification in either informant's words: it is the redundancy that made them ill. But the stories are made more dramatic by the implicit injustice of what happened. Both informants construct themselves as much more than mere workers. The innovations FH piloted and the loyalty on the part of NM make their redundancy at the very least heartless and themselves undeserving of it. One could speculate that the construction of the loss of work as injustice serves as the additional 'justification' for the depression. After all it was not just any job. It was *the* job the two speakers were made redundant from. In the next extract the significance of work in a man's life is made even clearer. Even though, the informant reverses the order (more in line with the extracts in the previous section), he constructs work as the basis of what kind of man he is:

Extract 9

DG: What did it mean to you: I am ill with depression?

GT: What did it mean to me? Well, that I lost my job, this I know. That I could not hold a managerial post because of this depression. Because [unclear] would not let me continue managing people or production. That I am dependent on my doctor. That many things, as before, I could not, or would not, or could not deal with. Now I cannot any more. I am no longer able, as before, to be an energetic, healthy man.

His inability to work as before, especially to manage people, and being dependent on his doctor means not only that he is ill, but, importantly, that he is no longer a dynamic man. And it is this dynamism which accounts for his health. Once again we see that depression is not about depressed mood. Health means to be able to fit into the dominant model of masculinity. It means to be able to do what is expected of a man, a 'real man', and predominantly it means to be able to be active and engaged in paid employment. This link between work and the ability to fulfil the duties of a man can also be seen in the next extract:

Extract 10

WT: I am not employed by [name] theatre, it's from a phone call to a phone call. When it rings I count the money earned on the basis of phone rings, I mean orders which are there. Sometimes the absence of these phone calls makes me feel low, because for the following months I will not have anything to pay with. But when they do call and my diary fills up for two months in advance, I can breathe easily and I know that for two months at least it a bit...I gambled a lot moving from [place] to [place], buying a flat here, two children, obviously, with needs, my wife didn't work for three years and everything was on my shoulders, credits, payments, in sum it was a lot monthly and I just could not bear it. It was too much for me.

The extract is one of very few instances when the informant is talking about low mood. Note, however, that the mood is hardly a pathological one. Not only is it constructed as transitory, episodic, but is also unrelated to the illness, which is implicitly referenced at the end of the extract ('I just could not bear. It was too much to for me'). And if anything, the low mood is the result of the problems he has. But it is them, the inability to have enough work to fulfil his duties as the breadwinner, it is uncertainty of freelance work which is putting the informant under pressure he cannot cope with.

I argued in Chapter 5 that depression is constructed around the notion of powerlessness, inability. Low mood as a problem, especially on its own, does not appear in the stories of the men I interviewed. The narratives here complement and make this picture of depression fuller. The informants' powerlessness should be seen in tandem with the stories of paid employment and what I called the imperative to work. This imperative, moreover, complements what I called the action-orientedness of my informants' stories.

Furthermore, the informants do not speak of work as a means to pay the bills. Work is the principle of life – one works, especially if one is a man, or, perhaps, precisely, because one is a man. If depression means inability to work, one might suspect that recovery should be linked to the opposite – the ability to get and hold full employment. And indeed, more than half of my informants linked recovery from depression to their ability to get work and it was the recovery-to-work motif which was the only clear *topos* in the corpus. The remainder of my informants made all sorts of statements without a clear pattern. Witness the following extracts:

Extract 11

DG: What would recovering from depression mean for you?

[...]

FH: Someone asked me this question before. For me it would be full return to paid employment.

Extract 12

> DG: [...] what would recovering from depression be for you?
>
> OC: [...] what would it be? Work every day [unclear].

Extract 13

> DG: What would have to happen for you to say: I am healthy.
>
> RP: I don't know. If I never came back here? If could stop my medication. And what is the most important, find a job. I have been looking for a job for two years.

It is interesting that the first two informants show going back to work in nominalised terms, as things rather than as actions. But I see the references to the 'return' and the 'work' more as attempts at trying to speak of an outcome, recovery, rather than as undermining of their agency. Incidentally, I would argue that despite the non-medical outcomes, the informants access medical discourse of disease outcomes, which are seen as a clear product, health, rather than a more negotiated nebulous result of psychiatric treatment (Davidson, 2003). It is also significant that RP in (13) is putting finding employment above the 'medical' recovery. I see this as supporting the argument that depression is more to do with inability to be active than recovering from its 'medical' form. This can be seen even more clearly in the following extract:

Extract 14

> AZ: I was in [hospital] and for three months they treated me there. Then I dumped all the medication and in two weeks I felt ready for work.

The quick treatment (the informant uses the word *przeleczyć* 'to treat' which connotes quick, cursory treatment, something which is done on the hoof) has only one result – the informant's readiness for work. Moreover, it is by giving up medicalisation that he is able to return work. It is work and work only which is the priority. But the desirability of work as the outcome of depression is put even more emphatically by the informant in the next extract. He sees going back in terms of normality:

Extract 15

DG: What would recovering from depression mean for you.

DE: Returning to normal life, to duties. I mean putting another burden on my back and pulling the cart on. Now I haven't got it, I do nothing, I don't function, right? I don't go to work, and I am so, I receive treatment.

DG: What would have to happen?

[...]

DE: I would harness, harness myself to life again, which was such a positive [laughs] stimulus in life for me. [...] For me I would have to get in the car and go to work in the morning for seven o'clock. Give instructions, take a few phone calls, manage things. Simple, in sum, simple things.

What is quite fascinating in the extract is that the informant talks about work in terms of a burden (literally, he uses the work *garb*, a hump, which in Polish is used as a cliché metaphor for a burden), admittedly a negative association, yet this is precisely what he strives for. This is the manifestation of the work imperative *par excellence*. The yoke is not an option, it is something one must do and which is in fact the 'positive stimulus' in life.

In Chapter 5, I demonstrated that the men I interviewed constructed themselves in terms of being unable to act. I juxtaposed it with the psychiatric formulation of one of the key diagnostic criteria of the depressive episode – 'loss of interest or pleasure in activities that are normally pleasurable' (WHO, 1993: 83) – and argued that this is not what my informants are talking about. It is even more clear in the case of Extract 15 in which the situation is reversed. The activity, or the drive to be active, does not come from the person, it comes from work. It is work which is the 'positive stimulus'. Such a formulation, if taken as a complement to my earlier argument, can be seen as significant for the kind therapy that could be offered to men in depression. Moreover, work is constructed in terms of reclaiming normality. Although I do not wish to engage in a discussion of what normality means, the reference thereto is quite interesting. For if the illness represents an aspect of abnormality, then normality in DE's narrative has nothing to do with a mental state. On the contrary it is represented in terms of the ability to work and thus fulfil the social expectations placed on men.

Conclusions

This chapter is a complement to my earlier argument about depression being more associated with the inability to perform masculinity on the part of the men I spoke to. The earlier evidence of powerlessness as a crucial aspect of men's depression is reinforced by that of the centrality of work in the narratives of men. I looked at the stories of work I collected through the perspective of what I have called the 'work imperative'. I have argued that even in those stories in which work is constructed in negative terms, resulting in too much stress, my informants underpinned it with the assumption that a man has no other option but to work. This imperative was also explicit in the stories in which getting a job was the preferred outcome of the psychiatric care.

But the conclusion that work is central to men's narratives of masculinity is hardly news. At the beginning of the chapter I made a brief review of the literature in which there is a consensus that paid employment is part of the very core of the dominant ideology of masculinity and also key in men's accounts of themselves and their lives. I would like to take it further. While the centrality of work in men's narratives might be expected in the case of men who are healthy, this is considerably less obvious in the case of ill men. At least theoretically, their illness should give them moral grounds on which to claim the inability to work (Charmaz, 1999). Even assuming that a mental illness is not perceived as sufficiently morally valid as, say, a heart attack from overworking, still, the work imperative is not obvious in the experience of depression. Thus, the anchorage of the narratives in the dominant model of masculinity is so strong that it sets the context also for the narratives of illness. Work seems to be central regardless of whether the man is or is not able to work. It remains the major frame of reference also for those who would not be expected to worry about it, having to worry about their health. Yet, the men do worry about work because they try to be normal.

Now, if one of the major judgements as to whether one is suffering from mental illness is that of 'normality' (Bolton and Hill, 2003; see also Sadler and Fulford, 2006), it immediately raises the problem of what exactly normality would be. Each perspective discussed by Verhaeghe (2004) (an average, an ideal, a developmental process) focuses upon the person who is assessed against whatever yardstick a researcher or practitioner chooses to take on board. It is significant that the men I spoke to do not take up the normality as laid out by psychiatry and its diagnostic criteria. Rather, the normality they anchor their stories in is that of the dominant gender ideology. Once again, the men I spoke to reject an 'illness identity' and take on the identity of men. Depression is not an illness, it is an assault on masculinity.

This conclusion has clear and significant implications at least for the men who are ill. If they can be persuaded that theirs is only a version of masculinity, at least some of the pressure would be taken off them (see also Kilmartin, 2005). If their families could be persuaded of that, probably most of the pressure would be removed (see, however, the stories of rejection by the family in the next chapter).

The second extension to the issue of the centrality of work in men's narratives is the explicit relationship between depression, depression outcomes and work. One of the striking aspects of the mainstream literature on mental illness, and that on depression is no different, is that there is very little written on recovery. Such major and authoritative publications on depressive disorders as Maj and Sartorius' *Depressive Disorders* (Maj and Sartorius, 2002) not only does not have a part, but also does not have a chapter on recovery from depression. The word 'outcome' is not even in the index! It focuses, rather, on diagnosis, on pharmaco- and psychotherapy and costs of depressive disorders. It explicitly, yet without any discussion, assumes that recovery means remission of symptoms (e.g. Bech, 2002). After all, if depression consists of the symptoms stipulated in the diagnostic criteria, then recovery must mean their absence!

But what if recovery from depression for men actually means being able to get a job, as the data I collected suggest? Now, admittedly, one can argue that getting a job will be the social outcome of reducing the symptoms my informants presented. Once the symptoms are eliminated, they will stand a good chance to get a job. But the question that I would like to pose here interrogates the reverse of that argument. What if the outcome of depression is getting a job and this is when the symptoms subside? Or, even more radically, what if the outcome of depression for men is simply getting a job?

Now, I do realise that by saying that every single man who suffers from depression needs a job to recover simplifies the argument considerably and I do not wish to propose it. However, work and, more generally, powerlessness as well as its link to recovery were at the very core of the men's accounts of their suffering, regardless of their individual experiences. Not a single informant failed to put paid to employment as one of the essential elements of their depression experiences and their suffering. While, obviously, there is a potential argument that the doctor, or indeed researcher or psychiatric policymaker, knows best and the patient is not the person to be trusted with the decision of what is best for them, I do not share that view. I have no doubt that my informants knew exactly what was the source of their suffering. Moreover, if my argument is too general and oversimplifying, which might be the case, the solution is hardly the one-fits-all approach taken by modern psychiatry. Rather, it seems, outcomes should match experiences, the actual suffering experienced by those who seek medical or psychological help.

Regardless of the outcome of such a debate, it is quite clear, I think, that while there are very few qualitative studies of recovery from mental illness (e.g. Davidson, 2003), it is quite difficult to make a firm judgement as to the extent of the argument's plausibility. More research is definitely needed.

The final point I would like to make, or rather reiterate, is the gendered nature of depression, and, more than likely, mental illness. And this gendering is not merely the way men or women are approached, diagnosed or treated by mental services, but, crucially, how they experience their psychological distress. Their experiences, or at least the experience of men, are deeply anchored within the dominant gender ideology. This conclusion has at least one significant consequence. As much as I agree with the critics of psychiatric casebooks (e.g. Busfield, 1996) for their blatant use of gender stereotypes, gender blindness in assessing and treating mental illness might actually be a mistake. This is to postulate sensitivity to gender and the kind of masculinity or femininity the patient espouses in his/her stories of their distress. Obviously, there are a number of extremely important questions about the extent to which discourses of class or age or ethnicity are also accessed by those who are ill and to what extent they interact with the experiences of mental illness. This, however, is outside the scope of this book.

In Chapter 10, I take up some of the most dramatic data I collected. I shall focus upon how my interviewees talked about their families. It will be a chapter about stigmatisation and, in the process, of rejection of mental illness.

10
Rejections. Men, Depression and the Family

Introduction

In the previous chapter I explored constructions of work in men's narratives. I argued that the relationship between work and depression is underpinned by what I called the 'imperative to work', requiring a 'real man', regardless of his illness, to have paid employment.

One of the major topics in my interviews was their families. I was interested in whether and how the informants talked to their wives and children about their illness, what their reaction was. The image of the family emerging from the narratives is quite dramatic. It shows rejection and lack of support. However, below, I shall not only show that my informants construct themselves as rejected by their families, but also show that they attempt to justify and 'naturalise' these rejections. I shall also show that family support is constructed predominantly in terms of logistic management of the condition which is unwanted and rejected. I shall also demonstrate that the informants construct their fatherhood as silent: while their children are mostly constructed outside any meaningful discourse of distress, any such discourse inevitably excludes those suffering.

Family and mental illness

It is a truism that mental illness puts an enormous stress upon the family. There is a considerable body of research showing that mental illness is associated with a significant burden carried by the family (e.g. Gubman and Tessler, 1987; Lefley, 1989), both subjective and objective (e.g. Baronet, 1999; Maurin and Boyd, 1990). It is also reported that the individual's level of functioning as well as his/her symptoms are related to the burden and its negotiation within the family (Loukissa, 1995).

Yet such research mostly focuses upon 'objective' measuring of the level of the burden and, as Lefley (1997) points out, there are as many as 21 instruments doing it. There are very few studies attempting to explore the lived experience of a family living with mental illness (Jones, 2002).

In a study of experiences of families in which there is a mentally ill person, Jones (2002) shows them experiencing contradictory feelings (including love, anger, despair, shame), which happen in the context of struggling over what is a family on the one hand and stigmatisation and marginalisation on the other (see also Karp, 1996; Muhlbauer, 2002). Karp (2001) aptly speaks of a *burden of sympathy*, obligations to care resulting from the illness which must not only be coped with but also negotiated with one's needs. Studies on mental illness and the family suggest that while families are conservative with labelling deviance (e.g. Tausig *et al.*, 2004), yet, inevitably, there comes a phase in which family life is disrupted and the mentally ill person is rejected (Cockerham, 2006), even if temporarily. As Goffman (1971) puts it, the mentally ill person threatens the meaningful existence within the family (see also Yang *et al.*, 2007). The strain of mental illness requires a number of strategies to manage the family's response, which, as Karp and Tanarugsachock (2000; also Karp, 2001) point out, typically moves on a slide from acceptance and empathy to anger and resentment, finally resulting in withdrawal without guilt. All this stress is situated within the context of the drain on the family's financial and time resources, disruption to its routines and constraints on social and leisure activities (Tausig *et al.*, 2004).

But in this chapter, I shall not focus on the family itself. Rather, I shall show it as represented by those who are mentally ill. I am therefore interested in how men in depression experience their position and role in the family, regardless of how the rest of the family would see it. As much as there is little research on the experiences of the mental illness within a family, I have not found research on how the mentally ill person experiences the family they live with (for a rare example of such a study using, however, standardised instruments to measure subjective rejection, see Richter and Richter, 1989). Indeed, although rejection has been taken up as a 'neglected phenomenon' in psychiatry (Hem and Heggen, 2004; also Hansen *et al.*, 2004), it is studied from the point of view of the medical staff, and not the experience of those being rejected.

Only in the negative

Before I present the data, I would like to discuss another excerpt from an interview with a woman. The interview comes from preliminary research into experiences of women whose husbands were suffering from depression, carried out in 2006 in the south-west of Poland. A convenience sample of seven women in long-term relationships with men diagnosed with (recurrent) depressive episode was interviewed.

The stories which the women offered were those of extreme strain on them and their relationships, the strain which affected every aspect of the family life and resulted, in one case, in a decision to file for divorce. One of the reasons the relationships were put under pressure was the changed image of the partner. The men were not who the women married, they were, in the words of one of the interviewees, transformed by the illness.

In the extract I am going to present here the speaking woman constructs the changes in her husband and their relationship resulting from the illness. Despite its starkness and extreme negativity, the extract is quite typical in that it shows the rejection of the ill men. To put it differently, the men's stories I am going to present below are set in this kind of context. What varies is only the level of negativity. The speaking woman is in her early fifties, lives in a city and has a clerical job. Her husband, diagnosed with recurrent depressive episode (ICD F33), was hospitalised at the time of the interview. The interviewer was a mature female student of psychology, in her fourth year of study. Consider the following:

> ML: I have now got used to it, but a few years ago, I saw a 180 degree turn. That now I must tell him everything, that, you know, he must do this or that, because he doesn't show initiative, right? That, maybe you will have your hair cut, maybe it has to be told him, right? That I must take over the initiative at home, I never cared, it used to be only the children, the dinner, because he will come and will be tired, so that it is cleaned, washed, and now I must decide about almost all things, right? Where he will go, what he will buy, you have to prompt him. You know, the only thing he takes care of is hygiene, he is not like that he does not wash or shave, I can't say he doesn't. But otherwise I must do all, what he is to buy, to do, perhaps paint, that he is to prepare dinner. So it was very hard to accept for me. Decide in certain things, because I did have to do it. He was the most important, the head of the family, as you say, right. But now everything changed and I must and must, it was hard to change.

What is immediately noticeable in the extract is that the woman views the changes that happened in the relationship with her husband in terms of traditional gender roles. The interviewee finds the expectation that she is to take charge of the household difficult. In addition to the housework she had to worry about, she had to take over running the family life. But the assumption of the role of the head of the family is imposed on her. The extract is full of the constructed compulsion with the interviewee speaking of her *having to* take over. Her entire story, moreover, is constructed in terms of her current agency, her husband's past agency and, crucially, his current passiveness and being merely an object of her actions. It seems that the man is not capable of taking a single decision or action. By accessing her voice speaking to the husband telling him to have a haircut, what to buy or what housework he is supposed to do, she dramatises and at the same time authenticates the narrative. We get to hear her having to instruct a grown-up in basic, mundane matters he is supposed to manage on his own. Even though the informant constructs a sort of 'grudging' agency, it completely disempowers the person she is speaking about.

The final point I would like to make refers to a little fragment within the extract:

> You know, the only thing he takes care of is hygiene, it is not like that he does not wash or shave, I can't say he doesn't.[1]

It is striking that the interviewee is talking about her husband's personal hygiene to a complete stranger. Normally, one does it either in reference to children, commenting on how well they take on the expected practices of hygiene or self-grooming, or people who are seriously ill, bed-bound or mentally incapacitated, as, say, in the latter stages of dementia. The informant's husband belongs to neither of these groups. He is reduced to someone whose private practices are not only subject to scrutiny and assessment, but are also discussed openly.

She introduces his hygiene practices by the word *jedyne* ('the only thing') constructing it as the 'last bastion' of the man's activity. Thus, it is not a positive construction – it is one to raise eyebrows and suggest that there are limits to inactivity and he has not crossed them yet. But then comes the most fascinating moment. The informant is introducing the fact that her husband does take care of himself with a double negative: 'It is not like that he does not wash.' It is as if giving him some minute credit for this minute agency is impossible within the discourse of family change. And she finishes with the 'I can't say he doesn't', showing herself as having a fair outlook on the husband's activities.

Now, it is extremely easy to score cheap points and show how stigmatising this account is. It would also be easy to forget what kind of upheaval a family whose breadwinner suddenly stops winning the bread goes through. I do not wish to pretend I understand the strain it puts on the partner, who suddenly needs to take on the duties the ill person had had. On the other hand, this blanket rejection is difficult even to begin to argue with. This is also the rejection my informants spoke of as a significant source of pain. Only two informants told me about their supportive families, yet even in their cases, as it turned out, things were somewhat more complicated. However, I want to stress that throughout the chapter I am not talking about 'how it really is or was in my informants' families'. What I am analysing is stories, accounts, and I do not wish to make any claims as to their truth. Yet, the aim of this book is to make men's voices heard.

In this chapter I am going to show the most dramatic and poignant stories. They are stories of heartache, of coping with being rejected by those one is closest to. This is also a chapter that, I hope, shows how difficult it is to be a man struck by depression.

Rejecting men

If generalisations are possible from qualitative research, I could say, men in depression feel rejected by their families, and most particularly by their partners. This rejection is not of illness or the situation, it is a rejection of the person, and more particularly of the man. The narratives of the men I interviewed construct the relationship between themselves and their wives in terms of complete lack of acceptance of a man in depression. And it is precisely masculinity which is constructed as the basis of the rejection. Witness the following extracts:

Extract 1

> EU: My wife didn't accept it at that moment. I was struggling, as I could not handle myself. My wife rejected it, because she did not want to accept into her consciousness that something of the sort was happening to me, saying that it was an unmasculine ailment and I should grit my teeth and get a grip of myself. What would happen if she said it? That she is also tired. That she also has problems, only different. That these problems are ours and that she can constantly grit her teeth and do things and I go to bed. And I go to bed and shake and I am scared to get out of bed, and I am unable to get out of bed, for example, I vomit.

Extract 2

> WT: I hate this state at the moment when my wife starts shouting that she didn't imagine a husband like that. That when I met you, you were a completely different man, what has been happening to you for a few years? One then, because it has been a few years, she can say, and then one falls into an even worse state [...] [wife's name], my wife, said that it is beyond bearing, that it is, what is it? We don't go out now, at the moment I am your mom, your nanny.

The two informants construct their wives as intentionally rejecting them. But we do not have to take their word for it – both equip their accounts with evidence for what they say, both extracts contain 'accessed voices' (Hartley, 1988) of their wives. They invoke them to offer a dramatised version of what their wives said, and through it, putting themselves in a position of a witness and so making the accounts more authentic (Hutchby, 2001). Yet, the two speakers construct their accounts showing themselves as not accepting, perhaps challenging, their wives' rejection. While EU clearly separates the perspectives of himself and his wife, WT explicitly presents what his wife said through his perspective and his hatred of her words. This was not common in the corpus.

Crucially, however, both informants construct their rejections in terms of gender. It is depression's 'unmasculinity' that is the main problem: the fact that the informants do not fulfil the roles of the stereotypical man. The references to getting a grip are accessing the parts of the dominant model of masculinity that see men 'toughing it out', getting on regardless. Implied is the model of a man who cannot be ill, and if he is, he is to disregard it and heroically march forward. But the projected reconstruction of the informants from a man to 'not a man' goes even further. WT's wife is represented as positioning her husband as a child, a baby. The final blow, it seems, consists in positioning depression as reducing the man into the role of a dependant.

The rejection shown in the extracts is just about complete. Not only is there no illness that the men could be ill with, as they have no right to be ill, but it is also a rejection of the 'core' of what the relationship between a woman and a man is. The man stops being a man and becomes a child, with all the connotations of asexuality and dependency that childhood carries with it. Thus, while men constructed depression as assaulting their masculinity, this picture is complemented by representations of their families, and particularly their wives. They too are experienced as situating their husbands outside the bipolar gender model.

Yet, in the following extract the informant actually accepts the rejection and takes it as his own. Consider the following:

Extract 3

> DG: And as regards those closest to you, have you talked about it to anyone?
>
> AZ: Well, my family are fed up with me. If only I could calm down, if only I could stop bothering them. Because I simply need help from someone. Right? So someone could give me a pill or something so something, but one simply, I start crying. I am pestering in general for my family, I'm making their life difficult and that's it. In 2004 I carried out a suicide attempt, by cutting my neck vessels.

Despite that the question asked was whether *he* talked to his family, not only does AZ immediately introduce the family's perspective, he shows them as a unity in opposition to him. The change of perspective when he introduces his cry for help is not a challenge, not even a view of reality or the illness that he has. Rather, it is an attempt to solicit the family's support. He continues speaking about himself, yet he incorporates his family's view into his own perspective. The pestering which the informant introduced as the way his family see him is taken as his own description of himself, as being annoying and making their lives difficult. From what is a family's rejection, the speaker moves to accepting it and reinforces the exclusion himself. But this time the exclusion was not only discursive, though. AZ attempted to commit suicide.

Self rejection

One of the most dramatic aspects of the narratives I collected was the fact that the informants actually took over the rejection and showed it as their own fault. Note the following extract in which the informants starts with an impersonal distance between himself and his family and moves to blaming himself for the situation.

Extract 4

> DG: And what is their [DE's family] attitude?
>
> DE: Well, it's not negative, in a way they don't treat me as the closest family, I mean my wife, my wife, my children. A certain distance has arisen between me and [my family] but more because I am unable,

shall I say, to function normally, I mean I am unable to perform the duties of a husband and wife, phew, husband, father [laughs] so this is why this distance arises, right? I am on the margin, I prefer to shut myself in a room, or lie down and do nothing. And this distance it arises, doesn't it? And the further family, it's normal, there was such a case in the family.

DG: What is the nature of this distance you were saying about?

DE: Lack of tenderness, sincerity perhaps. Such such this love, no, most probably, as I am saying, it more my fault than of the members of my family. Because they would not have moved away from me, but I did, I move away more than they.

There is hesitation right at the beginning of what DE says. The particle *no* (somewhat inadequately translated here as 'well') undermines the certainty of the unqualified statement of the family's non-negative (a choice interesting enough) attitude. And indeed what follows undermines the statement further. It is important that while no one is constructed as responsible for the distance between himself and his family, the informant justifies it and shows himself as difficult to live with. He accepts the distance. There is no reference to the illness, no reference to the fact that he has been disabled by depression, rather, also, he sees the justification in terms of not performing as a man should. It is noteworthy that implicitly he portrays the distance in his family as a sort of punishment for his failure in his manly duties. He does not perform, so he does not get the tenderness he speaks of moments later. It is a sad picture of an ill person who shows himself as undeserving of the affections of his family. Strikingly, he ends with a reversal of rejection and constructing himself as the agent of rejecting. Theirs was merely a reaction to what DE did.

Similarly, the informant in the following extract accepts his wife's rejection resulting from the way he is.

Extract 5

DG: It might be a difficult question [...] how did depression contribute to your marriage breaking up?

CW: Generally it's the problem of sex. Because all this medication I take now in large quantities causes a major decrease in libido. And it's a problem with a man who is constantly sad and constantly has a lot problems. It's difficult to bear it. I do realise it.

Despite taking his wife's position to describe himself as the incessantly sad man, he accepts her rejection of him. It is interesting that his decision to agree with his wife is not constructed in emotional terms. Rather, CW introduces a certain rationality into what he says. Reference to realising the state of affairs shows him as taking a measured assessment of the situation. But as much as it is a rational account on his part, by implication it also justifies his wife's attitude towards himself.

This is why I do not think of the self-rejections in terms of self-stigma (Corrigan and Watson, 2002; Hayward and Bright, 1997; Rüsch *et al.*, 2005): devaluation, shame or withdrawal from applying negative stereotypes of mental illness to oneself (Corrigan, 1998). The speakers negotiate the self-rejection by justifying what their families do, yet they do not explicitly espouse their views. What they do, I think, is attempting to save the family's face. If one accepts that illness gives people a certain moral status, albeit complex and problematic (Charmaz, 1999), then rejection of the ill person might be socially condemned. As much as the role of the man is to 'defend his family', as one of the informants told me, this is precisely what the speakers do here. Consequently, while they might be dealing with an experience of subjective stigma (Schulze and Angermeyer, 2003), still the pressure to defend is stronger.

The final fragment I would like to quote in this section is quite different and unique in the corpus. The informant reports a conversation he had with his adolescent son on his depression and his role in the son's life:

Extract 6

> BC: I walked two kilometres with my son [unclear] and I asked him whether he knew I was in depression, whether he knew what depression was. Whether he knew why I wanted, care about him being self-reliant quickly. He said yes. And that was really the whole conversation. I was not in a good form for a conversation. I was not in such a form to talk about it normally. Yesterday, there was one such day when I could talk to my wife about the future. Is she aware that this illness will have relapses and that can't be said how long it will last. With me it's like with a switch. It simply switches and I can talk normally, think normally, everything takes a real dimension, then click and everything taken a different dimension, such a depressive one. Strongly depressive.

The extract can be construed to refer to what is called *męska rozmowa* (men's talk) in Poland, a conversation on serious matters between (two) men, often between a father and a son, here on the father cutting himself off from his son's life. What is particularly significant is that there is no hint of any other relationship between the informant and his son. Instead, BC undermines himself even as someone who is capable of holding a 'men's talk'. The speaker seems to withdraw himself on the basis of his inability to provide for his son.

Silent fathers

During the interview, I asked my informants whether they talked about their depression with their families. The responses were normally in the affirmative, and mostly reported informing the closest family about the illness. Children, however, were a completely different matter. They were informed only when they were adult enough, which meant late teens. The decision not to inform the children of their father's mental illness was mostly based on their apparent inability to understand it. However, there were a few instances when children were actually told of the illness, yet it was not the man who told them. The fathers were silent. In the two extracts below the speakers attempt to counter the silence, though.

Extract 7

DG: Your elder daughter learnt about your diagnosis.

NP: The elder daughter did.

DG: What was her reaction?

NP: I actually don't know her reaction. I don't know her reaction because she learnt [unclear], her mother filled her in. I mean my wife. Nothing changed in her behaviour at any rate. We are very close and we understand each other well. I don't know whether it's a rule that a father and a daughter understand each other well or not. In any case, everything is OK. We talk, we joke, we have a laugh. Even at her fiancés, boyfriends, when there was a gig. She went to see [music band] or some other concert. So, I think that here it's a very good contact.

DG: You don't talk about it with her?

NP: We don't.

DG: Why not?

NP: I don't know. I don't want to, I mean, I don't want to, I don't seek to talk to her, and she doesn't ask.

DG: I see.

NP: I think she has had a thorough read about what it is all about.

Extract 8

DG: I understand you did talk to your wife. And the children?

GT: My daughter knows something that I go, but specially, or my wife, we don't talk, because she is only 13 years old.

DG: I see.

GT: So that she won't worry too much. So, here, it's usually with my wife.

In both extracts depression is constructed as outside the discourses in which those suffering from it can engage. In (7) the speaker tries to achieve two strategic goals. More important of the two, he shows that the news of his mental illness did not result in his daughter's rejection of him (he is one of the two informants who did not report rejection in his immediate family). He also shows that the fact that he does not speak of his illness to his daughter does not marginalise him and he is able to maintain a good relationship with her. In (8), on the other hand, the informant attempts first to show that talking to his daughter is a joint effort between him and his wife. He puts himself right in the middle of the family 'discourse of depression'. But, moments later, in the last move, the joint effort becomes his wife's only. Interestingly, he introduces the clause by *tak że* (translated here 'So'), which suggests that the statement is a consequence of the previous one, yet, clearly, it is not. In fact, the informant shifts from the construction of joint family conversations to those in which only his wife is engaged, even though also here he attempts to mitigate the constriction by using 'usually' (Polish *przeważnie*).

In the final extract that I would like to show in this subsection, the informant does talk to his daughter; yet, he presents it as talking about being ill, in general terms, rather than being ill of a mental illness.

Extract 9

DG: [daughter] she knows about your illness?

OC: Yes.

DG: And what is her reaction?

OC: She suffers, regrets, she is sorry, she would like to make me get better, because she wants a dad. I can't, I can't.

DG: Did you talk to your daughter about your illness?

OC: Yes, it's already.

DG: Can you tell me about that conversation?

OC: I mean, I was saying all the time that daddy is ill and why me, why it happened to me.

Not only is the conversation reported about the ambiguous 'being ill', significantly, it is not constructed as a conversation to tell one's child about one's illness. OC shows himself as engaging in a moral discourse about his illness (see Bennett *et al.*, 2003), as if mental illness was a retribution, a punishment or a direct result of what a person is or did (frequent traits in explanations of mental distress, e.g. Casey and Long, 2003; Kinderman *et al.*, 2006; Sayre, 2000). What transpires from OC's account is that in fact, his conversation was hardly one explaining his illness to his daughter.

The three extracts show the ill men outside the family 'depression talk', especially as regards their children. For whatever reason, paradoxically, someone else is more suitable to talk about the experiences they did not have and thus silencing those who suffer.

Invisible illness

Recall that in Extract 1 above, depression is constructed as depending on the decision of the informant: if only he gritted his teeth, got a grip! Depression is represented as an opt-out of duties, rather than a 'real illness', something the informants' partners could also decide to go for. Indeed, my informants also talked about rejection of the illness itself. Witness two other such extracts.

Extract 10

JS: And my fiancée seemed not to understand this too much. I remember when we were still, because the psychiatrist was from the health centre before I came here to the clinic, she asked that one of the visits be, so I come with my wife. After leaving, she said that I was like conspiring, that I with the psychiatrist were against her. This was her reaction.

Extract 11

NP.: When you are ill with laryngitis, you want to know what you are ill with. When my wife has tonsillitis, I want to know what she is ill with and what to treat her with. What I am to get from the pharmacy, [unclear] will tell you what antibiotic to take, this twice a day, give this to her, keep her warm, give her consommé, I don't know. And here one seems to be normal, one is sad, well, he is sad, but why doesn't he do anything? That he is sad does not interfere that he does not do anything. He could get a grip on himself and start working. Just as I was put in a bad mood last week. My family came and one of the aunts, accidentally: [informant's name], you get, you work on yourself, you get a grip on yourself. You get to work. I am a calm man, patient, I listened to that for an hour and a half, but I was boiling. This was only an hour and a half, but if you listen to this every day, for however many weeks, or months, or even years, you can imagine what kind of scenes happen then.

Whether it is a conspiracy between the informant and the doctor (as in (10)), or something you could get a grip on (as in (11)), depression is something one has the power of decision over. Once again, it is not an illness. In Extract 11, NP takes an outside perspective to describe the hypothetical man in depression who does not have any obvious symptoms, especially when contrasted with a person with laryngitis. He dramatises the account by accessing the voice of his aunt giving him the 'simple' advice of working on himself. Note that the low mood is again rejected as significant in depression – this time also within the external perspective of the family of the ill man. It is work which is crucial and, to reverse the argument, the core of the problem for a man in depression is that fact that he does not work. Obviously, even though the informant takes an outsider's perspective, it is still his relevancies that underpin what he is saying. It is his narrative, to put it differently, which puts work (or lack of it), and masculinity, at the heart of depression.

'Logistic' support

Yet, my informants also talked about the support they got from their families. Most of them told me about their wives urging them to go and see the doctor, to take their medication. I have decided to present this data in the chapter on rejection as I think it complements what I said about invisible depression. What I am going to show is that the support my informants talk about is reduced to smooth and efficient dealing with the problem of depression, and particularly its medicalisation. Consider the following extracts:

Extract 12

DG: Can you tell me what these conversations are like? What do you [and your wife] talk about?

GT: I mean my wife can see that I am going down, I am weakening psychologically. I am not interested in anything. I don't listen to the radio, television. I switch off, so she herself says I should go and see a doctor. So these conversations practically boil down to whether I feel unwell and: go to see the doctor today or tomorrow.

Extract 13

DG: What was your wife's reaction to starting the treatment?

KL: Well, she had to take care of me later. She had to make sure that I was getting the treatment. To make me go to see the doctor, because that's the problem. So, she had to urge me to go and see a doctor once a month. I mean I don't know whether you can call it treatment, I simply took medication.

Especially in (12) the speaker shows his wife's interest in his depression as limited to keeping the mood in check. The conversations, once again dramatised by 'role-playing' the partner, are reduced to a mere instruction to seek medical help. In Extract 13, the instructions seem more forceful as the informant is implied not be compliant. But the non-compliance is also implied not to be 'pathological', or a whim, rather, it stems from questioning pharmacotherapy as treatment. In this way, the informant adds negativity to the account of his wife's instructions. This logistic support eventually boils down to the irritation that the treatment does not work:

Extract 14

AZ: They [females] don't have anything against my treatment. On the contrary, if only it has effects. Because so far there hasn't been much effect. I don't feel in depression at the moment. Now I feel like

I was a normal man. I have not got a depressed mood. Just those fears bother me.

There is no other indication in what the informants say here (and it is typical of the corpus) that their partners' interest in their illness goes beyond the practicalities of a logistic operation. There were no stories of the partners actually talking about the experiences of the ill man. Rather, the situation is more as in the following extract where attempts to talk result in monologues:

Extract 15

JS: I tried to talk to my wife, but those conversations didn't contribute much.

DG: And could you tell me what they looked like?

JS: My wife usually didn't say much to what I was saying. So it was my monologue really.

Conclusions

In this chapter, I explored the narratives of how the men I interviewed construct their position in their families. I was interested in how a depressed man sees himself in his family, especially that depression is likely to put pressure on the stereotypical role of the 'head of the family'. And so, my informants constructed themselves predominantly in terms of rejection, lack of acceptance from their families. They are constructed as having failed, as inadequate, they are silenced within the family's depression discourse. Also the illness itself was rejected. The second kind of rejection is that of offering only the 'logistic' support in getting medical care. The men construct the help they receive in terms of efficiently getting medication which will keep the mood in check. What is most important for the discussion in this book is that the rejection is never merely of the illness, or the ill person, it is also a rejection of failed masculinity, from which, it seems, there is no escape. Depression, it seems again, reconfigures masculinity, introducing, as I said in Chapter 8, failure into it.

However, I do realise that as much as I try to avoid it, there is negativity in what I say. There are all these poor ill men who suffer the rejections of those horrible wives and families. I would not like to be understood in this way. Let me offer a story to make my point. During my internship,

I had an opportunity to watch (form behind a Venetian mirror) family consultations offered to patients who were hospitalised. The consultation is an attempt to make the relationships within the family explicit for the family members and might be an introduction to family therapy.

One of the consultations I witnessed was between a patient diagnosed with schizophrenia with a long-term psychiatric career – who was about to be discharged after suffering an acute psychotic episode – and his wife and son, who was about 11–12 years old. Right from the outset the consultation was not going very smoothly. The resistance of the wife to engage with the therapist (a very experienced one) was quite palpable, as was her unwillingness to talk about the man's homecoming. Eventually, the woman explained that she simply could not handle living with her husband in their house. Apart from the usual stories of stigmatisation and rejection of the community (the family lived in a village), she finally said that she just was not able to talk any more to her husband. According to her, he not only wanted to talk about his experiences and his illness, he wanted to talk all the time, regardless of the time of the day or the night, he wanted to talk, and talk, and talk. And then talk some more. As she was the one who ran the household, with most, if not all, household duties resting on her shoulders, the talking prevented her from cooking dinner, spending time with her son or simply relaxing. She then added that she simply would like sometimes to sit down with her husband and watch some television.

This was a very powerful story from the other side. Although I did witness families who refused to take psychotic patients home, as they wanted a respite, this was a story of a complete and systematic, albeit non-dramatic, disruption to the woman's and child's life. It was very difficult not to see her suffering due to her husband's illness or not to see her point and not to agree with her. I could not see anyone wanting to be in her shoes. Ever. And so, the consultation resulted in a stalemate. Although the woman did not refuse point blank to accept her husband back home, she was very insistent on him first going to live with his mother for a time. It would be even better if he could stay longer in hospital, after all as long as he was hospitalised, no decision actually had to be made.

The man, who came to the consultation in very high spirits, clearly expecting to be welcomed back home, left half the man he came. He became withdrawn, pensive and gave up his role as leader of the therapeutic community. There was nothing he waited for any more.

I have told this story to make the point again that I have offered only one side of the picture. As much as the narratives I collected are those of vulnerable men sometimes in desperate need of much help, their families also have to carry the burden of the illness. As I said at the outset of this chapter, mental illness is well known to affect entire families, both as a stigma and because living with a person whom life hurts and who is unable to contribute to the family as much as they used to is difficult in the extreme. The fact that the family from the story lived in a small community made things even more difficult (Angermeyer *et al.*, 2004). The logistic support might therefore be looked at as 'better than nothing' or as 'as good as it gets', given the stress the family as a whole is under. Yet, I have little doubt that it is also a rejection. It is a rejection of the person who has some extraordinary needs, which perhaps cannot be met. And it's a stalemate.

As I said at the beginning there were two informants who actually showed their wives as supportive. But their support did not come easy, it was quite hard won. The hell, as the informant puts it, ended when his wife accepted that he was actually ill.

Extract 16

NP: I mean when she [wife] learnt I was ill, she became, well, different, a caring woman, a caring wife. Until she didn't know I was ill, well, it was hell.

DG: Can you explain?

NP: Well, rows at home. You come and lie down and do nothing. This kind of stories. Because indeed I came from work, lay down on the bed, the television was on, me, eyes into the ceiling, perhaps a beer. And that was the extent of my life. It was necessary to go out for a walk. I don't feel like it. It was necessary to go to the river with the children on Sunday. I don't feel like it. Bicycle. I don't feel like it. So you won't be surprised that it was, as I say, hell.

DG: No. And it changed after the diagnosis?

NP: After the diagnosis, the first my wife did, she rushed to the computer, the Internet, what is it? And literally after several [between 10–20] hours, but I think that she is an exception in that matter.

It is only understanding, it seems, that brings relief, both to the ill person and to the family. And so, even though I present only one side of the story, I am not particularly interested in the 'truth' of the matter. I do not know and have no means of knowing what the situation in my informants' homes is. The picture painted in my informants' accounts is extremely bleak. It is a picture of loneliness in the face of an illness which takes away the very foundation upon which gender identities are built. The men who need a safe haven in their distress get nothing of the sort. They are rejected, stigmatised and are deprived of what is perceived as a core of their identity. Regardless of how good or bad their partners are, those men see themselves trapped in their situation. Surely, this is not conducive to their recovery, however that recovery will be understood.

The final point I would like to make is similar to that which I have made a number of times. What the stories I analysed in this chapter showed again is the extent of genderisation of depression. This time, however, it is not only the men themselves who frame their illness in terms of masculinity. This time they also construct others to do so. Not only do they see themselves as men, or failed men, it is also their families who do. And in effect they accept that frame, they become even more unworthy men. As gender is crucial in how men experience depression, it is also crucial in understanding men's relationships within their families. I think it is also safe to say that understanding of gender and its impact upon depression experience, especially within the family, is also crucial to how the family will function and thus how conducive it will be not only to the ill person's but also to its own recovery.

This chapter concludes my discussion of the constructed relationship between masculinity and depression. In the next one, I shall take stock of my entire exposition and try to comment on how to see what I have discussed so far.

11
Insight and Suffering: A Linguist's View of Psychopathology

The argument so far

Instead of a systematic summary of the book's argument, I would like to offer my view of what I perceive as the book's strengths. And so, these are the three main points which I would like the reader to come away from the book with.

Experience of depression

Primarily, my argument is about experiences of depression. But it is not designed to make the point of primacy of experience over universalising discourses of psychopathology – this is more than likely to be futile. However, I hope my contribution can show that experience of illness, especially studied with the finely tuned methods of discourse analysis, offers not only an interesting, but also an important insight into depression.

Psychopathology's focus on depression as a set of symptoms which can be harvested from the patient, who, if anything, is in the way of the process, can be juxtaposed with the complex experiences of those who suffer. Indeed, the evidence of my corpus questions the centrality of low mood in depression experience. Thus, the default insistence on the low mood, translated even into socially oriented literature at the level of a basic assumption (e.g. Martin, 2002), can be seen as unhelpful, to say the least. This universalness of symptomatology has very little reflection in what my informants said.

Indeed, not only have men chosen not to speak of low mood as having anything to do with what they experienced, but they, more generally, did not engage with the medical model of the illness. It was their social experience that by far dominated their accounts. Depression was 'naturalised' in autobiographies, distanced from in accounts of the self, de-medicalised through accounts of their 'timeless self'. It is never associated with the self in the narratives of my informants; when spoken of explicitly it is forever autonomous. My informants were certainly ill, by their own admission as well as in their practices, but then one could very easily ask the question, what exactly were those men ill of!

Discourses of depression

Second, this book is about discourse. Even though studies into discourses of mental illness, including depression, are not uncommon (although certainly not ubiquitous), linguistic discourse analyses are rare and I think that this is the first *linguistic* study of discourses of depression. Moreover, by focusing on the 'discourses of depression', I offer the opportunity to compare the mainstream discursive constructions of the depressive episode and those of the people who actually suffer from it. And the differences could not be more pronounced.

The micro-analytic insight into discursively constructed experience of depression shows a complex and uneasy relationship between the illness and those who are ill. Not only does this complexity show that the experience of mental illness escapes any possible attempt to describe by means of a few, quite ambivalent diagnostic criteria, but, and more importantly, my analyses show that insight into the experience of mental illness is significantly enhanced by explorations of its discursive and linguistic form. The argument and data I have presented here point to a need of systematic sensitivity to patients' discourses on the part of the clinician.

I also argued that recovery should be linked to how the illness is experienced rather than imposed by the clinician or the clinician's bosses and psychiatric policy makers. I reject the presumption that I do not know what it means for me to stop being in distress. I might not know how to achieve it (otherwise I would not have come for help); yet, I am likely to know, perhaps in a nebulous and badly articulated way, what it means for me to get better. It might make the job of the clinician more difficult, yet surely, it is the mirror side of what causes suffering where recovery should be sought. This is precisely where the distinction between getting a job and chemically enhancing my mood lies.

A linguistic discourse analysis also undermines the argument that focusing on experiences would not enable psychiatrists to communicate between one another, as I heard so many times in conversations with psychiatrists. One does not need to resort to arguments of intercultural psychiatry pointing out that, say, depression is a Western category that cannot be easily applied in other cultures (Jadhav, 2000). The analysis of the English and Polish versions of the ICD shows that the intercultural universality of communication is a myth. English-speaking psychiatrists speak of a different depression from those in Poland and just because of a translation! There is also discursive evidence that psychiatric discourses are a reflection of psychiatry as a set of social, discursive and institutional practices and as such it simply cannot be seen as internationally or interculturally universal.

Ideologies of depression

The experience of depression, finally, was profoundly gendered and throughout the book I have made the point that depression is a thoroughly gendered affair. For my informants, there is no depression outside the dominant model of masculinity. Regardless of whether the focus of my analyses was placed more towards the linguistic form or more towards the content of what my informants said, the dominant model of masculinity has always been an aspiration for my informants, a frame of reference in which to see themselves and their experiences.

It is gender ideology that shifts the lived experience of depression towards action orientation. My informants are interested in doing things, rather than experiencing low moods. They are failed doers and depression is an assault on masculinity, while it is work – not the reduction of one, more or even all the symptoms – which is the measure of recovery. On a number of occasions I pointed to the 'double jeopardy' of men's depression. Men suffer both from the illness and from the fact that they are ill men, particularly when they see their families as rejecting and undermining them. The dominant model of masculinity turns right against them.

Thus, on the one hand, the ideologies of depression are submerged into those of psychiatry, where the symptom rules, and depression is to do with something in the person, but, on the other, the stories of depression are underpinned by social expectations of what it is to be a man. If a diagnosis is an articulation of the key distinction between being abled and disabled (Barton, 1999), then it is difficult to see a point of overlap between a psychiatric diagnosis and the experience of men in depression. Moreover, if depression, as I argued, is an identity resource for the self and interacts with it, albeit only by introducing failure to masculinity, then universal psychopathology is at the least difficult, as it would have to incorporate a significant account of subjective suffering.

* * *

In the account above I have asked two questions that raise significant points for 'mainstream' psychopathology. By asking what exactly the men I interviewed are ill of, in part I am taking up the issue of insight, one of the significant, if somewhat ignored, categories with which illness experience is assessed. For if there is a hiatus between what psychiatry says about what the men suffer from, and what they themselves say, it raises the problem of their awareness of their illness.

The second point is the flip side of the issue. If the psychiatric diagnosis is geared towards translating the experience of distress into a clear diagnostic category on the basis of which a person is to be helped, then on the basis of the corpus I collected, it is difficult to see how it can be done. The clear de-medicalisation of depression in the narratives, together with the contextual importance of the linguistic form as offering insight into complex subjectivity, significantly undermines the possibility of psychopathology based on universal symptoms. This time, I raise the issue of suffering in psychopathology.

Obviously, this is not the point at which I am able to discuss the two issues in satisfactory detail. Rather, I am interested in opening spaces for discussions and suggesting avenues for potential research.

A linguist's insight into insight

In their meta-analysis of 40 studies of insight into schizophrenia, Mintz and her associates (2003; see also Amador and Kronengold, 2004; Baier *et al.*, 1998) define insight as consisting of five main elements: an awareness of mental disorder, its social consequences, its symptoms as well as the need for treatment, and the attribution of those symptoms to the mental disorder. Even though the diagnostic criteria of such illnesses as schizophrenia (ICD F20) or indeed depression (F32-33) do not have illness awareness in their diagnostic criteria, insight is occasionally seen as a symptom (e.g. Carroll *et al.*, 1999; Weiler *et al.*, 2000). It is also related to compliance with treatment (e.g. Keshavan *et al.*, 2004; Macpherson *et al.*, 1997; Rathod *et al.*, 2005). Although most literature on insight concerns schizophrenia (Sturman and Sproule, 2003), there are also attempts to conceptualise and measure insight in mood disorders (ibid., Dell'Osso *et al.*, 2002; Ghaemi *et al.*, 1997; Peralta and Cuesta, 1998). As might be expected, insight can be measured and a number of scales have been developed (e.g. Beck *et al.*, 2003; Markova *et al.*, 2003; Sturman and Sproule, 2003). As a thorough critique of what is proposed in the literature on insight is well beyond the scope of the chapter (see Hamilton and

Roper, 2006 for a well-made social critique of the concept; also Beck-Sander, 1998), here I would like to point to two issues useful for the discussion below.

First, insight is taken to be a characteristic of the patient. Patients *have* or are characterised by poor or good insight. Even though insight is dynamic, it can change via therapy, for example, still it remains a relatively stable attribute of the patient, so much so that it is used as a variable in research not only on medication compliance, but also on aspects of social life, such as interpersonal problems (Startup, 1998). One of the consequences of such conceptualisation of insight is that it backgrounds issue of the relationship between insight, power and resistance (Hamilton and Roper, 2006) of users of mental health services.

The second issue I would like to raise is the reliance of measuring instruments on the acontextual content of a number of statements. Thus when the Beck Insight Scale (Beck *et al.*, 2003: 328) asks people to choose answers from statements like the following:

3. Other people can understand the cause of my unusual experiences better than I can.
6. Some of the ideas I was certain were true turned out to be false.
13. I can trust my own judgment at all times.

The level of 'professionalisation' required of the patient to make the answers meaningful is extraordinary. The respondent must make exactly the same assumptions as to which people, experiences or ideas he/she refers to in (3) and (6). In (13) he/she must decide what exactly it means to trust one's judgement. For example, while I generally trust my judgement, I would trust it much to decide what running shoes I need, considerably less when it comes to buying a badminton racket, and I would not touch my car's engine with a barge pole (of course I trust my judgement that I should not trust my judgement with the car . . .). This is because I run a lot, play badminton a little, and never ever have repaired or want to repair a car. In other words, there is a spectrum of situations from those in which I can just about always trust my judgement, all the way to those in which it would not be appropriate to trust my judgement. However, for the most part I trust my judgement as to making the decision of whether I can trust my judgement. Unless, of course, I have had a drink or two, I am very tired, or reacting very angrily. But then I take precautions against such situations . . . and so on *ad infinitum*. But does this mean that if someone says that they can trust their judgement at all times, they are somehow lacking insight? Well, it depends precisely on the assumptions they make. As the paragraph above shows, questions of whether one trusts one's judgement is quite complex and simply cannot be answered with one simple sentence. Except, surely, most of us would like to say exactly what is in (13).

Hamilton and Roper (2006) put it aptly saying that even in the simplest of cases, the question of what is known by whom about 'the condition' is dynamic and might not overlap, while Perkins and Moodley (1993) add that the same individual might hold a number of mutually exclusive explanatory frameworks for what happens to them. On the other hand, Markova and her associates (2003) propose to start their instrument with the following:

(1) I am feeling different from my normal self.
(2) There is nothing wrong with me.
(3) I am ill.

It is difficult to imagine statements which are more ideologically contested, in need of the exact context and a story of the patient. When I tried to imagine completing the questionnaire, the number of variables of what it might mean that I feel different from my normal self was staggering. My knee hurts a bit after this morning's run, I need a haircut, I am quite tired as I have been working flat out on finishing this book for the last two months. All of these make me feel different, in a particular way. Yet, the list of the things that I could add is just about unlimited. And all these are the 'little things', things that I can actually pinpoint on some normality scale. There are also those which I cannot. So I actually would not know whether I feel my normal self or not. Incidentally, studies such as that by Benson and her associates (2003) show how medical personnel's positions with regard to their patients' aggression change within an interview; it is incomprehensible why that might not apply to patients.

Both instruments assume that there is a certain 'default' content of the items which the respondents will have access to and will be able to show their 'insight' clearly and transparently. I doubt such an assumption very much as neither instrument takes the perspective of the experience of the illness (see also Fulford, 2004), imposing the frame of what the researchers decided insight was. Yet, the problem I would like to raise as completely ignored by theorists and students of insight is that of the linguistic form.

One of the points I made throughout the first two parts of the book was that my informants never fully espoused depression. On the one hand, they constructed the illness as an independent force, largely unrelated to themselves, and on the other, they used strategies to distance themselves from the illness, or, 'tamed' it by showing it as a 'milestone', situating it in their lives rather than in themselves or constructing it as resulting from their 'true selves' and thus also de-medicalising it.

So, do they have insight? On the basis of the literature I quoted above, the answer is quite simple: yes, they do, and indeed it would be consistent with most research on insight into mood disorders as it shows that in such illnesses it is ubiquitous (Ghaemi and Rosenquist, 2004). If I had asked them directly, they would have said they were ill, they were aware of the consequences of their illness, they were voluntarily receiving treatment. It all seems quite unproblematic. But then, at the level of the linguistic form, their stories rejected the illness. They positioned themselves away from the illness, they rejected the illness-like status of their depression. These constructions, moreover, are systematic throughout the corpus and the individual informants' accounts. This is hardly insight!

And this is the first of the major points I would like to make in this concluding chapter. The data I have analysed throughout the book point to a twofold revision in the understanding of insight into mental illness. First, insight is not an attribute of the person, but, rather, it is an attribute of what they say. Insight is discursive. And this statement leads to a number of consequences, the most important of which, I think, is that insight is not only dynamic, it is dynamic within the context of a particularly communicative event. In other words, insight could change within the interview, and a number of times, depending on the particular story that the informant was telling. Such a formulation puts a significant question mark upon the possibility of studying insight with standardised instruments. What it opens, however, is the possibility of a much more nuanced and context-dependent understanding of the patient's distress and their relationship to it. An understanding which is not based upon 'our' psychiatric frame of reference (incidentally, the two instruments measuring insight are very significantly different!), but, rather, one based on lived experience of mental illness within its social context.

The second, and related, change in conceptualisation of insight is a significant focus on the form of what people say and not only on the content. If insight is discursive, then the discourse form is a crucial aspect of constructing insight. And it is precisely 'construction of insight' that one should speak about. Insight is done, not had, I could say. Such a performative understanding of insight not only allows placing the one who suffers right in the centre of the focus, but it also assumes the possibility of the patient's using insight strategically.

Suffering and psychopathology

The other major issue that I would like to flag up in this chapter is that
of suffering. Let me start with a definition of suffering. Frank (2001: 355)
wrote,

> Suffering involves experiencing yourself on the other side of life as
> it should be, and no thing, no material resource, can bridge that
> separation. Suffering is what lies beyond such help. Suffering is the
> unspeakable, as opposed to what can be spoken; it is what remains
> concealed, impossible to reveal; it remains in darkness, eluding illu-
> mination; and it is dread, beyond what is tangible even if hurtful.
> Suffering is loss, present or anticipated, and loss is another instance
> of no thing, an absence. We suffer the absence of what was missed
> and now is no longer recoverable and the absence of what we fear
> will never be. At the core of suffering is the sense that something is
> irreparably wrong with our lives, and wrong is the negation of what
> could have been right. Suffering resists definition because it is the
> reality of what is not.

I would like to use this definition as a reference for a brief account
of suffering useful for me here. First, Frank says that suffering means
'experiencing oneself on the other side of life' and likening suffering
to an assault on the self is commonplace. Cassell (2004) speaks of a
threat to the intactness of the person; Morse (2000), who distinguishes
between suffering (emotional) and enduring (emotionless), speaks of
a threat to oneself (see also Rodgers and Cowles, 1997). In that sense
suffering cannot be 'objective' as proposed by van Hooft (1998; for a
critique see Edwards, 2003). Second, Frank talks of unspeakability of
suffering. Once again, this is a ubiquitous description of suffering. Radley (2004) says that suffering is mute, Morris (1997) says it is voiceless,
Candib (2002) uses the adjective 'wordless'. All these authors make
the point that those who suffer cannot put their suffering in words
totally; Morris (1997) says that there is a core of suffering that is beyond language. Frank's third point is that of an absence – suffering results
from something that is not. Younger (1995) talks about lack of control
over one's existence. Morse and Penrod (1999) say that suffering results
from an overwhelming past which alters the future, making the present
unbearable.

At least two of the elements of this account of suffering (which is
by no means comprehensive, see Wilkinson, 2005) can be useful in the

description of informants' experiences of depression. First, they all found themselves on 'the other side of life', with their selves assaulted by the illness; they all constructed themselves as men under threat, failed men. Second, depression meant for them the absence of what the dominant masculinity required – their activity, work, but also respect from their families. As I have been arguing throughout the book, the main source of suffering for my informants was the gender ideology, and not their mood, loss of interest or decreased energy.

Where is the psychopathology in it then? As I have demonstrated before, there is a clear disparity between what the diagnostic criteria stipulate with regard to the depressive episode and what my informants chose to say about their experiences of the illness. Moreover, while the depressive episode will be treated by the reduction of symptoms, alleviating the suffering of the men I spoke to would be a different thing altogether. This is not to say that the symptoms stipulated by psychopathological nosology cannot be observed – it means that they might not be the problem, or indeed the source of suffering. If 'pain is what the patient says it is', as Price and Cheek (1996: 216) say in reference to physical pain, this principle must also apply to mental illness. Distress does not necessarily translate into a disorder (Kleinman, 1988a), while the presence of depressive symptoms does not necessarily result from a psychiatric disease (Kleinman, 1995). In other words, the perennial question of what came first, chicken or egg, is definitely not solved, but it is the focus upon suffering that could in fact provide the clinician with some answers.

Now, I have not yet commented on the third element of Frank's description of suffering – its unspeakability. I do not wish to engage in a discussion on whether there is an element of suffering that is beyond words and what exactly it would mean: there are all sorts of shades and aspects to the proposed inability to tell about suffering – from language, not being able to handle it, to its being too personal and traumatic. While I have some problems with accepting the former (and the fact that people do say that something is beyond words is not necessarily evidence), I have no difficulty with the latter. Yet, for my discussion here, this is a point which is relatively marginal.

The men I interviewed told me a number of stories about their experiences of depression, whatever this depression was for them. I have no way of knowing to what extent they censored themselves, made sure not to tell me too much, too little. I have little doubt that they managed the contents of what they said, sometimes explicitly excluding a topic from our conversation (and, incidentally, explicitly including it towards the end of the interview). This is inevitable, regardless of the kind of research, including quantitative. Still, instead of attempting to frame their experiences into someone else's system of symptoms, the informants were able to tell stories with their relevancies, emphases, experiences. By approaching their stories discourse analytically, I accessed aspects over which the speakers had practically no control: the linguistic form. By trying to access those relevancies, I attempt to show the suffering from the perspective of the sufferer. The focus upon the suffering and its discursive expression reduces its 'professional transformation' (Kleinman and Kleinman, 1991). As with insight, it puts the patient, not the model of illness with all its more or less unspoken assumptions, in the centre of considerations.

And it is precisely those relevancies constructed in the patients' stories that should be attended to – for they show my informants as gendered subjects and suffering itself as gendered. And it is these gendered meanings of illness, very much ignored by psychiatry, that are crucial at least for the informants who participated in the research I carried out. The focus upon stories of suffering or, as in this book, discourses of depression allows one to see distress in its constructed social context, one which is lived as important by those who come for help.

The focus on suffering, or more precisely now, the focus upon the relevancies constructed in the stories of mental illness, not only allows for more complexity of mental distress, by interrogating the possibility of its non-pathological nature (Moreira, 2003), but also encompasses the perspective in which depression can be seen as a positive project for understanding oneself (Fee, 2000b; Martin, 1999). Moreover, just as I said that insight is context-bound, so is depression and its story. I have no doubt that in order to understand my informants' depression, one needs to understand what it does to them, their identities or, more generally, to their life-stories. Only then, do we as researchers, and they as clinicians, have a more fulsome picture of what it means, here and now, to be depressed and what it means to recover. One might also argue that this suffering that I think should be the dominant focus of psychiatric practice should probably also include the suffering of those closest to the patient.

But the focus on suffering I am advocating does not only allow a focus on experience. Even though still hardly taken up by dominant discourses of psychopathology, calls to see the person in their context (Agar, 2003), which could be transformed into the person in his/her narratives, have been made many times. What I am suggesting here goes beyond that. It is a call to see the narrative as a discursive construction of the person's experience and reality, not only at the level of the context but, crucially, at the level of the linguistic form. While the point is quite obvious within the social sciences and particularly discourse studies, it has hardly penetrated psychiatry, and particularly psychiatric practice.

Thus, I am not proposing to go along the lines of discursive psychology and its focus upon medical interactions or the lines of a Foucauldian analysis of discourse (for a brief review of discourse analytic methods in health psychology, see Willig, 2004), but a more systematic analysis of the lexico-grammatical form of discourse as having a significant social dimension. It is precisely the systematic analysis of the linguistic form that shows the entanglement of the experiences of depression in the dominant models of masculinity. I am therefore advocating a significantly more sensitive attention to how a person speaks, not only at the level of 'marked' (i.e. out of place, extraordinary), but at the level of ordinary. A discursive focus on suffering also shows its socialness and opens the space for a qualitative epidemiology, as Agar (2003) suggested. One which allows the patient perspective both on his/her illness and on the recovery which stems from the suffering, rather than from the current supposedly atheoretical model of a particular disease unit.

To put it more radically, I am putting forward linguistics and tools for discourse analysis as a significant resource not merely for research into illness experience, but for clinical practice. As psychiatrists and clinical psychologists listen to and make sense of their patients' or clients' stories, I suggest that they avail themselves of systematic tools with which to expedite their analyses more deeply and systematically. In this sense the discourse analysis I am advocating here is not only a tool for describing and understanding illness experiences academically, it is also a powerful toolkit for a practitioner with which to unpick the experiences of those who are at their most vulnerable. This unpicking, which I hope to have shown throughout this book, can lead to more nuanced and hence better strategies to understand the patient's distress and plan his/her recovery.

The final word

I would like to finish with a couple of postulates. But let me start with a final story. During one of the interviews, after some 20 minutes I looked at my watch. As I never set a time-frame for the interview, it always lasted for as much as was needed, looking at the watch had no particularly reason; I simply checked the time, as one does, a barely intentional gesture. My informant, who was speaking at the time, noticed it and immediately stopped. In a perhaps somewhat guilty tone, he asked, 'we are finishing, right?' I said we were not, and added that I just looked at my watch, nothing to it. Yet I could see the implication he drew from my gesture – he had talked too much, had taken too much of my time. It took some time, before he relaxed again.

This has been the most difficult project I worked on. I met people who suffered so much that, more often than not, I could not even begin to understand it; my own experiences paled in contrast. Life hurt them so much that some of them had tried to end it. Some more than once. Our conversations were extremely difficult, perhaps more for me, as I was on the receiving end of all this suffering. I started wondering how the psychiatrists do it, seeing considerably more patients daily. I thought that perhaps this was indeed why they tended not to focus on the patients' suffering – it would be unbearable.

But in all this anguish most informants spontaneously thanked me for talking to them, they said the conversations helped them. A conversation like that helped, I was quite astonished. But then I remembered the guilty look on the face of the informant I have just mentioned. It occurred to me that it was probably one of the few occasions in which they could talk as much as they wanted, no strings attached, and I was happy to listen to whatever they had to say. And here is my first postulate: let them talk. Men do talk.

The second postulate is that of context. My interpretations of the informants' narratives in terms of gender ideologies, the plea for a focus on suffering and other analyses have the common denominator of context. There is no psychiatry outside gender, probably class, age. To see a man as a man is a start. But to see a balding man with a beard, using a cane while walking very straight, and listen to his story is quite a different thing. There is so much more to us men than just wearing our trousers. Some of us are bad, very bad, but some are kind, some of us are ill, and some of us lost their jobs. Understanding that might help getting us back on track to boldly go where no one has gone before. Because we're worth it!

Notes

1 Men, depression and discourse analysis

1. http://www.who.int/mental_health/management/depression/definition/en/.

2 Discourses of depression

1. The Polish original reads: 'Epizod depresyjny trwa przez co najmniej 2 tygodnie.'
2. A. Spełnione ogólne kryteria epizodu depresyjnego (F32). B. Występują co najmniej dwa z następujacyh trzech objawów.

3 The experience of autonomy (of depression)

1. As I am presenting translations, I am not following the usual transcription conventions and I am marking only fragments of the extracts which were unclear [unclear] and fragments which I chose to delete [...], occasionally I offer some other information also in square brackets. Also, I have decided to delete backchannel responses of the interviewer (noises such as 'mhm'), it is just about impossible to position them accurately in a translated interaction.

9 Men's imperatives. Men, depression and work

1. The research was carried out in the Institute of Psychology at the University of Opole in Poland by Aleksandra Zarosa for her MA dissertation. She interviewed women whose husbands either were unemployed, or earned considerably less than their wives. I am indebted to her for making this extract available to me. The quoted extract is my translation of the Polish original.
2. (http://forum.gazeta.pl/forum/72,2.html?f=99&w=57854601).

10 Rejections. Men, depression and the family

1. The Polish original is even more interesting: *no jedyne co dba no to o higienę nie jest taki wie pani że że tam się nie myje czy tam nie goli czy to to nie mogę powiedzieć nie.*

References

Aben, I., Verhey, F., Lousberg, R., Lodder, J., and Honig, A. (2002). Validity of the Beck Depression Inventory, hospital anxiety and depression scale, SCL-90, and Hamilton depression rating scale as screening instruments for depression in stroke patients. *Psychosomatics*, 45, 386–393.

Addis, M.E. and Mahalik, J.R. (2003). Men, masculinity, and the contexts of help seeking. *American Psychologist*, 58 (1), 5–14.

Agar, M. (2003). Toward a qualitative epidemiology. *Qualitative Health Research*, 13, 974–986.

Amador, X.F. and David, A. (eds) (2004). *Insight and Psychosis* (2nd edn), Oxford: Oxford University Press.

Amador, X.F. and Kronengold, H. (2004). The description and meaning of insight in psychosis. In: Amador and David, 2004, pp. 15–32.

American Psychiatric Association (2000). *Diagnostic and Statistical Manual of Mental Disorders* (4th edn, text revision), Washington, DC: American Psychiatric Association.

Aneshensel, C., Estrada, A.L., Hansell, M.J., and Clark, V.A. (1987). Social psychological aspects of reporting behavior. *Journal of Health and Social Behaviour*, 28, 232–246.

Angermeyer, M.C., Beck, M., Dietrich, S., and Holzinger, A. (2004). The stigma of mental illness. *International Journal of Social Psychiatry*, 50, 153–162.

Angermeyer, M.C. and Dietrich, S. (2006). Public beliefs about and attitudes towards people with mental illness. *Acta Psychiatrica Scandinavica*, 113, 163–179.

Angermeyer, M.C. and Matschinger, H. (1997). Social distance towards the mentally ill. *Psychological Medicine*, 27, 131–141.

Angermeyer, M.C. and Matschinger, H. (1999). The public's attitude toward drug treatment of schizophrenia. In: Guimo, J., Fischer, W., and Sartorius, N. (eds). *The Image of Madness* (pp. 152–161), Basel: Karger.

Angermeyer, M.C. and Matschinger, H. (2003). The stigma of mental illness. *Acta Psychiatrica Scandinavica*, 108, 304–309.

Angermeyer, M.C. and Matschinger, H. (2004). Public attitudes to people with depression. *Journal of Affective Disorders*, 83, 177–182.

Angst, J. and Dobler-Mikola, A. (1984). The definition of depression. *Journal of Psychiatric Research*, 18, 401–406.

Annandale, E. and Clark, J. (1996). What is gender? *Sociology of Health & Illness*, 18, 17–44.

Apple, M.W. and Christian-Smith, L.K. (eds) (1991). *The Politics of the Textbook*, New York: Routledge.

Atkinson, P. (1997). *The Clinical Experience*, Aldershot: Ashgate.

Baier, M., Murray, R.L.E., and McSweeney, M. (1998). Conceptualization and measurement of insight. *Archives of Psychiatric Nursing*, 12, 32–40.

Baker, C. (1997). Membership categorization and interview accounts. In: Silverman, D. (ed.). *Qualitative Research: Theory, Method and Practice* (pp. 130–143), London: Sage.

Ballard, K. and Elston, M.A. (2005). Medicalisation. *Social Theory & Health*, 3, 228–241.

Barclay, C.R. and DeCooke, P.A. (1988). Ordinary everyday memories: some of the things of which selves are made. In: Neisser, U. and Winograd, E. (eds). *Remembering Reconsidered* (pp. 91–126), Cambridge: Cambridge University Press.

Barilan, Y. and Weintraub, M. (2001). The naturalness of the artificial and our concepts of health, disease and medicine. *Medicine, Health Care and Philosophy*, 4, 311–325.

Barker, C. and Galasiński, D. (2001). *Cultural Studies and Discourse Analysis*, London: Sage.

Baronet, A.-M. (1999). Factors associated with caregiver burden in mental illness. *Clinical Psychology Review*, 19, 819–841.

Barrett, R.J. (1996). *The Psychiatric Team and the Social Definition of Schizophrenia*, Cambridge: Cambridge University Press.

Barrett, F. (2001). The organizational construction of hegemonic masculinity. In: Whitehead and Barrett, 2001b, pp. 77–99.

Barroso, J. and Sandelowski, M. (2001). In the field with the Beck Depression Inventory. *Qualitative Health Research*, 11, 491–504.

Barton, E.L. (1999). The social work of diagnosis. In: Kovarsky, D., Duchan, J., and Maxwell, M. (eds). *Constructing (In) Competence* (pp. 257–288), Mahawah: Lawrence Erlbaum.

Bauman, R. (1986). *Story, Performance, and Event*, Cambridge: Cambridge University Press.

Bavelas, J.B., Black, A., Chovil, N., and Mullett, J. (1990). *Equivocal Communication*, Newbury Park: Sage.

Beautrais, A., Joyce, P., and Mulder, R. (1998). Unemployment and serious suicide attempts. *Psychological Medicine*, 28, 209–218.

Bech, P. (2002). Pharmacological treatments of depressive disorders. In: Maj and Sartorius, 2002, pp. 89–198.

Beck, A.T. (1962). Reliability of psychiatric diagnoses: a critique of systematic studies. *American Journal of Psychiatry*, 119, 210–216.

Beck, A.T. (1976). *Cognitive Therapy and the Emotional Disorders*, New York: International Universities Press.

Beck, A.T., Baruch, E., Balter, J.M., Steer, R.A., and Warman, D.M. (2003). A new instrument for measuring insight. *Schizophrenia Research*, 68, 319–329.

Beck, A.T. and Beamesderfer, A. (1974). Assessment of depression. In: Pichot, P. and Oliver-Martin, R. (eds). *Modern Problems in Pharmacopsychiatry: Vol. 7. Psychological Measurements in Psychopharmacology* (pp. 151–169), Basel: Karger.

Beck, A.T., Rush, A.J., Shaw, B.F., and Emery, G. (1979). *Cognitive Therapy Depression*, New York: Guilford.

Beck, A.T., Steer, R.A., and Brown, G.K. (1996). *Beck Depression Inventory II*, San Antonio: The Psychological Corporation.

Beck, A.T., Steer, R.A., and Garbin, M.G. (1988). Psychometric properties of the Beck Depression Inventory. *Clinical Psychology Review*, 8, 77–100.

Beck, A.T., Ward, C.H., Mendelson, M., Mock, J., and Erbaugh, J. (1961). An inventory for measuring depression. *Archives of General Psychiatry*, 4, 561–571.

Beck, A.T., Ward, C.H., Mendelson, M., Mock, J., and Erbaugh, J.K. (1962). Reliability of psychiatric diagnoses. *American Journal of Psychiatry*, 119, 351–357.

Becker, G. (1997). *Disrupted Lives*, Berkeley: University of California Press.

Beckham, E.E. and Leber, W.R. (1995). *Handbook of Depression*, New York: Guilford Press.

Beckham, E.E., Leber, W.R., and Youll, W.R. (1995). The diagnostic classification of depression. In: Beckham and Leber, 1995, pp. 37–60.

Beck-Sander, A. (1998). Is insight into psychosis meaningful? *Journal of Mental Health*, 7, 25–34.

Bennett, D. and Bauman, A. (2000). Adolescent mental health and risky sexual behaviour. *British Medical Journal*, 321, 251–252.

Bennett, S., Coggan, C., and Adams, P. (2003). Problematising depression: young people, mental health and suicidal behaviours. *Social Science & Medicine*, 57, 289–299.

Benson, J. (1997). *Prime Time*, London: Longman.

Benson, A., Secker, J., Balfe, E., Lipsedge, M., Robinson, S., and Walker, J. (2003). Discourses of blame: accounting for aggression and violence on an acute mental health inpatient unit. *Social Science & Medicine*, 57, 917–926.

Benwell, B. and Stokoe, E. (2006). *Discourse and Identity*, Edinburgh: Edinburgh University Press.

Beresford, P. (2005). Social approaches to madness and distress. In: Tew, 2005, pp. 32–52.

Berganza, C.E., Mezzich, J.E., and Pouncey, C. (2005). Concepts of disease. *Psychopathology*, 38, 166–170.

Bertelsen, A. (1999). Reflections on the clinical utility of the ICD-10 and DSM-IV classifications and their diagnostic criteria. *Australian and New Zealand Journal of Psychiatry*, 33, 166–173.

Beynon, J. (2002). *Masculinities and Culture*, Buckingham, Philadelphia: Open University Press.

Billig, M., Condor, S., Edwards, D., Gane, M., Middleton, D., and Radley, A.R. (1988). *Ideological Dilemmas*, London: Sage.

Blair, A. (1993). Social class and the contextualization of illness experience. In: Radley, A. (ed.). *Worlds of Illness* (pp. 27–48), London: Routledge.

Blatt, S.J. (2004). *Experiences of Depression*, Washington, DC: American Psychological Association.

Blaxter, M. (1993). Why do victims blame themselves? In: Radley, A. (ed.). *Worlds of Illness. Biographical and Cultural Perspectives on Health and Disease*, London: Routledge.

Blommaert, J., Collins, J., and Slembrouck, S. (2005). Spaces of multilingualism. *Language & Communication*, 25, 197–216.

Bolton, D. and Hill, J. (2003). *Mind, Meaning, and Mental Disorder*, Oxford: Oxford University Press.

Bordo, S. (1997). *Twilight Zones*, Berkeley: University of California Press.

Bourdieu, P. (1984). *Distinction*, London: Routledge & Kegan Paul.

Boyle, M. (2002). *Schizophrenia* (2nd edn), London: Routledge.

Bräher, E. and Maier, H. (2001). Men's health. In: Smelser, N.J. and Baltes, P.B. (eds). *International Encyclopedia of the Social & Behavioral Sciences* (pp. 9625–9628), Oxford: Elsevier.

Brittan, A. (1989). *Masculinity and Power*, Oxford, NY: Basil Blackwell.

Brockmeier, J. (2000). Autobiographical time. *Narrative Inquiry*, 10, 51–73.

Brown, G.W. (1991). Epidemiological studies of depression. In: Becker, J. and Kleinman, A. (eds). *Psychosocial Aspects of Depression* (pp. 1–37), Hillsdale: Lawrence Erlbaum.

Brown, G.W. and Harris, T. (1978). *Social Origins of Depression*, London: Routledge.

Brown, G.W. and Harris, T.O. (1989). *Life Events and Illness*, London: Unwin Hyman.

Brown, P. and Levinson, S. (1987). *Politeness*, Cambridge: Cambridge University Press.

Brownhill, S., Wilhelm, K., Barclay, L., and Schmied, V. (2005). 'Big build': hidden depression in men. *Australian and New Zealand Journal of Psychiatry*, 39, 921–931.

Bucholtz, M., Liang, A.C., and Sutton, L.A. (eds) (1999). *Reinventing Identities*. New York: Oxford University Press.

Burr, V. and Butt, T. (2000). Psychological distress and postmodern thought. In: Fee, 2000, pp. 186–206.

Burr, J. and Chapman, T. (2004). Contextualising experiences of depression in women from South Asian communities. *Sociology of Health & Illness*, 26, 433–452.

Bury, M. (1982). Chronic illness as biographical disruption. *Sociology of Health & Illness*, 4, 167–182.

Bury, M. (1991). The sociology of chronic illness. *Sociology of Health & Illness*, 13, 451–468.

Bury, M. (2001). Illness narratives. *Sociology of Health & Illness*, 23, 263–285.

Busfield, J. (1996). *Men, Women and Madness*, Basingstoke: Macmillan.

Butler, J. (1990). *Gender Trouble*, London: Routledge.

Cameron, D. (1997). Performing gender identity: young men's talk and the construction of heterosexual masculinity. In: Johnson and Meinhof, 1997, pp. 47–64.

Cameron, D. (1998). Gender, language, and discourse. *Signs: Journal of Women in Culture and Society*, 23, 945–973.

Candib, L.M. (2002). Working with suffering. *Patient Education and Counselling*, 48, 43–50.

Canguilhem, G. (2000 [1966]). *Normalne i patologiczne* (Polish transl. of *Le normal et le pathologigue*, Presses Universitaires de France), Gdansk: Wydawnictwo slowo/obraz terytoria.

Cape, J. (2001). How general practice patients with emotional problems presenting with somatic or psychological symptoms explain their improvement. *British Journal of General Practice*, 51, 724–729.

Cape, J. and McCullough, Y. (1999). Patients' reasons for not presenting emotional problems in general practice consultations. *British Journal of General Practice*, 49, 875–879.

Caplan, P.J. and Cosgrove, L. (eds) (2004). *Bias in Psychiatric Diagnosis*, Lanham: Jason Aronson.

Carbaugh, D. (1999). Positioning as display of cultural identity. In: Harré and van Langenhove, 1999a, pp. 160–177.

Carricaburu, D. and Pierret, J. (1995). From biographical disruption to biographical reinforcement. *Sociology of Health & Illness*, 17, 65–88.

Carroll, A., Fattah, S., Clyde, Z., Coffey, I., Owens, D.G.C., and Johnstone, E.C. (1999). Correlates of insight and insight change in schizophrenia. *Schizophrenia Research*, 35, 247–253.

Casey, B. and Long, A. (2002). Reconciling voices. *Journal of Psychiatric and Mental Health Nursing*, 9, 603–610.

Casey, B. and Long, A. (2003). Meanings of madness. *Journal of Psychiatric and Mental Health Nursing*, 10, 89–99.

Cassell, E.J. (2004). *The Nature of Suffering and the Goals of Medicine* (2nd edn), Oxford: Oxford University Press.

Chapman, R. (1988). The great pretender: variations on the new man theme. In: Chapman, R. and Rutherford, J. (eds). *Male Order. Unwrapping Masculinity* (pp. 225–249), London: Lawrence & Wishart.

Chapple, A. and Ziebland, S. (2002). Prostate cancer: embodied experience and perceptions of masculinity. *Sociology of Health & Illness*, 2, 820–841.

Charmaz, K. (1983). Loss of self: a fundamental form of suffering in the chronically ill. *Sociology of Health & Illness*, 5, 168–195.

Charmaz, K. (1991). *Good Days, Bad Days*, New Brunswick: Rutgers University Press.

Charmaz, K. (1999). Stories of suffering. *Qualitative Health Research*, 9, 362–382.

Charmaz, K. (2002). Stories and silences. *Qualitative Inquiry*, 8, 302–328.

Chatwin, J. (2006). Patient narratives. *Communication & Medicine*, 3, 113–123.

Cheshire, J. and Ziebland, S. (2005). Narrative as a resource in accounts of the experience of illness. In: Coates, J. and Thornborrow, J. (eds). *The Sociolinguistics of Narrative* (pp. 17–40), Amsterdam: John Benjamins.

Chouliaraki, L. and Fairclough, N. (1999). *Discourse in Late Modernity*, Edinburgh: Edinburgh University Press.

Clare, A. (2001). *On Men. Masculinity in Crisis*, London: Arrow Books.

Clark, L.A. and Watson, D. (1988). Mood and the mundane. *Journal of Personality and Social Psychology*, 54, 296–308.

Clatterbaugh, K. (1997). *Contemporary Perspectives on Masculinity*, Boulder, Oxford: Westview Press.

Coates, J. (1997). One-at-a-time: the organization of men's talk. In: Johnson, S. and Meinhof, U.H. (eds). *Language and Masculinity* (pp. 107–129), Oxford: Blackwell.

Coates, J. (1999). Changing femininities. In: Bucholtz, *et al.*, 1999, pp. 123–144.

Cochran, S.V. (2006). Struggling for sadness: a relational approach to healing men's grief. In: Englar-Carlson, M. and Stevens, M. (eds). *In the Room with Men: A Casebook of Therapeutic Change* (pp. 91–108), Washington, DC: American Psychological Association.

Cochran, S.V. and Rabinowitz, F.E. (2000). *Men and Depression*, San Diego: Academic Press.

Cochran, S.V. and Rabinowitz, F.E. (2003). Gender-sensitive recommendations for assessment and treatment of depression in men. *Professional Psychology*, 34, 132–140.

Cockerham, W.C. (2006). *Sociology of Mental Disorder* (7th edn), Upper Saddle River: Pearson Education.

Collinson, D.L. and Hearn, J. (2005). Men and masculinities in work, organizations and management. In: Kimmel, *et al.*, 2005, pp. 289–310.

Commission for Healthcare Audit (2007). *Count Me In*, London: Commission for Healthcare Audit and Inspection.

Connell, R.W. (1995). *Masculinities*, Cambridge: Polity.

Connell, R.W. (2000). *The Men and The Boys*, Cambridge: Polity.

Connell, R.W. (2002). *Gender*, Cambridge: Polity.

Conrad, F., Blair, J., and Tracy, E. (1999). Verbal Reports Are Data! Federal Committee on Statistical Methodology Research Conference in Arlington, USA.

Cooper, R. (2004). What is wrong with the DSM? *History of Psychiatry*, 15, 5–25.

Corbin, J. and Strauss, A. (1987). Accompaniments to chronic illness. *Research in the Sociology of Health Care*, 6, 249–281.

Corin, E. (1996). Cultural comments on organic and psychotic disorders. In: Mezzich and Fabrega, 1996, pp. 63–69.

Corin, E., Rangaswami, T., and Padmavati, R. (2004). Living through a staggering world: the play of signifiers in early psychosis in South India. In: Jenkins, J.H. and Barrett, R.J. (eds). *Schizophrenia, Culture, and Subjectivity* (pp. 110–145), Cambridge: Cambridge University Press.

Corrigan, P.W. (1998). The impact of stigma on severe mental illness. *Cognitive and Behavioral Practice*, 5, 201–222.

Corrigan, P.W. and Matthews, A.K. (2003). Stigma and disclosure. *Journal of Mental Health*, 12, 235–248.

Corrigan, P.W. and Watson, A.C. (2002). The paradox of self-stigma and mental illness. *Clinical Psychology*, 9, 35–53.

Corrigan, P.W., Kerr, A., and Knudsen, L. (2005). The stigma of mental illness. *Applied and Preventive Psychology*, 11, 179–190.

Courtenay, W.H. (2000). Constructions of masculinity and their influence on men's well-being. *Social Science & Medicine*, 50, 1385–1401.

Courtenay, W.H. and Keeling, R.P. (2001). Men, gender, and health. *Journal of American College Health*, 48, 243–246.

Coyle, A. and Pugh, D. (1998). Discourse analysis in clinical research and practice. *Clinical Psychology Forum*, 114, 22–24.

Coyne, J.C. (1994). Self-reported stress: analog or ersatz depression. *Psychological Bulletin*, 118, 29–45.

Coyne, J.C. and Gotlib, I.H. (1983). The role of cognition in depression: a critical appraisal. *Psychological Bulletin*, 94, 472–505.

Crowe, M. (2000). Constructing normality: a discourse analysis of the DSM-IV. *Journal of Psychiatric and Mental Health Nursing*, 7, 69–77.

Crowe, M. (2002). Reflexivity and detachment: a discursive approach to women's depression. *Nursing Inquiry*, 9, 126–132.

Crowe, M. and Alavi, C. (1999). Mad talk: attending to the language of distress. *Nursing Inquiry*, 6, 26–33.

Crowe, M. and Luty, S. (2005). Recovery from depression: a discourse analysis of interpersonal psychotherapy. *Nursing Inquiry*, 12, 43–50.

Cunningham Owens, D.G.C. (2000). The challenges of diagnosis and continuing patient assessment. *International Journal of Psychiatry in Clinical Practice*, 4 (Suppl. 1), S13–S18.

Dahlstrom, W.G., Brooks, J.D., and Peterson, C.D. (1990). The Beck Depression Inventory: item order and the impact of response sets. *Journal of Personality Assessment*, 55, 224–233.

Davidson, L. (2003). *Living Outside Mental Illness*, New York: New York University Press.

Dell'Osso, L., Pini, S., Cassano, G.B., Mastrocinque, C., Seckinger, R.A., Saettoni, M., Papasogli, A., Yale, S.A., and Amador, X.F. (2002). Insight into illness in patients with mania, mixed mania, bipolar depression and major depression with psychotic features. *Bipolar Disorders*, 4, 315–322.

Demorest, A., Crits-Christoph, P., Hatch, M., and Luborsky, L. (1999). A comparison of interpersonal scripts in clinically depressed versus nondepressed individuals. *Journal of Research in Personality*, 33, 265–280.

Denscombe, M. (1998). *The Good Research Guide: For Small-Scale Social Research Projects*, Buckingham: Open University Press.

Denzin, N.K. (1989). *The Research Act: A Theoretical Introduction to Social Methods*, London: Prentice Hall.

Denzin, N.K. and Lincoln, Y.S. (eds) (2000). *Handbook of Qualitative Research*, London: Sage.

Donsbach, W. (1997). Survey research at the end of the twentieth century. *International Journal of Public Opinion Research*, 9, 17–28.

Drennan, G., Levett, A., and Swartz, L. (1991). Hidden dimensions of power and resistance in the translation process. *Culture, Medicine and Psychiatry*, 15, 361–381.

Drew, M.L., Dobson, K.S., and Stam, H.J. (1999). The negative self-concept in clinical depression: a discourse analysis. *Canadian Psychology*, 40, 192–204.

Dutton, G.R., Grothe, K.B., Jones, G.N., Whitehead, D., Kendra, K., and Brantley, P.J. (2004). Use of the Beck Depression Inventory-II with African American primary care patients. *General Hospital Psychiatry*, 26, 437–442.

Edgar, A. (2005). The expert patient. *Medicine, Health Care and Philosophy*, 8, 165–171.

Edley, N. (2001) Analysing masculinity: interpretative repertoires, ideological dilemmas and subject positions. In: Wetherell, M., Taylor, S., and Yates, S.J. (eds). *Discourse as Data* (pp. 189–228), London: Sage.

Edwards, T. (1997). *Men in the Mirror*, London: Cassell.

Edwards, S.D. (2003). Three concepts of suffering. *Medicine, Health Care and Philosophy*, 6, 59–66.

Elias, N. (1978). *The History of Manners*, Oxford: Blackwell.

Elias, N. (1982). *State Formation and Civilization*, Oxford: Blackwell.

Emslie, C. (2005). Women, men and coronary heart disease. *Journal of Advanced Nursing*, 51, 283–395.

Emslie, C., Ridge, D., Ziebland, S., and Hunt, K. (2006). Men's accounts of depression. *Social Science & Medicine*, 62, 2246–2257.

Endler, N.S., Macrodimitris, S.D., and Kocovsky, N.L. (2000). Depression: the complexity of self-report measures. *Journal of Applied Biobehavioral Research*, 5, 26–46.

Erdner, A., Magnusson, A., Nystro, M., and Lütze, K. (2005). Social and existential alienation experienced by people with long-term mental illness. *Scandinavian Journal of Caring Sciences*, 19, 373–380.

ESEMeD/MHEDEA 2000 Investigators (2004). 12-month comorbidity patterns and associated factors in Europe. *Acta Psychiatrica Scandinavica*, 109 (Suppl. 420), 28–37.

Fabrega, H. (1996). Cultural and historical foundations of psychiatric diagnosis. In: Mezzich and Fabrega, 1996, pp. 3–14.

Fabrega, H. (2005). Psychiatric conditions and the social sciences. *Psychopathology*, 38, 223–227.

Faircloth, C.A., Boylstein, C., Rittman, M., Young, M.E., and Gubrium, J. (2004). Sudden illness and biographical flow in narratives of stroke recovery. *Sociology of Health & Illness*, 26, 242–261.

Fairclough, N. (1989). *Language and Power*, London: Longman.

Fairclough, N. (1992). *Discourse and Social Change*, Oxford: Polity Press.

Fairclough, N. (1995). *Critical Discourse Analysis*, London: Longman.

Fairclough, N. (2003). *Analysing Discourse*, London: Routledge.

Fairclough, N. and Wodak, R. (1997). Critical discourse analysis. In: van Dijk, T.A. (ed.). *Discourse as Social Interaction* (pp. 258–284), London: Sage.

Falicov, C.J. (2003). Culture, society and gender in depression. *Journal of Family Therapy*, 25, 371–387.

Faludi, S. (2000). *Stiffed: The Betrayal of the American Man*, London: Vintage.

Faravelli, C., Albanesi, G., and Poli, E. (1986). Assessment of depression. *Journal of Affective Disorders*, 11, 245–253.

Farr, P. (1987). *Work, Unemployment and Mental Health*, Oxford: Clarendon Press.

Fee, D. (ed.) (2000). *Pathology and the Postmodern*, London: Sage.

Fee, D. (2000a). The broken dialogue. Mental illness as discourse and experience. In: Fee, 2000, pp. 1–17.

Fee, D. (2000b). The project of pathology. In: Fee, 2000, pp. 74–99.

Filc, D. (2004). The medical text: between biomedicine and hegemony. *Social Science & Medicine*, 59, 1275–1285.

Fine, J. (2006). *Language in Psychiatry*, London: Equinox.

Fischer, W. and Goblirsch, M. (2007). Biographical structuring. In: Bamberg, M. (ed.). *Narrative – State of the Art* (pp. 37–46), Amsterdam: John Benjamins.

Flax, J. (1993). *Disputed Subjects*, London: Routledge.

Fong, G., Frost, D., and Stansfeld, S. (2001). Road rage: a psychiatric phenomenon? *Social Psychiatry Psychiatric Epidemiology*, 36, 277–286.

Foucault, M. (1977). *Discipline and Punish*, London: Allen Lane.

Fowler, R. (1985). Power. In: van Dijk, T.A. (ed.). *Handbook of Discourse Analysis*, Vol. 4 (pp. 61–82), London: Academic Press.

Fowler, R. (1991). *Language in the News*, London: Routledge.

Fowler, R. (1996). On critical linguistics. In: Caldas-Coulthard, R.C. and Coulthard, M. (eds). *Texts and Practices* (pp. 3–14), London: Routledge.

Fowler, R., Hodge, B., Kress, G., and Trew, T. (eds) (1979). *Language and Control,* London: Routledge.

Fox, N. and Ward, K. (2006). Health identities: from expert patient to resisting consumer. *Health*, 10, 461–479.

Frances, A.J. and Link Egger, H.L. (1999). Whither psychiatric diagnosis. *Australian and New Zealand Journal of Psychiatry*, 33, 161–165.

Frank, A.W. (1995). *The Wounded Story-Teller*, Chicago: University of Chicago Press.

Frank, A.W. (2006). Health stories as connectors and subjectifiers. *Health*, 10, 421–440.

Fredriksson, L. and Lindström, U.A. (2002). Caring conversations – psychiatric patients' narratives about suffering. *Journal of Advanced Nursing*, 40, 396–404.

Freund, P.E.S., Maguire, M., and Podhurst, S. (2003). *Health, Illness and the Social Body* (4th edn), London: Prentice Hall.

Friedman, C., Brownson, R.C., Peterson, D.E., and Wilkerson, J.C. (1994). Physician advice to reduce chronic disease risk factors. *American Journal of Preventive Medicine*, 10, 367–371.

Fulford, K.W.M. (1989). *Moral Theory and Medical Practice*, Cambridge: Cambridge University Press.

Fulford, K.W.M. (2004). Insight and delusion. In: Amador and David, 2004, pp. 51–100.

Fulford, K.W.M., Morris, K., Sadler, J.Z., and Stanghellini, G. (eds) (2003). *Nature and Narrative*, Oxford: Oxford University Press.

Furnham, A. and Kuyken, W. (1991). Lay theories of depression. *Journal of Social Behavior and Personality*, 6, 329–342.

Gaillie, D., Marsh, C., and Vogler, C. (eds) (1994). *Social Change and the Experience of Unemployment*, Oxford: Oxford University Press.

Galasiński, D. (1992). *Chwalenie się jako perswazyjny akt mowy*, Kraków: Instytut Języka Polskiego PAN.

Galasiński, D. (2000). *The Language of Deception*, Thousand Oaks, CA: Sage.

Galasiński, D. (2004). *Men and the Language of Emotions*, Basingstoke: Palgrave Macmillan.

Galasiński, D. (2008). Constructions of the self in interaction with the Beck Depression Inventory. *Health*, 12 (4).

Galasiński, D. (forthcoming). Niezwykła lekkość psychopatologii. In: Duszak, A. and Fairclough, N. (eds). *Krytyczna analiza dyskursu*. Kraków: Universitas.

Galdas, P.M., Cheater, F., and Marshall, P. (2005). Men and health help-seeking behaviour. *Journal of Advanced Nursing*, 49, 616–623.

Gary, L.E. (1985). Correlates of depressive symptoms among a select population of black men. *American Journal of Public Health*, 75, 1220–1222.

Gask, L., Rogers, A., Oliver, D., May, C., and Roland, M. (2003). Qualitative study of patients' perceptions of the quality of care for depression in general practice. *British Journal of General Practice*, 53, 278–283.

Geertz, C. (1979). From the native's point of view. In: Rabinow, P. and Sullivan, W.M. (eds). *Interpretive Social Science* (pp. 225–241), Berkeley: University of California Press.

Georgakopoulou, A. (2006). The other side of the story: towards a narrative analysis of narratives-in-interaction. *Discourse Studies*, 8, 235–257.

Gergen, K.J. (1989). Warranting voice and the elaboration of the self. In: Shotter, J. and Gergen, K.J. (eds). *Texts of Identity* (pp. 70–81), London: Sage.

Gergen, K.J. (1991). *The Saturated Self*, New York: Basic Books.

Gergen, K.J. (2000). The self: transfiguration by technology. In: Fee, 2000, pp. 100–115.

Gergen, K. and Gergen, M. (1988). Narrative and self as relationship. In: Berkowitz, L. (ed.). *Advances in Experimental Social Psychology* (pp. 17–56), New York: Academic Press.

Ghaemi, S.N. and Rosenquist, K.J. (2004). Insight in mood disorders. In: Amador and David, 2004, pp. 101–115.

Ghaemi, S.N., Sachs, G.S., Baldassano, C.F., and Truman, C.J. (1997). Insight in seasonal affective disorder. *Comprehensive Psychiatry*, 38, 345–348.

Gibbons, J. (ed.) (1994). *Language and the Law*, London: Longman.

Giddens, A. (1984). *The Constitution of Society*, Cambridge: Polity.

Giddens, A. (1991). *Modernity and Self-identity*, Cambridge: Polity.

Gillham, B. (2000). *Developing a Questionnaire*, London: Continuum.

Goffman, E. (1959). *The Presentation of Self in Everyday Life*, Garden City: Doubleday.

Goffman, E. (1971). *Relations in Public*, New York: Basic Books.

Goffman, E. (1990). *Stigma*, London: Penguin Books.

Good, B.J. (1994). *Medicine, Rationality, and Experience*, Cambridge: Cambridge University Press.

Gotlib, I.H. and Hammen, C.L. (2002). *Handbook of Depression*, New York: Guilford Press.

Gottschalk, S. (2000). Escape from insanity. 'Mental disorder' in the postmodern moment. In: Fee, 2000, pp. 18–48.

Grant, A., Mills, J., Mulhern, R., and Short, N. (2004). *Cognitive Behavioural Therapy*, London: Sage.

Greenlagh, T. and Hurwitz, B. (1998). Why study narrative? *Narrative Based Medicine* (pp. 3–16), London: BMJ.

Grice, H.P. (1975). Logic and conversation. In: Cole, P. and Morgan, J. (eds). *Speech Acts (Syntax and Semantics 3)* (pp. 41–58), New York: Academic Press.

Grossman, M. and Wood, W. (1993). Sex differences in intensity of emotional experience. *Journal of Personality and Social Psychology*, 65, 1010–1022.

Grove, B., Secker, J., and Seebohm, P. (eds) (2005). *New Thinking About Mental Health and Employment*, Oxford: Radcliffe Publishing.

Gubman, G.D. and Tessler, R.C. (1987). The impact of mental illness on families. *Journal of Family Issues*, 8, 226–245.

Guilfoyle, M. (2001). Problematizing psychotherapy. *Culture & Psychology*, 7 (2), 151–179.

Gurevich, M., Bishop, S., Bower, J., Malka, M., and Nyhof-Young, J. (2004). (Dis)embodying gender and sexuality in testicular cancer. *Social Science & Medicine*, 58 (9), 1597–1607.

Gutmann, M.C. (1997). Trafficking in men. *Annual Review of Anthropology*, 26, 385–409.

Gwyn, R. (2002). *Communicating Health and Illness*, London: Sage.

Haidet, P. and Paterniti, D.A. (2003). 'Building' a history rather than 'taking' one. *Archives of Internal Medicine*, 163, 1134–1140.

Hall, S. (1981). Encoding/decoding. In: Hall, S., Hobson, D., Lowe, A., and Willis, P. (eds). *Culture, Media, Language* (pp. 128–138), London: Hutchinson.

Hall, S. (1990). Cultural identity and diaspora. In: Rutherford, J. (ed.). *Identity*, London: Lawrence & Wishart.

Hall, S. (1992). Cultural Studies and its Theoretical Legacies. In: Grossberg, L., Nelson, C., and Treichler, P. (eds). *Cultural Studies* (pp. 277–294). London: Routledge.

Hall, S. (1996). For Allon White: metaphors of transformation. In: Morley, D. and Chen, D.-K. (eds). *Stuart Hall*, London: Routledge.

Hall, S. (1997). The work of representation. In: Hall, S. (ed.). *Representation: Cultural Representation and Signifying Practices*, London and Thousand Oaks: Sage.

Hall, S. and du Gay, P. (eds) (1996). *Questions of Cultural Identity*, London: Sage.

Halliday, M.A.K. (1978). *Language as Social Semiotic*, London: Edward Arnold.

Halliday, M.A.K. (1994). *An Introduction to Functional Grammar* (2nd edn), London: Edward Arnold.

Halliday, M.A.K. and Hasan, R. (1985). *Language, Context, and Text*, Oxford: Oxford University Press.

Hamilton, B. and Roper, C. (2006). Troubling 'insight': power and possibilities in mental health care. *Journal of Psychiatric and Mental Health Nursing*, 13, 416–422.

Hammen, C.L. and Padesky, C.A. (1977). Sex differences in the expression of depressive responses on the Beck Depression Inventory. *Journal of Abnormal Psychology*, 86, 609–614.

Hänninen, V. and Aro, H. (1996). Sex differences in coping and depression among young adults. *Social Science & Medicine*, 43, 1453–1460.

Hansen, T., Hatling, T., Lidal, E., and Ruud, T. (2004). The user perspective: respected or rejected in mental health care. *Journal of Psychiatric and Mental Health Nursing*, 11, 292–297.

Hardin, P.K. (2003). Constructing experience in individual interviews, autobiographies, and on-line accounts. *Journal of Advanced Nursing*, 41, 536–544.

Harper, D. (1995). Discourse analysis and 'mental health'. *Journal of Mental Health*, 4, 347–357.

Harper, D. (1998). Discourse analysis and psychiatric medication. *Clinical Psychology Forum*, 114, 19–21.

Harré, R. (ed.) (1986). *The Social Construction of Emotions*, Oxford: Basil Blackwell.

Harré, R. (1998). *The Singular Self*, London: Sage.

Harré, R. (2005). Positioning and the discursive construction of categories. *Psychopathology*, 38, 185–188.

Harré, R. and Gillett, G. (1994). *The Discursive Mind*, Thousand Oaks: Sage.

Harré, R. and Parrott, W.G. (eds) (1996). *The Emotions*, London, Thousand Oaks, New Delhi: Sage.

Harré, R. and van Langenhove, L. (eds) (1999a). *Positioning Theory*, Oxford: Blackwell.

Harré, R. and van Langenhove, L. (1999b). Reflexive positioning. In: Harré and van Langenhove, 1999a, pp. 60–73.

Harré, R. and van Langenhove, L. (1999c). The dynamics of social episodes. In: Harré and van Langenhove, 1999a, pp. 1–13.

Harré, R. and Slocum, N. (2003). Disputes as complex social events. In: Harré, R. and Moghaddam, F. (eds). *The Self and Others* (pp. 123–136), Westport-London: Praeger.

Harré, R. and Stearns, P. (eds) (1995). *Discursive Psychology in Practice*, London, Thousand Oaks, New Delhi: Sage.

Hartley, J. (1988). *Understanding News*, London: Routledge.

Hawton, K. (2000). Sex and suicide: gender differences in suicidal behaviour. *British Journal of Psychiatry*, 177, 484–485.

Hays, R.D., Wells, K.B., Sherbourne, C.D., Rogers, W., and Spritzer, K. (1995). Functioning and well-being outcomes of patients with depression compared with chronic general medical illnesses. *Archives of General Psychiatry*, 52, 11–19.

Hayward, P. and Bright, J.A. (1997). Stigma and mental illness. *Journal of Mental Health*, 6, 345–354.

Hearn, J. and Kolga, V. (2006). Health. In: Hearn and Pringle, 2006a, pp. 170–183.

Hearn, J. and Pringle, K. (eds) (2006a). *European Perspectives on Men and Masculinities*, Basingstoke: Palgrave Macmillan.

Hearn, J. and Pringle, K. (2006b). Studying men in Europe. In: Hearn and Pringle, 2006a, pp. 1–19.

Heesacker, M., Wester, S.R., Vogel, D.L., Wentzel, J.T., Mejia-Millan, C.M., and Goodholm, C.R. Jr. (1999). Gender-based emotional stereotyping. *Journal of Counselling Psychology*, 46, 483–492.

Heifner, C. (1987). The male experience of depression. *Perspectives in Psychiatric Care*, 33, 10–18.

Heifner, C. (1997). The male experience of depression. *Perspectives in Psychiatric Care*, 33, 10–18.

Heinimaa, M. (2000). Ambiguities in the psychiatric use of the concepts of the person. *Philosophy, Psychiatry and Psychology*, 7 (2), 125–136.

Hem, M.H. and Heggen, K. (2004). Rejection – a neglected phenomenon in psychiatric nursing. *Journal of Psychiatric and Mental Health Nursing*, 11, 55–63.

Henn, M., Weinstein, M., and Foard, N. (2006). *A Short Introduction to Social Research*, London: Sage.

Hepworth, J. (1999). *The Social Construction of Anorexia Nervosa*, London: Sage.

Hepworth, M. and Featherstone, M. (1982). *Surviving Middle Age*, Oxford: Basil Blackwell.

Hepworth, M. and Featherstone, M. (1998). The male menopause. In: Nettleton, S. and Watson, J. (eds). *The Body in Everyday Life* (pp. 276–301), London: Routledge.

Herzlich, C. (1973). *Health and Illness*, London: Academic Press.

Higgs, R. (1999). Depression in general practice. In: Dowrick, C. and Frith, L. (eds). *General Practice and Ethics* (pp. 134–149), London: Routledge.

Hodge, R. and Kress, G. (1988). *Social Semiotics*, Oxford: Polity Press.

Hodge, R. and Kress, G. (1993). *Language as Ideology*, London: Routledge.

Honkalampi, K., Hintikka, J., Tanskanen, A., Lehtonen, J., and Viinamaki, H. (2000). Depression is strongly associated with alexithymia in the general population. *Journal of Psychosomatic Research*, 48, 99–104.

Hood, J.C. (ed.) (1993). *Men, Work, and Family*, Newbury Park, London, New Delhi: Sage.

Horrocks, R. (1994). *Masculinity in Crisis*, New York: St Martin's Press.

Hurwitz, B., Greenlagh, T., and Skultans, V. (2004). *Narrative Research in Health and Illness*, London: BMJ Books.

Hutchby, I. (2001). Witnessing: the use of first-hand knowledge in legitimating lay opinions on talk radio. *Discourse Studies*, 3, 481–497.

Hyden, L.-C. (1997). Illness and narrative. *Sociology of Health & Illness*, 19, 48–69.

Ingleby, D. (2006). Transcultural mental health care. In: Double, D.B. (ed.). *Critical Psychiatry* (pp. 61–78), Basingstoke: Palgrave Macmillan.

Jablensky, A. (1999). The nature of psychiatric classification. *Australian and New Zealand Journal of Psychiatry* and 33, 137–144.

Jadhav, S. (2000). The cultural construction of western depression. In: Skultans and Cox, 2000, pp. 41–65.

Jaeger, S.M. (2003). World travelling as a clinical methodology of psychiatric care. *Philosophy, Psychiatry and Psychology*, 10, 227–231.

Jansz, J. (2000). Masculine identity and restrictive emotionality. In: Fischer, A.H. (ed.). *Gender and Emotion* (pp. 166–186), Cambridge: Cambridge University Press.

Jenkins, J.H. and Kleinman, A. (1991). Cross-cultural studies of depression. In: Becker, J. and Kleinman, A. (eds). *Psychosocial Aspects of Depression* (pp. 67–99), Hillsdale: Lawrence Erlbaum.

Johannsen, W.J. (1969). Attitudes towards mental patients. *Mental Hygiene*, 25, 218–228.

Johnson, S. (1997). Theorizing language and masculinity. In: Johnson and Meinhof, 1997, pp. 8–26.

Johnson, S. and Meinhof, U.H. (eds) (1997). *Language and Masculinity*, Oxford: Blackwell.

Johnstone, L. (2000). *Users and Abusers of Psychiatry* (2nd edn), London: Brunner-Routledge.

Jones, L. (1991). Unemployed fathers and their children: implications for policy and practice. *Child and Adolescent Social Work Journal*, 8, 101–116.

Jones, D.W. (2002). *Myths, Madness, and the Family*, Basingstoke: Palgrave Macmillan.

Jorm, A.F., Angermeyer, M.C., and Katschnig, H. (2000a). Public knowledge of and attitudes to mental disorders. In: Andrews, G. and Henderson, S. (eds). *Unmet Need in Psychiatry* (pp. 399–341), Cambridge: Cambridge University.

Jorm, A.F., Medway, J., Christensen, H., Korten, A.E., Jacomb, P.A., and Rodgers, B. (2000b). Attitudes towards people with depression. *Australian and New Zealand Journal of Psychiatry*, 34, 612–618.

Joseph, J.E. (2004). *Language and Identity*, Basingstoke: Palgrave Macmillan.

Kadam, U.T., Croft, P., McLeod, J., and Hutchinson, M. (2001). A qualitative study of patients' views on anxiety and depression. *British Journal of General Practice*, 51, 375–380.

Kangas, I. (2001). Making sense of depression: perceptions of melancholia in lay narratives. *Health*, 5, 76–92.

Karp, D. (1994). Living with depression: illness and identity turning points. *Qualitative Health Research*, 4, 6–30.

Karp, D.A. (1996). *Speaking of Sadness*, New York: Oxford University Press.

Karp, D.A. (2001). *The Burden of Sympathy*, Oxford: Oxford University Press.

Karp, D.A. and Tanarugsachock, V. (2000). Mental illness, caregiving, and emotion management. *Qualitative Health Research*, 10, 6–25.

Kasper, S., den Boer, J.A., and Ad Sitsen, J.M. (2003). *Handbook of Depression and Anxiety* (2nd edn), New York: Marcel Dekker.

Katz, R., Shaw, B.F., Vallis, T.M., and Kaiser, A.S. (1995). The assessment of severity and symptom patterns in depression. In: Beckham and Leber, 1995, pp. 61–85.

Kelly, B.D. (2006). The power gap: freedom, power and mental illness. *Social Science & Medicine*, 63, 2118–2128.

Kelvin, P. and Jarrett, J.E. (1985). *Unemployment*, Cambridge: Cambridge University Press.

Kendell, R.E. (2002). Much diversity, many categories, no entities. In: Maj and Sartorius, 2002, pp. 52–54.

Kennedy, S.H., Lm, R.W., Nutt, D.J., and Thase, M.E. (2004). *Treating Depression Effectively*, London: Martin Dunitz.

Kennedy, G., Metz, H., and Lowinger, R. (1995). Epidemiology and inferences regarding the etiology of late life suicide. In: Kennedy, G. (ed.). *Suicide and Depression in Late Life* (pp. 3–22), New York: Wiley.

Kerfoot, D. (2001). The organization of intimacy: mangerialism, masculinity and masculine subject. In: Whitehead and Barrett, 2001b, pp. 233–252.

Keshavan, M.S., Rabinowitz, J., DeSmedt, G., Harvey, P.D., and Schooler, N. (2004). Correlates of insight in first episode psychosis. *Schizophrenia Research*, 70, 187–194.

Kessler, R.C., House, J.S., and Turner, J.B. (1987). Unemployment and health in a community sample. *Journal of Health and Social Behavior*, 28, 51–59.

Keys, C.F. (1985). The interpretive basis of depression. In: Kleinman and Good, 1985, pp. 153–174.

Kilian, R. and Angermeyer, M.C. (1999). Quality of life in psychiatry as an ethical duty. *Psychopathology*, 32, 127–134.

Kilmartin, C. (2005). Depression in men. *Journal of Men's Health and Gender*, 2, 95–99.

Kimmel, M.S., Hearn, J., and Connell, R.W. (eds) (2005). *Handbook of Studies of Men & Masculinities*, Thousand Oaks: Sage.

Kinderman, P., Setzu, E., Lobban, F., and Salmon, P. (2006). Illness beliefs in schizophrenia. *Social Science & Medicine*, 63, 1900–1911.

King, N. (2000). *Memory, Narrative, Identity*, Edinburgh: Edinburgh University Press.

Kirk, S.A. (2005). *Mental Disorders*, New York: Columbia University Press.

Kirk, S.A. and Hsieh, D.K. (2004). Diagnostic consistency in assessing conduct disorder. *American Journal of Orthopsychiatry*, 74, 43–55.

Kirk, S.A. and Kutchins, H. (1988). Deliberate misdiagnosis in mental health practice. *Social Service Review*, 62, 225–237.

Kirk, S.A. and Kutchins, H. (1994). The myth of reliability of DSM. *Journal of Mind and Behavior*, 15, 71–86.

Kirmayer, L.J. (2005). Culture, context and experience in psychiatric diagnosis. *Psychopathology*, 38, 192–196.

Kitzinger, C. (2000). Doing feminist conversation analysis. *Feminism and Psychology*, 10, 163–193.

Kleinman, A. (1986). *Social Origins of Distress and Disease*, New Haven: Yale University Press.

Kleinman, A. (1987). Anthropology and psychiatry. *British Journal of Psychiatry*, 151, 447–454.

Kleinman, A. (1988a). *Rethinking Psychiatry*, New York: Free Press.

Kleinman, A. (1988b). *The Illness Narratives*, New York: Basic Books.

Kleinman, A. (1995). *Writing at the Margin*, Berkeley: University of California Press.

Kleinman, A. (1996). How is culture important for DSM-IV? In: Mezzich and Fabrega, 1996, pp. 15–25.

Kleinman, A., Das, V., and Lock, M. (eds) (1997). *Social Suffering*, Berkeley: University of California Press.

Kleinman, A. and Good, B. (eds) (1985). *Culture and Depression*, Berkeley: University of California Press.

Kleinman, A. and Kleinman, J. (1991). Suffering and its professional transformation. *Culture, Medicine and Psychiatry*, 15, 275–301.

Klose, M. and Jacobi, F. (2004). Can gender difference in the prevalence of mental disorders be explained by sociodemographic factors? *Archives of Women's Mental Health*, 7, 133–148.

Kozłowska, O. (2004). *Żyć bezrobociem: analiza dyskursu bezrobotnych*. MA dissertation, Institute of Psychology, University of Opole, Poland.

Kraus, A. (2003). How can the phenomenological-anthropological approach contribute to diagnosis and classification in psychiatry. In: Fulford, *et al.*, 2003, pp. 199–216.

Kress, G. and van Leeuwen, T. (1996). *Reading Images*, London: Routledge.

Kutchins, H. and Kirk, S.A. (1999). *Making Us Crazy*, London: Constable.

Lacasse, J.F. and Gomory, T. (2003). Is graduate social work education promoting a critical approach to mental health practice? *Journal of Social Work Education*, 39, 383–408.

Lakoff, R. (1973). Language and woman's place. *Language in Society*, 2, 45–80.

Lam, R.M., Michalak, E.E., and Swinson, R.P. (2005). *Assessment Scales in Depression, Mania and Anxiety*, London: Taylor and Francis.

Lasa, L., Ayuso-Mateos, J.L., Vazquez-Barquero, J.L., Diez-Manrique, F.J., and Dowrick, C.F. (2000). The use of the Beck Depression Inventory to screen for depression in the general population: a preliminary analysis. *Journal of Affective Disorders*, 57, 261–265.

Launer, J. (1999). A narrative approach to mental health in general practice. *British Medical Journal*, 318, 117–119.

Lawton, J. (2003). Lay experiences of health and illness. *Sociology of Health & Illness*, 25 (Silver Anniversary Issue), 21–49.

LeDoux, J. (1998). *The Emotional Brain*, London: Phoenix.

Lee, C. and Owens, R.G. (2002). Issues for a psychology of men's health. *Journal of Health Psychology*, 7, 209–217.

Lefley, H.P. (1989). Family burden and family stigma in major mental illness. *American Psychologist*, 44, 556–560.

Lefley, H. (1997). Consumer recovery vision. *American Journal of Orthopsychiatry*, 67, 210–219.

Lepine, J.P., Gastpar, M., Mendlewicz, J., and Tylee, A. (1997). Depression in the community: the first pan-European study DEPRES. *International Clinical Psychopharmacology*, 12, 12–29.

Lester, H. and Tritter, J.Q. (2005). 'Listen to my madness': understanding the experiences of people with serious mental illness. *Sociology of Health & Illness*, 27, 649–669.

Levant, R.F. (1996). The new psychology of men. *Professional Psychology*, 7, 259–265.

Levant, R.F. (1998). Desperately seeking language. In: Pollack and Levant, 1998, pp. 35–56.

Levine, R.R.J. (2005). Social class of origin, lost potential, and hopelessness in schizophrenia. *Schizophrenia Research*, 76, 329–335.

Levitt, H., Korman, Y., and Angus, L. (2000). A metaphor analysis is in treatments of depression: metaphor as a marker of change. *Counselling Psychology Quarterly*, 13 (1), 23–35.

Lewis, S. (1995). A search for meaning: making sense of depression. *Journal of Mental Health*, 4, 369–382.

Lewis, B. (2000). Psychiatry and postmodern theory. *Journal of Medical Humanities*, 21, 71–84.

Link, B.G., Phelan, J.C., Bresnahan, M., Stueve, A., and Pescosolido, B.A. (1999). Public conceptions of mental illness. *American Journal of Public Health*, 89, 1328–1333.

Lloyd, M. (1999). 'Performativity, Parody, Politics', *Theory, Culture and Society*, 16, 195–213.

Lloyd-Williams, M., Dennis, M., and Taylor, F. (2004). A prospective study to compare three depression screening tools in patients who are terminally ill. *General Hospital Psychiatry*, 26, 384–389.

Lorencz, B. (1991). Becoming ordinary. In: Morse and Johnson, 1991a, pp. 140–200.

Loukissa, D. (1995). Family burden in chronic mental illness: a review of research studies. *Journal of Advanced Nursing*, 21, 248–255.

Lupton, D. (1998). *The Emotional Self*, London: Sage.

Lupton, D. (2003). *Medicine and Culture* (2nd edn), London: Sage.

Lutz, C. (1985). Depression and the translation of emotional worlds. In: Kleinman and Good, 1985, pp. 63–100.

Lutz, B.J. and Bowers, B.J. (2005). Disability in everyday life. *Qualitative Health Research*, 15, 1037–1054.

Lyons, A.C. and Willott, S. (1999). From suet pudding to superhero: representations of men's health for women. *Health*, 3, 283–302.

Lysaker, P.H., Lancaster, R.S., and Lysaker, J.T. (2003). Narrative transformation as an outcome in the psychotherapy of schizophrenia. *Psychology and Psychotherapy*, 76, 285–299.

Macpherson, R., Jerrom, B., and Hughes, A. (1997). Drug refusal among schizophrenic patients treated in the community. *Journal of Mental Health*, 6, 141–147.

Maj, M. (1998). Critique of the DSM-IV operational diagnostic criteria for schizophrenia. *British Journal of Psychiatry*, 172, 458–460.

Maj, M. and Sartorius, N. (2002). *Depressive Disorders*, Chichester: John Wiley.

Mann, J.J. (1989). *Models of Depressive Disorders*, New York: Plenum Press.

Manson, S.M. (1996). Culture and DSM-IV. In: Mezzich and Fabrega, 1996, pp. 99–113.

Markova, I.S., Roberts, K.H., Gallagher, C., Boos, H., McKennab, P.J., and Berrios, G.E. (2003). Assessment of insight in psychosis. *Psychiatry Research*, 119, 81–88.

Martin, M.W. (1999). Depression: illness, insight, identity. *Philosophy, Psychiatry and Psychology*, 6, 271–286.

Martin, M.W. (2002). On the evolution of depression. *Philosophy, Psychiatry and Psychology*, 9, 255–259.

Masse, R. (2000). Qualitative and quantitative analyses of psychological distress: methodological complementarity and ontological incommensurability. *Qualitative Health Research*, 10, 411–423.

Mattingly, C. (1998). *Healing Dramas and Clinical Plots: The Narrative Structure of Experience*. Cambridge: Cambridge University Press.

Mattinson, J. (1988). *Work, Love, Marriage: The Impact of Unemployment*, London: Duckworth.

Maurin, J.T. and Boyd, C.B. (1990). Burden of mental illness on the family: a critical review. *Archives of Psychiatric Nursing*, 4, 99–107.

McCreight, B.S. (2004). A grief ignored: narratives of pregnancy loss from a male perspective. *Sociology of Health & Illness*, 26, 326–350.

McIlvenny, P. (ed.) (2002). *Talking Gender and Sexuality*, Amsterdam, Philadelphia: John Benjamins.

McIlvenny, P. (2002a). Researching talk, gender and sexuality. In: McIlvenny, P. (ed.). *Talking Gender and Sexuality* (pp. 1–48), Amsterdam, Philadelphia: John Benjamins.

McIlvenny, P. (2002b). Critical reflections on performativity and the 'un/doing' of gender and sexuality in talk. In: McIlvenny, P. (ed.). *Talking Gender and Sexuality* (pp. 111–150), Amsterdam, Philadelphia: John Benjamins.

McMullen, L.M. (2003). 'Depressed' women's constructions of the deficient self. In: Stoppard and McMullen, 2003, pp. 17–38.

McMullen, L.M. and Stoppard, J.M. (2003). Conclusion. In: Stoppard and McMullen, 2003, pp. 207–215.

McMullen, L.M. and Stoppard, J.M. (2006). Women and depression: a case study of the influence of feminism in Canadian psychology. *Feminism & Psychology*, 16, 273–288.

McPherson, S. and Armstrong, D. (2006). Social determinants of diagnostic labels in depression. *Social Science & Medicine*, 62, 50–58.

Meinhof, U.H. and Galasiński, D. (2005). *The Language of Belonging*, Basingstoke: Palgrave Macmillan.

Menz, F. (1989). Manipulation strategies in newspapers. In: Wodak, R. (ed.). *Language, Power and Ideology* (pp. 227–249), Amsterdam: John Benjamins.

Mey, J.L. (2001). *Pragmatics* (2nd edn), Oxford: Blackwell.

Mezzich, J.E. (1999). Ethics and comprehensive diagnosis. *Psychopathology*, 32, 135–140.

Mezzich, J.E. and Berganza, C.E. (2005). Purposes and models of diagnostic systems. *Psychopathology*, 38, 162–165.

Mezzich, J.E. and Fabrega, H. (eds) (1996). *Culture and Psychiatric Diagnosis*, Washington, DC: American Psychiatric Press.

Middleton, P. (1992). *The Inward Gaze. Masculinity and Subjectivity in Modern Culture*, London and New York: Routledge.

Mill, N., Busuttil, V., Harper, R., King, N., Lillstone, C., Manners, A.-M., Shipsey, C., and Short, M. (2001). *Social Focus on Men*, London: The Stationery Office.

Miller, R.B. (2005). Suffering in psychology. *Journal of Psychotherapy Integration*, 15, 299–336.

Miller, J. and Bell, C. (1996). Mapping men's mental health. *Journal of Community & Applied Social Psychology*, 6, 317–327.

Mintz, A.R., Dobson, K.S., and Romney, D. (2003). Insight in schizophrenia. *Schizophrenia Research*, 61, 75–88.

Mischler, E. (2006). Narrative identity: the double arrow of time. In: De Fina, A., Schiffrin, D., and Bamberg, M. (eds). *Discourse and Identity* (pp. 30–47), Cambridge: Cambridge University Press.

Mishler, E.G. (1991). *Research Interviewing*, Cambridge: Harvard University Press.

Mishler, E.G., Amara Singham, L.R., Osherson, S.T., Hauser, S.T., Waxler, N.E., and Liem, R. (1981). *Social Contexts of Health, Illness and Patient Care*, New York: Cambridge University Press.

Misztal, B. (2003). *Theories of Social Remembering*, Maidenhead: Open University Press.

Mohr, W.K. (1999). Deconstructing the language of psychiatric hospitalization. *Journal of Advanced Nursing*, 29, 1052–1059.

Möller-Leimkühler, A.M. (2002). Barriers to help-seeking by men. *Journal of Affective Disorders*, 71, 1–9.

Möller-Leimkühler, A.M. (2003). The gender gap in suicide and premature death or: Why are men so vulnerable? *European Archives of Psychiatry and Clinical Neuroscience*, 253, 1–8.

Möller-Leimkühler, A.M., Bottlender, R., Strauss, A., and Rutz, W. (2004). Is there evidence for a male depressive syndrome in inpatients with major depression? *Journal of Affective Disorders*, 80, 87–93.

Monks, J.A. (2000). Talk as social suffering: narratives of talk in medical settings. *Anthropology & Medicine*, 7, 15–38.

Moreira, V. (2003). The ideological meaning of depression in the contemporary world. *International Journal of Critical Psychology*, 9, 143–159.

Morgan, D.H.J. (1992). *Discovering Men*, London and New York: Routledge.

Morris, D.B. (1997). About suffering: voice, genre and moral community. In: Kleinman, *et al.*, 1997, pp. 25–45.

Morse, J.M. (2000). Responding to the cues of suffering. *Health Care for Women International*, 21, 1–9.

Morse, J.M. (2001). Toward a Praxis Theory of Suffering. *Advances in Nursing Science*, 24, 47–59.

Morse, J. and Johnson, J.J. (1991a). *The Illness Experience*, Newbury Park: Sage.

Morse, J. and Johnson, J.J. (1991b). Towards a theory of illness. In: Morse and Johnson, 1991a, pp. 315–342.

Morse, J.M. and Penrod, J. (1999). Linking concepts of enduring, uncertainty, suffering, and hope. *Image: Journal of Nursing Scholarship*, 31, 145–150.

Moscicki, E. (1997). Identification of suicide risk factors using epidemiologic studies. *Psychiatric Clinics of North American*, 20, 499–517.

Muhlbauer, S.A. (2002). Navigating the storm of mental illness. *Qualitative Health Research*, 12, 1076–1092.

Mulac, A., Bradac, J.J., and Gibbons, P. (2001). Empirical support for the gender-as-culture hypothesis. *Human Communication Research*, 27, 121–152.

Murray, M. (2000). Levels of narrative analysis in health psychology. *Journal of Health Psychology*, 5, 337–347.

Murray, M. (ed.) (2004). *Critical Health Psychology*, Basingstoke: Palgrave Macmillan.

Nathan, P.E. and Langenbucher, J.W. (1999). Psychopathology: Description and classification. *Annual Review of Psychology*, 50, 79–107.

Nazroo, J.Y., Edwards, A.C., and Brown, G.W. (1997). Gender differences in the onset of depression following a shared life event. *Psychological Medicine*, 27, 9–19.

New, C. (2001). Oppressed and oppressors? The systematic mistreatment of men. *Sociology*, 35, 729–748.

Nezu, A.M., Nezu, C.M., McClure, K.S., and Zwick, M.L. (2002). Assessment of depression. In: Gotlib and Hammem, 2002, pp. 61–85.

Ng, S.H. and Bradac, J.J. (1993). *Power in Language*, Newbury Park: Sage.

NICE (2004). *Depression: Management of Depression in Primary and Secondary Care*. Clinical Guideline 23, London.

Nicholson, J., Nason, M.W., Calabresi, A.O., and Yando, R. (1999). Fathers with severe mental illness. *American Journal of Orthopsychiatry*, 69, 134–141.

Nicolson, P. (1995). Qualitative research, psychology and mental health. *Journal of Mental Health*, 4, 337–346.

Nolen-Hoeksema, S. (2001). Gender differences in depression. *Current Directions in Psychological Science*, 10, 173–176.

Nonn, T. (2001). Hitting bottom: homelessness, poverty, and masculnity. In: Kimmell, M.S. and Messner, M.A. (eds). *Men's Lives* (pp. 242–251), Boston: Allyn and Bacon.

O'Brien, M., Singleton, N., Sparks, J., Meltzer, H., and Brugha, T. (2002). *Adults with a Psychotic Disorder Living in Private Households*, London: The Stationery Office.

O'Brien, R., Hunt, K., and Hart, G. (2005). 'It's caveman stuff, but that is to a certain extent how guys still operate': men's accounts of masculinity and help seeking. *Social Science & Medicine*, 61, 503–516.

Ochs, E. (1992). Indexing gender. In: Duranti, A. and Goodwin, C. (eds). *Rethinking Context* (pp. 335–358), Cambridge: Cambridge University Press.

Oleś, P.K. (2000). *Psychologia przelomu polowy zycia*, Lublin: Towarzystwo Naukowe KUL.

Oliffe, J. (2005). Constructions of masculinity following prostatectomy-induced impotence. *Social Science & Medicine*, 60, 2249–2259.

Oliffe, J. (2006). Embodied masculinity and androgen deprivation therapy. *Sociology of Health & Illness*, 28, 410–432.

ONS (2007). *Social Trends No 37*, Basingstoke: Palgrave Macmillan.

Paechter, C. (2003). Masculinities and femininities as communities of practice. *Women's Studies International Forum*, 26, 69–77.

Page, S. and Bennesch, S. (1993). Gender and reporting differences in measures of depression. *Canadian Journal of Behavioral Science*, 25 (4), 579–589.

Papakostas, G.I., Petersen, P., Mahal, Y., Mischoulon, D., Nierenberg, A.A., and Fava, M. (2004). Quality of life assessments in major depressive disorder. *General Hospital Psychiatry*, 26, 13–17.

Parker, G. (2004). Critique of the guidelines for the treatment of depression. *Australian and New Zealand Journal of Psychiatry*, 38, 885–890.

Parker, I. (1992). *Discourse Dynamics*, London: Routledge.

Parker, G., Hilton, T., Hadzi-Pavlovic, D., and Bains, J. (2001). Screening for depression in the medically ill. *Australian and New Zealand Journal of Psychiatry*, 35, 474–480.

Parker, I., Georgaca, E., Harper, D., McLaughlin, T., and Stowell-Smith, M. (1995). *Deconstructing Psychopathology*, London: Sage.

Parsons, T. (1951). *The Social System*, London: Routledge & Kegan Paul.

Paykel, E.S. (ed.) (1992). *Handbook of Affective Disorders*. Edinburgh: Churchill Livingstone.

Paykel, E.S., Brugha, T., and Fryers, T. (2005). Size and burden of depressive disorders in Europe. *European Neuropsychopharmacology*, 15, 411–423.

Peralta, V. and Cuesta, M.J. (1998). Lack of insight in mood disorders. *Journal of Affective Disorders*, 49, 55–58.

Perkins, R. and Moodley, P. (1993). The arrogance of insight? *Psychiatric Bulletin*, 17, 233–234.

Phillips, A. (2005). *Going Sane*, London: Penguin.

Phillips, J. (2003). Psychopathology and the narrative self. *Philosophy, Psychiatry and Psychology*, 10, 313–328.

Phillips, J. (2005). Idiographic formulations, symbols, narratives, context and meaning. *Psychopathology*, 38, 180–184.

Pierret, J. (2003). The illness experience. *Sociology of Health & Illness*, 25 (Silver Anniversary Issue), 4–22.

Pilgrim, D. (2007). The survival of psychiatric diagnosis. *Social Science & Medicine*, 65, 536–547.

Pilgrim, D. and Bentall, R. (1999). The medicalisation of misery: a critical realist analysis of the concept of depression. *Journal of Mental Health*, 8, 262–276.

Pilgrim, D. and Rogers, A. (1997). Mental health, critical realism and lay knowledge. In: Ussher, 1997, pp. 33–49.

Pilgrim, D. and Rogers, A. (1999). *A Sociology of Mental Health and Illness*, Buckingham: Open University Press.

Pinnock, C., O'Brien, B., and Marshall, V.R. (1998). Older men's concerns about their urological health: a qualitative study. *Australian and New Zealand Journal of Public Health*, 22, 368–373.

Plummer, K. (1995). *Telling Sexual Stories*, London: Routledge.

Pollock, K. (2007). Maintaining face in the presentation of depression. *Health*, 11, 163–180.

Pollack, W.S. (1998). Mourning, melancholia, masculinity. In: Pollack and Levant, 1998, pp. 147–166.

Pollack, W.S. and Levant, R.F. (eds) (1998). *New Psychotherapy for Men*, New York: John Wiley.

Porter, R. (ed.) (1997). *Rewriting the Self*, London: Routledge.

Potts, M.K., Burnam, M.A., and Wells, K.B. (1991). Gender difference in depression detection. *Psychological Assessment*, 3, 609–615.

Pound, P., Gompertz, P., and Ebrahim, S. (1998). Illness in the context of older age. *Sociology of Health & Illness*, 20, 489–506.

Power, M. (ed.) (2004). *Mood Disorders: A Handbook of Science and Practice*, Chichester: John Wiley.

Price, K. and Cheek, J. (1996). Pain as a discursive construction. *Social Sciences in Health*, 2, 212–217.

Prior, L. (2003). Belief, knowledge and expertise. The emergence of the lay expert in medical sociology. *Sociology of Health & Illness*, 25 (Silver Anniversary Issue), 41–57.

Prior, L., Wood, F., Lewis, G., and Pill, R. (2003). Stigma revisited: disclosure of emotional problems in primary care consultations in wales. *Social Science & Medicine*, 56, 2191–2200.

Prior, P.M. (1999). *Gender and Mental Health*, Basingstoke: Macmillan.

Pujolar, J. (2000). *Gender, Heteroglossia and Power*, Berlin: Mouton de Gruyter.

Puskar, K., Sereika, S., Lamb, J., Tusaie-Mumford, K., and McGuiness, T. (1999). Optimism and its relationship to depression, coping, anger and life events in rural adolescents. *Issues in Mental Health*, 20, 115–130.

Pyke, K.D. (1996). Class-based masculinities. *Gender & Society*, 10, 527–579.

Rabkin, J.G. (1972). Opinions about mental illness. *Psychological Bulletin*, 77, 153–177.

Radden, J. (2000). *The Nature of Melancholy*, Oxford: Oxford University Press.

Radley, A. (1994). *Making Sense of Illness*, London: Sage.

Radley, A. (2004). *Suffering*. In: Murray, 2004, pp. 31–43.

Radley, A. and Billig, M. (1996). Accounts of health and illness. *Sociology of Health & Illness*, 18, 220–240.

Rathod, S., Kingdon, D., Smith, P., and Turkington, D. (2005). Insight into schizophrenia. *Schizophrenia Research*, 74, 211–219.

Real, T. (1998). *I Don't Want to Talk About It: Men and Depression*, Dublin: Newleaf.

Regier, D.A., Kaelber, C.T., Rae, D.S., Farmer, M.E., Knauper, B., Kessler, R.C., and Norquist, G.S. (1998). Limitations of diagnostic criteria and assessment instruments for mental disorders. *Archives of General Psychiatry*, 55, 109–115.

Richter, G. and Richter, J. (1989). Social relationships reflected by depressive inpatients. *Acta Psychiatrica Scandinavica*, 80, 573–578.

Richter, P., Werner, J., Heerlein, A., Kraus, A., and Sauer, H. (1998). On the validity of the Beck Depression Inventory. *Psychopathology*, 31, 160–168.

Ridge, D.T. and Ziebland, S. (2006). 'The old me could never have done that': how people give meaning to recovery following depression. *Qualitative Health Research*, 16, 1038–1053.

Riska, E. (2002). From type a man to the hardy man. *Sociology of Health & Illness*, 24, 347–358.

Riska, E. (2004). *Masculinity and Men's Health*, Lanham: Rowman & Littlefield.

Robbins, A. (2004). Introduction to men's mental health. *Journal of Men's Health and Gender*, 1, 359–364.

Robbins, C. (2002). *Real World Research. A Resource for Social Scientists and Practitioner-Researchers*, Oxford: Blackwell.

Roberts, B. (2004). Health narratives, time perspectives and self-images. *Social Theory & Health*, 2, 170–183.

Rodgers, B.L. and Cowles, K.V. (1997). A conceptual foundation for human suffering in nursing care and research. *Journal of Advanced Nursing*, 25, 1048–1053.

Rogers, A. and Pilgrim, D. (2003). *Mental Health and Inequality*, Basingstoke: Palgrave Macmillan.

Rogers, A., May, C., and Oliver, D. (2001). Experiencing depression, experiencing the depressed. *Journal of Mental Health*, 10, 317–333.

Rogers, W.H., Adler, D.A., Bungay, K.M., and Wilson, I.B. (2005). Depression screening instruments made good severity measures in a cross-sectional analysis. *Journal of Clinical Epidemiology*, 58, 370–377.

Rose, N. (1989). *Governing the Soul*, London: Routledge.

Rose, N. (1990). Psychology as a social science. In: Parker, I. and Shotter, J. (eds). *Deconstructing Social Psychology* (pp. 103–116), London: Routledge.

Rose, N. (1996). Identity, genealogy, history. In: Hall and du Gay, 1996, pp. 128–150.

Rose, N. (1997). Assembling the modern self. In: Porter, 1997, pp. 224–248.

Rosenfeld, D. and Faircloth, C.A. (eds) (2006). *Medicalised Masculinities*, Philadelphia: Temple University Press.

Roter, D.L. and Hall, J.A. (1997). *Doctors Talking with Patients/Patients Talking with Doctors*, Westport: Praeger.

Rottenberg, J. and Gotlib, I.H. (2004). Socioemotional functioning in depression. In: Power, 2004, pp. 61–77.

Rowe, D. (1978). *The Experience of Depression*, Chichester: John Wiley.

Rubin, D.C. (ed.) (1988). *Autobiographical Memory*, Cambridge: Cambridge University Press.

Rudge, T. and Morse, K. (2001). Re-awakenings? A discourse analysis of the recovery from schizophrenia after medication change. *Australian and New Zealand Journal of Mental Health Nursing*, 10, 66–76.

Rüsch, N., Angermeyer, M.C., and Corrigan, P.W. (2005). Mental illness stigma. *European Psychiatry*, 20, 529–539.

Rutherford, J. (1988). Who's that man? In: Chapman, R. and Rutherford, J. (eds). *Male Order* (pp. 21–67), London: Lawrence & Wishart.

Rutz, W., Walinder, J., von Knorring, L., Rihmer, Z., and Pihlgren, H. (1997). Prevention of depression and suicide by education and medication. *International Journal of Psychiatry in Clinical Practice*, 1, 39–44.

Ryba, M. (2003). *Narracje Mężczyzn Zarabiających Mniej Od Swoich Żon*. MA dissertation, Institute of Psychology, University of Opole, Poland.

Sabat, S. and Harré, R. (1999). Positioning and the recovery of social identity. In: Harré and van Langenhove, 1999a, pp. 87–101.

Sabo, D. (2005). The study of masculinities and men's health. In: Kimmel, *et al.*, 2005, pp. 326–352.

Sabo, D. and Gordon, D.F. (1995). Rethinking men's health and illness. In: Sabo, D. and Gordon, D.F. (eds). *Men's Health and Illness* (pp. 1–21), Thousand Oaks: Sage.

Sadler, J.Z. (2005a). *Values and Psychiatric Diagnosis*, Oxford: Oxford University Press.

Sadler, J.Z. (2005b). Social context and stakeholders' values in building diagnostic systems. *Psychopathology*, 38, 197–200.

Sadler, J.Z. (2007). The psychiatric significance of the personal self. *Psychiatry*, 70, 113–129.

Sadler, J.Z. and Fulford, B. (2006). Normative warrant in diagnostic criteria. *Journal of Personality Disorders*, 20, 170–180.

Salmon, P. and Manyande, A. (1996). Good patients cope with their pain. *Pain*, 68, 63–68.

Sanders, C., Donovan, J., and Dieppe, P. (2002). The significance and consequences of having painful and disabled joints in older age. *Sociology of Health & Illness*, 24, 227–253.

Santor, D.A. and Coyne, J.C. (2001). Evaluating the continuity of symptomatology between depressed and nondepressed individuals. *Journal of Abnormal Psychology*, 110, 216–225.

Sayre, J. (2000). The patient's diagnosis. *Qualitative Health Research*, 10, 71–83.

Scattolon, Y. (2003). I just went on ... There was no feeling better, there was no feeling worse. In: Stoppard and McMullen, 2003, pp. 162–182.

Schegloff, E. (1997). Whose text? Whose context? *Discourse & Society*, 8, 165–187.

Schieffelin, E.L. (1985). The cultural analysis of depressive affect. In: Kleinman and Good, 1985, pp. 101–152.

Schmolke, M. (1999). Ethics in psychiatric diagnosis from a psychodynamic perspective. *Psychopathology*, 32, 152–158.

Schofield, T., Connell, R.W., Walker, L., Wood, J.F., and Butland, D.L. (2000). Understanding men's health and illness. *Journal of American College Health*, 48, 247–256.

Schotte, C.K.W., Maesc, M., Cluydts, R., De Doncker, D., and Cosyns, P. (1997). Construct validity of the Beck Depression Inventory in a depressive population. *Journal of Affective Disorders*, 46, 115–125.

Schulze, B. and Angermeyer, M.C. (2003). Subjective experiences of stigma. *Social Science & Medicine*, 56, 299–312.

Schuman, H. and Presser, S. (1981). *Questions and Answers in Attitude Surveys*, New York: Academic Press.

Schwarz, N. (1999). Self-reports. *American Psychologist*, 54, 93–105.

Segal, Z., Williams, J., and Teasdale, J. (2002). *Mindfulness-Based Cognitive Therapy for Depression: A New Approach to Preventing Relapse*, New York and London: The Guilford Press.

Seidler, V.J. (1989). *Rediscovering Masculinity*, London: Routledge.

Seidler, V.J. (1994). *Unreasonable Men*, London: Routledge.

Seymour-Smith, S., Wetherell, M., and Phoenix, A. (2002). 'My wife ordered me to come!': a discursive analysis of doctors' and nurses' accounts of men's use of general practitioners. *Journal of Health Psychology*, 7, 253–267.

Shaw, I. (2002). How lay are lay beliefs? *Health*, 6, 287–299.

Shilling, C. (2003). *The Body and Social Theory* (2nd edn), London: Sage.

Singleton, N., Bumpstead, R., O'Brien, M., Lee, A., and Meltzer, H. (2000). Psychiatric Morbidity among Adults living in Private Households, Summary Report. London: Office for National Statistics.

Singleton, N., Bumpstead, R., O'Brien, M., Lee, A., and Meltzer, H. (2001). *Psychiatric Morbidity among Adults Living in Private Households, 2000*, London: The Stationery Office.

Skultans, V. (2000). Narrative illness and the body. *Anthropology and Medicine*, 7, 5–13.

Skultans, V. and Cox, J. (eds) (2000). *Anthropological Approaches to Psychological Medicine*, London: Jessica Kingley.

Smith, B. (1999). The abyss: exploring depression through a narrative of the self. *Qualitative Inquiry*, 5, 264–279.

Smith, B. and Sparkes, A.C. (2004). Men, sport, and spinal cord injury. *Disability & Society*, 19, 613–626.

Smith, C.D. (1998). 'Men don't do this sort of thing': a case study of the social isolation of househusbands. *Men and Masculinities*, 1, 138–172.

Socall, D.W. and Holtgraves, T. (1993). Attitudes toward the mentally ill. *Sociological Quarterly*, 33, 435–445.

Speed, E. (2006). Patients, consumers and survivors. *Social Science & Medicine*, 62, 28–38.

Speer, S. (2002). 'Natural' and 'contrived' data: a sustainable distinction? *Discourse Studies*, 4 (4), 511–525.

Startup, M. (1998). Insight and interpersonal problems in long-term schizophrenia. *Journal of Mental Health*, 7, 299–308.

Steer, R.A., Ball, R., Ranieri, W.F., and Beck, A.T. (1999). Dimensions of the Beck Depression Inventory-II in clinically depressed patients. *Journal of Clinical Psychology*, 55 (1), 117–128.

Steer, R.A., Beck, A.T., and Brown, G. (1989). Sex differences on the revised Beck Depression Inventory for outpatients with affective disorders. *Journal of Personality Assessment*, 53, 693–702.

Steer, R.A., Cavalieri, T.A., Leonard, D.M., and Aaron, T.B. (1999). Use of the Beck Depression Inventory for primary care to screen for major depression disorders. *General Hospital Psychiatry*, 21, 106–111.

Stefanis, C.N. and Stefanis, N.C. (2002). Diagnosis of depressive disorder. In: Maj and Sartorius, 2002, pp. 1–51.

Stewart, A.L., Greenfield, S., Hays, R.D., Wells, K., Rogers, W.H., Berry, S.D., McGlynn, E.A., and Ware Jr., J.E. (1989). Functional status and well-being of patients with chronic conditions. *Journal of American Medical Association*, 262, 907–913.

Stokoe, E.H. and Smithson, J. (2001). Making gender relevant. *Discourse & Society*, 12, 217–244.

Stoppard, J.M. (1997). Women's bodies, women's lives and depression. In: Ussher, 1997, pp. 10–32.

Stoppard, J.M. (2000). *Understanding Depression*, London: Routledge.

Stoppard, J.M. and Gammell, D.J. (2003). Depressed women's treatment experiences. In: Stoppard and McMullen, 2003, pp. 39–61.

Stoppard, J.M. and McMullen, L.M. (2003). *Situating Sadness*, New York: New York University Press.

Strain, J.J. (2005). Psychiatric diagnostic dilemmas in the medical setting. *Australian and New Zealand Journal of Psychiatry*, 39, 764–771.

Strandmark, K.M. (2004). Ill health is powerlessness. *Scandinavian Journal of Caring Sciences*, 18, 135–144.

Strauss, A. (1992). Turning points in identity. In: Clark, C. and Robboy, H. (eds). *Social Interaction* (pp. 149–155), New York: St Martin's Press.

Sturman, E.D. and Sproule, B.A. (2003). Toward the development of a mood disorders insight scale. *Journal of Affective Disorders*, 77, 21–30.

Sundquist, K., Johansson, L.-M., Johansson, S.-E., and Sundquist, J. (2004). Social environment and psychiatric illness. *Social Psychiatry and Psychiatric Epidemiology*, 39, 39–44.

Svenaeus, F. (2000). Das unheimliche – towards a phenomenology of illness. *Medicine, Health Care and Philosophy*, 3, 3–16.

Szymczak, J.E. and Conrad, P. (2006). *Medicalising the Aging Male Body*. In: Rosenfeld and Faircloth, 2006, pp. 89–111.

Talbot, M., Atkinson, K., and Atkinson, D. (2003). *Language and Power in the Modern World*, Edinburgh: Edinburgh University Press.

Tannen, D. (1998). Talk in the intimate relationships. In: Coates, J. (ed.). *Language and Gender* (pp. 435–445), Malden: Blackwell.

Tannen, D. (1999). The display of (gendered) identities in talk at work. In: Bucholtz, *et al.*, 1999, pp. 221–240.

Tausig, M. (1999). Work and mental health. In: Aneshensel, C.S. and Phelan, J.C. (eds). *Handbook of the Sociology of Mental Health* (pp. 255–274), New York: Kluwer Academic.

Tausig, M., Michello, J., and Subedi, S. (2004). *A Sociology of Mental Illness* (2nd edn), Upper Saddle River: Pearson Education.

Taylor, B. (2006). *Responding to Men in Crisis*, London: Routledge.

Teasdale, J.D. and Dent, J. (1987). Cognitive vulnerability to depression. *British Journal of Clinical Psychology*, 26, 113–126.

Tew, J. (ed.) (2005). *Social Perspectives in Mental Health*, London: Jessica Kingsley.

The Men's Health Forum (2006). The report of the Gender Equity Project. (http://www.dh.gov.uk/en/Publicationsandstatistics/Publications/Publications PolicyAndGuidance/DH_075467).

Thomas, P. and Bracken, P. (2005). *Postpsychiatry*, Oxford: Oxford University Press.

Thomas-McLean, R. and Stoppard, J.M. (2004). Physicians' constructions of depression: inside/outside the boundaries of medicalization. *Health*, 8, 275–293.

Timms, D. (1998). Gender, social mobility and psychiatric diagnoses. *Social Science & Medicine*, 46, 1235–1247.

Titscher, S., Meyer, M., Wodak, R., and Vetter, E. (2000). *Methods of Text and Discourse Analysis*, London: Sage.

Ucok, O. (2005). From diagnostic to aesthetic. In: Duchan, J. and Kovarsky, D. (eds). *Diagnosis as Cultural Practice* (pp. 65–79), Berlin: Mouton de Gruyter.

Ussher, J.M. (ed.) (1997). *Body Talk*, London: Routledge.

Van Dijk, T.A. (1993). Principles of critical discourse analysis. *Discourse & Society*, 4, 249–283.

Van Dijk, T.A. (1998). *Ideology*, London: Sage.

van Dongen, E. (2000). Anthropology and psychiatry. In: Skultans and Cox, 2000, pp. 123–144.

van Hooft, S. (1998). Suffering and the goals of medicine. *Medicine, Health Care and Philosophy*, 1, 125–131.

Van Langenhove, L. and Harré, R. (1993). Positioning and autobiography. In: Coupland, N. and Nussbaum, J.F. (eds). *Discourse and Lifespan Identity* (pp. 81–99), Newbury Park: Sage.

Van Leeuwen, T. (1996). The representation of social actors. In: Caldas-Coulthard, C.R. and Coulthard, M. (eds). *Texts and Practices* (pp. 32–70), London: Routledge.

van Leeuwen, T. and Wodak, R. (1999). Legitimizing immigration control. *Discourse Studies*, 1, 83–118.

Van Praag, H. and Plutchik, R. (1987). Interconvertability of five self-report measures of depression. *Psychiatry Research*, 22 (3), 243–256.

van Praag, H.M. (2002). Flaws in the current diagnosis of depression. In: Maj and Sartorius, 2002, pp. 59–63.

Van Staden, C.W. (2002). Linguistic markers of recovery. *Philosophy, Psychiatry and Psychology*, 9 (2), 105–121.

Vedel Keesing, L. (2005). Gender differences in patients presenting with a single depressive episode according to ICD-10. *Social Psychiatry and Psychiatric Epidemiology*, 40, 197–201.

Verbrugge, L.M. (1989). The twain meet: empirical explanations of sex differences in health and mortality. *Journal of Health and Social Behavior*, 30, 282–304.

Verhaeghe, P. (2004). *On Being Normal and Other Disorders*, New York: Other Press.

Waddington, D., Critcher, C., and Dicks, B. (1998). 'All jumbled up': employed women with unemployed husbands. In: Popay, J., Hearn, J., and Edwards, J. (eds). *Men, Gender Division and Welfare* (pp. 231–256), London: Routledge.

Wakefield, J.C., Pottick, K.J., and Kirk, S.A. (2002). Should the DSM-IV diagnostic criteria for conduct disorder consider social context? *American Journal of Psychiatry*, 159, 380–386.

Walker, K. (1994). 'I'm not friends the way she's friends': ideological and behavioral constructions of masculinity in men's friendships. *Masculinities*, 2, 38–55.

Wallace, J. and Pfohl, B. (1995). Age-related differences in the symptomatic expression of major depression. *Journal of Nervous and Mental Disease*, 183 (2), 99–102.

Warren, L.W. (1983). Male intolerance of depression. *Clinical Psychology Review*, 3, 147–156.

Weiler, M.A., Fleisher, M.H., and McArthur-Campbell, D. (2000). Insight and symptom change in schizophrenia and other disorders. *Schizophrenia Research*, 45, 29–36.

Weisman, C.S. and Teitelbaum, M.A. (1989). Women and health care communication. *Patient Education and Counselling*, 13, 183–199.

Werner, A., Widding Isaksen, L., and Malterud, K. (2004). 'I am not the kind of woman who complains of everything': illness stories on self and shame in women with chronic pain. *Social Science & Medicine,* 59, 1035–1045.

West, C. and Zimmerman, D.H. (1987). Doing gender. *Gender & Society,* 1 (2), 125–151.

Wetherell, M. (1998). Positioning and interpretative repertoires. *Discourse & Society,* 9, 387–412.

White, A. (2001). How men respond to illness. *Men's Health Journal,* 1 (1), 18–19.

White, R. (2002). Social and political aspects of men's health. *Health,* 6 (3), 267–285.

Whitehead, S.M. (2002). *Men and Masculinities,* Cambridge: Polity.

Whitehead, S.M. and Barrett, F.J. (2001a). The Sociology of Masculinity. In: Whitehead and Barrett, 2001b, pp. 1–26.

Whitehead, S.M. and Barrett, F.J. (eds) (2001b). *The Masculinities Reader,* Cambridge: Polity.

Wiggins, S. (2001). Construction and action in food evaluation. *Journal of Language and Social Psychology,* 20 (4), 445–463.

Wilkinson, I. (2005). *Suffering,* Cambridge: Polity.

Williams, S.J. (2000). Chronic illness as biographical disruption or biographical disruption as chronic illness? *Sociology of Health & Illness,* 22, 40–67.

Williams, G. (1984). The genesis of chronic illness. *Sociology of Health & Illness,* 6, 175–200.

Williams, R.A. (2007). Masculinities fathering and health. *Social Science & Medicine,* 64, 338–349.

Williams, S. (2000). Chronic illness as biographical disruption or biographical disruption as chronic illness? Reflections on a core concept. *Sociology of Health and Illness,* 22, 40–67.

Williams, S.J. (2005). Parsons revisited. *Health,* 9, 123–144.

Willig, C. (2004). Discourse analysis and health psychology. In: Murray, 2004, pp. 155–169.

Willis, P. (2000). *Ethnographic Imagination,* Cambridge: Polity.

Willott, S. and Griffin, C. (1996). Men, masculinity and the challenge of long-term unemployment. In: Mac an Ghaill, M. (ed.). *Understanding Masculinities* (pp. 77–92), Buckingham: Open University Press.

Willott, S. and Griffin, C. (1997). 'Wham Bam, am I a Man?': unemployed men talk about masculinities. *Feminism & Psychology,* 7, 107–128.

Willott, S. and Griffin, C. (2004). Redundant men: constraints on identity change. *Journal of Community & Applied Social Psychology,* 14, 53–69.

Wilson, S. (2007). When you have children, you're obliged to live' motherhood, chronic illness and biographical disruption. *Sociology of Health & Illness,* 29, 610–626.

Winkler, D., Pjrek, E., and Kaper, S. (2005). Gender-specific symptoms of depression and anger attacks. *Journal of Men's Health and Gender,* 3, 19–24.

Winkler, D., Pjrek, E., Heiden, A., Wiesegger, G., Klein, N., Konstantinidis, A., and Kasper, S. (2004). Gender differences in the psychopathology of depressed inpatients. *European Archives of Psychiatry and Clinical Neuroscience,* 254, 209–214.

Wodak, R. (1999). Critical discourse analysis at the end of the 20th century. *Research on Language and Social Interaction,* 32, 185–193.

World Health Organisation (1992). *The ICD-10 Classification of Mental and Behavioural Disorders: Clinical Descriptions and Diagnostic Guidelines,* New York: World Health Organisation.

World Health Organisation (1993). *The ICD-10 Classification of Mental and Behavioural Disorders: Diagnostic Criteria for Research,* New York: World Heatlh Organisation.

World Health Organisation (1998). *Klasyfikacja zaburzeń psychicznych i zaburzeń zachowania w ICD-10. Badawcze kryteria diagnostyczne (Polish translation of WHO, 1993),* Kraków-Warszawa: Vesalius-IPiN.

Yang, L.H., Kleinman, A., Phelan, B.G., Leed, S., and Good, B. (2007). Culture and stigma: adding moral experience to stigma theory. *Social Science & Medicine,* 64, 1524–1535.

Younger, J.B. (1995). The alienation of sufferer. *Advances in Nursing Science,* 17, 53–72.

Zachar, P. (2000). Psychiatric disorders are not natural kinds. *Philosophy, Psychiatry and Psychology,* 7, 167–182.

Zimmerman, M. (1994). *Interview Guide for Evaluating DSM-IV Psychiatric Disorders and the Mental Status Examination,* East Greenwich: Psychological Products Press.

Zuroff, D.C., Mongrain, M., and Santor, D.A. (2004). Conceptualizing and measuring personality vulnerability to depression. *Psychological Bulletin,* 130, 489–511.

Index

autobiography, 91

Beck Depression Inventory, 33–42
biographical disruption, 90–2, 102–4

depression
  agency of, 44–57
    and failed agents, 48
    and autobiography, 90–105
    in culture, 3–5
    diagnostic criteria of, 2–3, 26–9,
      32, 87
    and discourse, 55
    experience of, *passim*
      and the BDI, 41
      and the ICD, 29
    literature on, 11–14
      in men, 13–14
    and family, 151–68
    and gender, 73, 88
    and masculinity, 54, 83
    in men, *see* men, and depression
    prevalence, 3
    in psychiatry, 2–3
      critiques of, 4–5
    social dimension of, 56, 84
    and work, 136–50
diagnostic manuals, 24–6
discourse
  analysis, 14–16
  experience, 18
  and mental illness, 17–19
  of psychiatry, 23–4
distancing, 58–74
  definition of, 59

face, 72

gender, 5–6
  in psychiatry, 54, 86, 178

ICD-10, 23–32, 41–2
  modality in, 26–7, 30

identity, 106–7
illness
  experience of, 59
  and identity, 91–2, 101
  vs. disease, 19
insight, 172–5

life events, 94, 103, 104, 106, 119

masculinity, 53
  definition, 6–7
  and illness, 9, 73
  model of, 73, 77–8
medicalisation, 41, 101–2
men
  and depression, 10–11
  and health, 7–10
  and mental health, 8–10
  and powerlessness, 53–4
  and suicide, 10–11
  and unemployment, 87
  and work, 85–8
mental illness
  and family, 151–2
  and work, 85–6

normality, 104–5, 147–9
  and mental illness, 148–9

psychiatry
  and language, 55–6

recovery, 86, 145–6, 149–50
  and work, 149–50

stigmatisation, 53, 55, 73
  and labelling, 45–6
  self-, 159
suffering, 176–9
  definition of, 176

tellability, 102